Alcibiades at the Door

ALCIBIADES AT THE DOOR

*Gay Discourses in
French Literature*

LAWRENCE R. SCHEHR

*Stanford University Press
Stanford, California* *1995*

Stanford University Press
Stanford, California
© 1995 by the Board of Trustees of the
Leland Stanford Junior University

Printed in the United States of America
CIP data are at the end of the book

Stanford University Press publications are
distributed exclusively by Stanford
University Press within the United States,
Canada, Mexico, and Central America;
they are distributed exclusively by
Cambridge University Press throughout
the rest of the world.

*To the memory of
my grandparents
and for their
great-grandson,
Eddie.*

Preface

This book is a study of several twentieth-century French narratives dealing with homosexuality. Though in no way a sequel to *The Shock of Men*, it does form a complement to it. In that volume, I concentrated on how Marcel Proust, Roland Barthes, Renaud Camus, and Michel Tournier develop the structures of homosexuality as means and grounds for interpretation and how they use homosexuality as a liberating hermeneutics for understanding. Focusing on works by René Crevel, Jean-Paul Sartre, Roland Barthes, and Hervé Guibert, this study examines how the figures of homosexuality function at the limits of narrative, as part of the deep structures of narrative, and at the border between public and private discourses.

Each chapter explores the figures that define the limits of one or several texts that engage homosexuality. The introductory chapter starts with the famous image of Alcibiades arriving at the door in Plato's *Symposium*. Even in his joyful dance, Alcibiades occupies a liminal position until the diners are sure of who he is. At that point he reorients the dynamics and dances his way into a newly energized situation. I thus take Alcibiades as an emblematic figure mediating between inside and outside.

The second chapter examines the writing of René Crevel in the singular context that was his: that of an openly homosexual writer who was part of the officially heterosexual Surrealist circle. The general opposition to homosexuality, albeit with several interesting exceptions, that was the official position of Breton and others ambiguously and contradictorily both included and excluded Crevel. The material discussed includes both Surrealist pronouncements about homosexuality, especially Breton's, and Crevel's *Mon corps et moi*, his most sustained attempt to negotiate the problems of inside and outside and of public and private personae.

The next chapter focuses on the writing of Jean-Paul Sartre in the thirties and forties. Sartre's interest in homosexuality is well known, and the study of Genet is testimony to that interest. Yet long before concentrating on Genet, Sartre repeatedly dealt with the subject. The figures and forms of homosexuality in Sartre's work relate to a phenomenology of perception, to an insistence on the relation between vision and knowledge, and to a set of narrative ploys that recast Sartre's own relation to the subject. Not merely an accident, the homosexual component in Sartre's work is an essential function of his project, his thought, his narrative approach, and his philosophy.

The fourth chapter outlines the rhetoric of representation of the other as it is figured in several works by Gide and in Barthes's diary, entitled *Incidents*, which is about a trip to Morocco. The discourses of homosexuality are related to discourses about social power, dominant structures, and a model of colonialism deployed by both Gide and Barthes. Looking at the public and private discourses of homosexuality in their work, I examine how Gide negotiates the idea of freedom and how Barthes plays with semiosis in order to sustain or to subvert the models of knowledge and power that relate to the definitions and uses of homosexuality.

The final chapter is devoted to Hervé Guibert, who died at the end of 1991. Many of Guibert's last books are a meditation and exploration of AIDS, this most public of private phenomena. This chapter examines the changing relation between public and private, between the outside world and Guibert's inner world, and between the singularity of literary writing and the nomothetic nature of the public document, all of which undergo change in a world and in an individual affected by AIDS. I also look at Guibert's notorious introduction of the figure of Michel Foucault as a character and the implications of that event for our understanding of public and private discourses on homosexuality.

Earlier portions of part of this book have appeared as "Guibert under Bureaucratic Quarantine," in *L'Esprit Créateur*, and as "Roland Barthes's Semierotics," in the *Canadian Review of Comparative Literature*. I thank both journals for allowing me to reuse the material.

I am most grateful for the support of my writing provided by my chairperson, Bernard J. Quinn; his encouragement and endorsement have given me the wherewithal to do this work. As always, there are many other people to thank for support, for encouragement, for opportunities to speak, for commentaries and readings, for good conversation, for stimulating questions: Martine Antle, George Bauer, David Bell, Sharon Bissell, Ross Chambers, John Coker, Dominique Fisher, Jean-François Fourny, Robert Harvey, Anne Herrmann, Caryl Lloyd, Ralph Sarkonak, Alain Vizier, and Stephen Whitworth. I thank them one and all.

L.R.S.

Contents

Abbreviations

The following abbreviations and acronyms are used throughout the text and notes. Full forms of citations and complete publication data may be found in the Works Cited.

AR	Sartre, *L'Age de raison*
Ami	Guibert, *A l'ami qui ne m'a pas sauvé la vie*
Baby	Crevel, *Babylone*
Baud	Sartre, *Baudelaire*
CM	Sartre, *Cahiers pour une morale*
CMV	Guibert, *Cytomégalovirus*
D	Crevel, *Détours*
"E"	Sartre, "Erostrate," in *Le Mur*
"EC"	Sartre, "L'Enfance d'un chef," in *Le Mur*
ECR	Crevel, *L'Esprit contre la raison et autres écrits surréalistes*
EJ	Sartre, *Ecrits de jeunesse*
EN	Sartre, *L'Etre et le néant*
EVF	Crevel, *Etes-vous fous?*
HCR	Guibert, *L'Homme au chapeau rouge*
"I"	Sartre, "Intimité," in *Le Mur*

IF	Sartre, *L'Idiot de la famille*
MA	Sartre, *La Mort dans l'âme*
MCM	Crevel, *Mon corps et moi*
MLV	Guibert, *Mauve le vierge*
N	Sartre, *La Nausée*
PC	Guibert, *Le Protocole compassionnel*
PP	Crevel, *Les Pieds dans le plat*
RC	Crevel, *Le Roman cassé et derniers écrits*
Rech	Pierre, ed. *Recherches sur la sexualité*
S	Sartre, *Le Sursis*
SG	Sartre, *Saint Genet*
S4	Sartre, *Situations, IV*

Alcibiades at the Door

Introduction:
Alcibiades at the Door

History has handed down two archetypal stories of dance performances accompanied by music. The first one we recall is Salome's dance. Called upon to please Herod, she withholds performing her dance until he agrees to grant her any wish she may have. What she asks for, at her mother's bidding, is the head of John the Baptist. Herod can do nothing but comply. The truth is gradually unveiled during Salome's dance, and, as Françoise Meltzer has so admirably shown, what is revealed is Salome's "pure meaning" (42). This meaning, hidden by Salome's veils, covered by the fictions of company, family drama, and performance, is desire, or more specifically, desire and death: Salome's request for the head of John the Baptist, Herodias's desire for John's death, Herod's undoubtedly less than pure motives for wanting his stepdaughter Salome to dance. As Salome's dance gradually unveils the truth, we find an image of death at the heart of her dance, the death both of the individual John and of the family unit whose libidinal dynamics are awry. The death of John is not singular, for the dance writes its traces of death everywhere. To reveal the truth is to reveal death both for the self and for the other, for Salome, Herod, Herodias, and John together. Yet Salome's dance is part of a cycle of life, much as, in Hindu culture, Siva's dance of destruction is the prelude to a rebirth. So, too, within the larger New

Testament story, Salome's dance is seen as the promise of a life to come, the promise of redemption through the Messiah of whom John is the forerunner, the promise of an eternal life to come in the kingdom of heaven.

Salome's dance takes place entirely in a series of enclosures. Salome performs in a little familial theater that inscribes the father's lust, the mother's ambition, and the daughter's vulnerability within the enclosed spaces that can barely contain an excess of desire. The circles remain separate even within the enclosure, for Herod's speech and Salome's dance stay isolated from one another. More important, the outside does not enter except teleologically: it is the space in which John is beheaded and in which John will be reborn. To come into the outside world means to go elsewhere, removed from the spaces of enclosure and from the discourses of familial oppression.

Now there is another aspect to Salome's dance as it unfurls in the seraglio-like space of family drama: Salome's dance of death is gendered as a heterosexual space. It is the space of reproduction, of mothers and daughters, of the economic institution of marriage, and the insistence of the viability of that economy for the perpetuation of the group. Then as now, Herod's lust may have been considered an abominable behavior that hints at incest and child molestation. Yet that seems to be part and parcel of the heterosexual familial model, not only in biblical times but in the age of bourgeois modernity as well. Salome's dance is every heterosexual family's dirty little secret, kept veiled, and unveiled in the family closet, not available for viewing in the outside world.

More recently, the retelling of the Salome story has produced a revisionist view of gender as the heterosexual space of Salome's dance was rewritten many times in the nineteenth century as a space of homosexual desire. As Kevin Kopelson has so admirably pointed out (42–43), there were an extraordinary number of versions of the Salome story at the end of the nineteenth century. These versions, and especially that of Oscar Wilde, exploded the sordid drama and brought its closure into a space of excess; there the decadent embellishments of the newly transcribed story, such as Salome French-kissing Jokanaan's severed head (Kopelson 43), establish a dynamic of homoeroticism and homophobia by what Kopelson calls "perverse attachments to beautiful men" (43).

I have started with the well-known story of Salome's dance because it is a useful illustration of the way in which we capture an image and force it to perform an ongoing task in writing. Salome's dance is fixed for all time in a Christian model of representation and interpretation. What has been captured is murder, death, and illicit desire. When the space is seen as that of the figural forerunner of the Passion it becomes a space of hope and redemption. Alternatively, when the space is opened up by the aesthetics of decadence, the heterosexual drama takes on strong homoerotic overtones. Yet without a redemption that negates the theatricality of the drama as such, whether one continues to see the story as a heterosexual one or whether one integrates decadent revisionism to read it homoerotically, Salome's dance of death remains inscribed as the dance of destruction, wherein some secrets are too heinous to be directly revealed.

Recalling Salome's dance, which I see as an allegory of concealment and revelation, is a way of remembering another dance that has been veiled in its own way. It too hides a meaning and a figure of complex desire. Just as the beginning of Christianity is heralded by a dance, there is another such notable performance at the beginning of philosophy. We move from Herod's Jerusalem to Socrates' Athens as we consider a scene in Plato's *Symposium*. After a night of conversation about love, the convivial guests at Agathon's banquet find themselves suddenly interrupted by a wild, boisterous Alcibiades, accompanied by a flute-girl. Alcibiades teeters in and weaves about to the sound of music. If he is not exactly dancing, he is moving to music, and that is close enough.

While Alcibiades has been out carousing, the men at the banquet have been discoursing nobly on the philosophy and meaning of love. These deipnosophists take the lofty tones suitable to this weighty subject. At their most earnest, they find themselves interrupted by Alcibiades' rowdy entrance. After an evening of wild entertainment, far from the civilized discussions of the men at the banquet, Alcibiades shows up to interrupt their feast. Philosophically, Alcibiades is the eruption of the real within the realm of the theoretical, the interruption of the statically discursive by the illustration of movement. Alcibiades weaves in and out, weaves inside and outside together, and weaves his way to the heart of the discussion: Socrates himself. In contrast with the destruction and ultimate rebirth that will be symbolized by Salome's dance, Alcibiades' entrance evokes nothing but praise, encomia, joy, and even rapture. Alcibiades' performance needs no promise of rebirth, but is a joyful dance here and now. Alcibiades' dance and the discourses of the guests are two versions of the same story: two threads that come together as outside and inside meet in the *Symposium*. Alcibiades practices what the others preach. He comes in to praise, to talk, and to stir up the festivities; the diners allow the outside interruption to come in at a suitable moment, the end of Socrates' speech that is a "eulogy bestowed on Love" (*Sym.* 212D). Together the two parties, performer and listeners, actor and viewers, agent and speakers, join to form the figure of the performative dance. Plato gives us language and action, separated at first, but then intermingled in a joyful mixture of sound, sense, and movement. Garlanded by the very figure of the dance, the worlds of inside and outside begin to merge for these men.

Now, just as Herod, Herodias, and even John are included in Salome's dance as the spectators and victim who are a part of that very movement, so too do the men at the banquet become part of Alcibiades' dance. As we make that analogy we realize that whereas the dance of Salome is a heterosexual and vaguely incestuous scenario, the dance of the *Symposium* is resolutely homosexual. Even if some of the discourses offered in the *Symposium* have been about the love of men for women, the dance of Alcibiades enacts a scenario in which there are no women save the attendant, ancillary flutist. Enchanted by Alcibiades, the speakers at the banquet insist on exchange and love, but those figures are within the structure of homosexual desire, homoerotic bonds, and homosocial contexts. Beyond this bachelors' party is the simple fact that at the heart of this dance is Socrates. As Herod would wish Salome to dance for him, Alcibiades dances *for* Socrates: to please him, to perform for him, to have him. The dance expresses the full desire of the dancer as subject, not as one subjected. As he sobers, Alcibiades seconds his dance with a description of Socrates as the seductive other; for Alcibiades, Socrates is a satyr resembling Marsyas, a desirable Silenus-like figure, with pipes in hand (215B–C). It matters little that Socrates is not the handsomest of men, for he can ravish and seduce as can the most attractive. Socrates' seductive charm is so complete and so overpowering that he might well be a favorite instead of a lover (222B). Against the eventual discourse of death, one reads the all-affirming, protean discourse of life; against an eventual surfeit of incestuous heterosexuality, one reads an encomium to Greek pederastic behavior. Against the closure of the space in which dirty little secrets will be told, here is a space of exchange opened to the outside world. And at the heart of all this is the father of philosophy, midwife to ideas, and the so-called corrupter of the youth of Athens.

A revisionist reading of the story of Alcibiades would undoubtedly stress the repression of the homosexual motif in the received history of the acceptance of the text. Consider that Aristophanes' criticisms of Socrates and his band in *The Clouds* have been considered partially responsible, if not for the condemnation of Socrates, then at least for the turn of public opinion against the pederastic model that Socrates espouses. Consider as well that as Thucydides points out (VI.15), Alcibiades himself was put to death in part because of "his lawless and sensual self-indulgence in his manner of living" that was feared by the masses (*phobethentes gar hoi polloi*). The deaths of Socrates and of Alcibiades are certainly candidates for the category of some anachronistic homophobia. More important, however, for me is that there has been a process of selective memory in the inscription of the *Symposium*: if philosophy has recognized the undeniable homoeroticism of this story, the received knowledge about the discourses of love has often tended to forget the enactment of the scene as one suffused with homoeroticism. In other words, everyone clearly remembers that it was, ironically, the same Aristophanes who developed the theory of the beings that, once split, looked for their other half, men looking for women (and vice versa), but also men looking for men and women for women (189C–193E). Moreover, at the very moment of Alcibiades' entrance, it is again Aristophanes who is different from the others: he is speaking anew and not applauding. Even more important is the fact that these discourses are given in the context of an all-male gathering, a constant reminder of the pederastic model: Aristophanes and Socrates and all the others talk about love and sex among men, to men, with the approval of men, as a homoerotic bond seals and supports the discourse.

Still, the reader may be surprised that even this context of homoeroticism is not ultimately what interests me, precisely because, from the clear-sighted position of the late twentieth century, such an argument is predictably doxological. One could easily rehearse and repeat tired arguments and litanies about homoeroticism and homophobia. On the contrary, what does interest me is the image of Alcibiades in a world that is anything but "heterocratic" and "homophobic." What does his dance of liberation mean when it is not considered as a fight against a hostile world? For me, Alcibiades' dance is the point at which practice and theory meet; inside and outside touch with his arrival at the banquet. His very presence on the threshold produces a meeting between inside and outside, between a world of language and a world of action, between a world of select, idealized behavior epitomized by discourses of love and a world with economic considerations, an outside world that may contain an intimate (212D) or someone unknown, perhaps even someone hostile. The outside world is mixed, the inside world, a metonymy for civilization itself, is uniform and safe. Alcibiades opens up the inside to the outside. His presence is instrumental in joining the two places: he brings in the mixture from the outside world; he opens up the ideal space of the symposium to multiple influences, potentially dangerous, probably not.

Why have I begun this study of twentieth-century French narratives about homosexuality with an appeal to Athens on the one hand and to Jerusalem on the other? By quickly playing off two stories of dances against each other we have been able to see what is at stake in such a performance: how, *pace* Yeats, there is an enormous difference between the dancer and the dance. The spectators of the dance, and even the readers of that act, are part of the dance as well. By using these two dance tales allegorically, I am trying to suggest several things, not the least of which is the complex relation of the individual to the performance. One must gauge the audience: Is it a private group, slightly apprehensive, yet ultimately sympathetic? Is the performance in a public sphere where the interpreter is reduced to his or her dance? Or is it a closed-off world, the world of the seraglio or even the bourgeois family, where the role of the individual is to reproduce the structure in which, and from which, he or she gets his or her identity?

The works that I am considering all share in these aspects of a loosely defined dance. In most cases, we will find that the presumed rhetorical audience, though initially apprehensive, is deemed to be a sympathetic one. Still, one never knows what to expect when theory passes to action. Moreover, at every turn, there is potentially another audience, the invisible, hostile stranger that might have come in instead of Alcibiades. I am also suggesting that the model for reading is not one of shame versus open abandon, the Salome-like model of repression that keeps her repressed (by Herod) even as she dances and expresses desire, be it hers, his, or her mother's. Rather, much more sympathetically, the model is that of the open door through which Alcibiades eventually enters. From that entrance, the discourses of love are enchantingly actualized.

My understanding, then, of the works I shall be examining is that they are situated in the spaces connecting public and private spheres, between announcement and closure, and between repression and expression. When we compare the two allegories, not for their allegorical value of dance as performance, but for their comparative organization of materials and dynamics, one other thing stands out that is relevant to the works in question. Even if there is a change of discourse between public and private worlds, even if, for example, there is a critique of Socrates' pederasty within the context of the classical tradition—I am thinking again of Aristophanes' *The Clouds*—homosexuality is not defined essentially as being secondary to heterosexuality. For despite the critique of Socrates in *The Clouds*, Plato's version of Aristophanes does not seem to be inimical to pederasty. As I have noted above, it is Plato's version of Aristophanes who, in his famous speech in *The Symposium* (189C–193D), says that there were originally three sorts of beings. Eventually they were divided and each seeks its former half: those that came from "men-women" (*androgynon*) seek a member of the opposite sex, but those that came from men seek their *symbolon*, which is another man; those that came from women seek theirs, which is another woman.

I recall Aristophanes' famous story of the descent of the sexes (or genders) to underscore the sense of Alcibiades' entrance. He is not entering into a closed-off society, a secret world of pederasty, but rather is crossing the line between public and private space. Against this allegory of two kinds of spaces, we can briefly reread the story of Salome. Shut off to everything but the reinscription of the family drama, the world of Herod, Herodias, and Salome is the world of secrets, the world of unavowed sexuality, one of whose forms is Herod's semi-incestuous desire for his stepdaughter. Reading these two tales against one another, we may realize that far from being heterosexuality's dirty little secret, homosexuality can define a world on its own terms, can construct its own borders, and can exercise *parrhesia*, or free speech. Certainly, homosexuality will be forced to occupy the space of that secret, but it is a space opened up within heterosexuality for a congeries of sexualities considered to be unorthodox. And again, that is one of the reasons that there can be slippage from the incest motif of the biblical version of the story to the homoeroticism of the decadent version: in a sense, all aberrant sexualities become equated in the mind of the collective and fearful other already mentioned by Thucydides as instrumental in Alcibiades' death. Translated into the terms of modernity—that is to say, the bourgeois state and its mechanisms—the opposition is not between heterosexuality and homosexuality but between the reproductive, economic model of sexuality and whatever does not fit within its confines. When not forced into the interstices created as the generic, nonreproductive, secondary, other sexuality, homosexuality has not sought the opening of the closet door, but some differentiation of itself and some sign of safety in the outside world in general.

Let us turn from these allegories of the sexual dance to the discourse of sexuality: the language used to tell the tales, what Alcibiades might have said after the dinner, what Herod might have told his friends the next day if only he had been able. I am referring, obviously, to the semipublic, semiprivate tales of narratives of sexual conquest. Men tell other men stories, women tell other women stories; the gender of the vanquished is secondary. If the apostrophes of love are alternately hetero- or homosexual, the discourse about sexuality is structured as homosexual, sign of a shared lust or a remembered chagrin. Now, obviously there are cases in which, for example, a male narrator tells a story to a female listener, or vice versa. Still, even in cases like that there is a homosexual dimension. If the woman listens to a man telling a tale, she is asked to identify with the other woman, so that she too will get turned on, so to speak. Or, alternatively, as is the case with Mme de Merteuil's reading of Valmont's seduction of the Présidente de Tourvel, one could say that she identifies with Valmont and is a lesbian voyeur in that case. And in the case

in which a female confidante listens to a man tell of his love for another man (or a male confidant listens to a women tell of her love for
another woman), the story, by definition, already comes under the
sign of the homosexual.

Thus there is always a homosexual component to heterosexual
discourses about sex. Already at the beginning of these discourses, at
the beginning of philosophy's tales of love, Plato reminds us that the
structure of the discourses of sexuality will be among men (or among
women), as the deipnosophists extend their banquet into a symposium on love. The story of Salome shows us that the discourses between the sexes are reduced to closets within closets, tales of lust
never spoken. Again we wonder if the figure of the closet, the metaphor of gay liberation of the last twenty years, should not itself be
turned on its head: Is it not heterosexuality that is really locked in a
closet of its own devising and that forces a similar closet on homosexuality out of spite?

Now, I am aware that this idealized parrhesia and this liberty of
behavior are a far cry from the structures in which homosexuality, as
often as not, is acted out. I am not denying the existence in modern
times of the acts of repression and the secrets of the night with which
homosexuality has become associated. Yet to jump from there to an
image of opposition and closure is to do a disservice to the acts and
discourses of homosexual sex. I am not denying that the figure of the
closet has operated as a powerful tool on homosexual individuals and
on homosexuals as an amorphous group, as Eve Sedgwick has admirably shown. I am saying that the closet itself is a heterosexual
construct foisted on homosexuality. This is readily apparent in the
concepts of social constructivism that gender studies have offered: If
sexual and gender identity are only products of the crisscrossings of
instruments, structures, and discourses of power, how could homosexuality not be in a "closet"? Then again, how could any sexuality
not be in a closet? Even as white male heterosexuality thinks it is free
because each individual instance identifies with the doxological discourses of social construction, is it not at that moment that sexuality
is in its deepest, most tightly locked closet?

All questions of the appropriateness of a modern vocabulary aside
—and I ask the reader to allow me this conceit since I am still in the
realm of timeless allegory—I like to see in Alcibiades the first figure

of gay liberation that history records. It is not that the Greek concept of homosexuality is the same as our modern occidental one: I am not proposing that Alcibiades be viewed as the herald of some Stonewall riots that will occur over two thousand years in the future. Not at all; still, as the figure of freedom, Alcibiades literally joins the inner discussion of homosexuality or the Greek equivalent of ephebophilia to the outside praxis and exemplification of that behavior. Alcibiades is not opening a closet door; he is joining public and private spaces, he is joining theory and praxis. At the edge between outside and inside, Alcibiades shows that praxis and theory can be interwoven: having been in the outside world, he will talk at this revived symposium. And he will undoubtedly go out into the world again to revel anew.

I have discussed various implications of the allegory of these two dances and how I see them as being a possible means of illumination of modern homosexual discourses. And I have briefly mentioned the semipublic, semiprivate exchange of discourses and stories. I would now like to turn to the official acts of exchange of representation. Again, Françoise Meltzer has shown that the story of Salome is allegorically the story of the dance of representation. We have also seen that, in its own way, Alcibiades' dance is also representation, a parodic reproduction of an act of seduction. Now, in a more contemporary forum, we have often forgotten the latter in favor of the former: the problem with Alcibiades' dance is that he veils nothing. The good thing about Salome's dance—at least within the repressive model to which we often unwittingly turn—is that the act of representation veils the images and closes off desire from the surface.

Having internalized the models of closure instead of seeing the openness of a literary work, we have often been drawn to safe conclusions about the figure of homosexuality within a cultural space. Our conclusions depend on our understanding of the dominance of male heterosexuality, whose forms and structures have organized representation in the Western world. Moreover, male heterosexuality has lent its power to the dominant discursive structures and to the praxes that are accepted and acceptable. Male heterosexuality provides the adequation between the truth and the discourses promulgated in the name of truth. Faced with the omnipotence of that discursive and juridico-political machine, voices of women, voices of people of color, voices of the impoverished and the disenfranchised, and voices of nonofficialdom in general have repeatedly and continuously been repressed.

With the development of the modern world in the eighteenth century, women's voices begin to have semiofficial standing; testifying to that fact is not only the rise of the novel as a genre but especially the large numbers of novels written by women who, in one way or another, had often been marginalized in the canonical forms of the drama and the poem. The developing genre of the novel was often considered to be nonserious amusement; thus it was not problematic for women to write such stuff. Retrospectively, of course, we have accorded the novel a far more central and serious role, as that genre has proven to be the defining genre of its age, the perfect vehicle, as Ian Watt shows, to embody the ideology of the rising middle-class society and bourgeois exchange systems. In the novel, the freely floating signifiers of exchange made women's participation more viable than it had been. Before that, in France, for example, women's voices were present in the literature of the court: Mme de Lafayette, Mme de Sévigné, Mlle de Scudéry come to mind. Yet the space of this writing was at a remove from the world of direct or verisimilar representation and a far cry from the writing imbued with power represented by the canonical dramatists, among others. It is only with the development of the bourgeois novel that women's voices move a bit closer to center stage.

As Michel Foucault demonstrates in *The History of Sexuality*, the notion that sexuality continued to be repressed in the nineteenth century is a specious hypothesis when there is a mountain of evidence to suggest that it was anything but repressed. If one takes Foucault to the limit, people seem to have done nothing but write about sex. Treatise after treatise told readers how to combat nymphomania, hysteria, dangerous proclivities, and the worst offender of them all, masturbation. In Victorian England, names of things or behaviors were changed in order not to suggest or offend. Evidence suggests that the surface of the Victorian bowdlerization of culture covered a far more heterogeneous world than the neat repressive model we have come to assume. Later, Freud could talk about sex not because he was unleashing the dogs of reason against a forceful, silencing repression, but because sex was already visibly and invisibly present in word, deed, and symptom.

Two models seem to be competing here: one is a model of repression; another is a model of construction. In the first model, a type of praxis is either not allowed or endlessly marginalized. At a given moment, because the dynamics of the world or of textuality have changed, the marginal flickering gradually moves from the Ultima Thule of representation into a roped-off area where the act of representation is supposed to repeat the generous bestowal of the right to speech: novels by women are supposed to talk about the repression and emancipation of women; novels by African-Americans are supposed to talk about the African-American experience. Perhaps in this continued, though sophisticated, version of marginalization in a high-tech closet within the panopticon, the marginal discourse is supposed to repeat the doxology of the dominant discourse. In the model of social construction, the discourses are not repressed but controlled. Sometimes there is open access to loci of enunciation; sometimes the discourses circulate through another system, heterogeneous, vaguely underground. In this view of the interrelation of discourses, there is no suggested reorganization of contents the way there is in the repressive model. Thus, what might be considered an extreme of discourse (though one ironically now at center stage in the ongoing discussion of Michel Foucault), that is, a sadomasochistic discourse, could circulate freely, could comment on anything; sometimes it could be heard in official circles but more often only in nonofficial ones.

These two models exist side by side and have been institutionally sanctioned, as any reader of this work knows. In one model, one might have a powerful official conference, whether it is a big gathering (the MLA, for example) or a small group of very visible people. In such conferences, perhaps the official model allows for the presence of some underrepresented or marginalized discourses. More often than not, the space allotted is one in which the individual discourses are asked to respond to their marginality, or their status, and asked politely not to talk about something else. The other model can be found in a conference off the beaten path, where everyone is perfectly, freely happy to talk about a plenitude of things. Yet this conference may go unmentioned in the official newsletters of the more visible organizations.

I mention this version of institutionalization for two reasons. At the level of theory, it is in these institutions of higher learning that the battles about gender theory are taking place before they move further into public view. So there is an intimate relationship, at least in the universities of North America and Europe, between the discourses of minority voices and the means of representing them institutionally. Second, it so happens that the works I have chosen to look at all interrelate and question the public and private spheres of discourse and sexuality. It behooves us, then, to look closely at the models we explicitly or implicitly choose.

What some will find striking and others heretical is that I cannot fully accept the implications of either one of those models. Without becoming an essentialist, I would like to suggest that the public-private division is perhaps more useful in elucidating the status of homosexual aesthetic expression than either the repressive model or the model of control. To put it roughly, I would say that homosexual discourse is always there and, more often than not, at center stage. Sometimes we choose to read the homosexual aspect publicly, sometimes privately. And when it is read privately by some, others do not read it at all.

Homosexuality has its own path, distinct from the more clearly repressed voices of minorities and women, and even distinct from the general discourse of sexuality. Why is this important or even significant? Over the past two decades, it has been convenient to associate the various voices seeking liberation; that association, the solidarity it produces, and the empowerment it seeks are all laudable on the scale of action, event, and deed. Yet when political activity is institutionalized as discipline, there may be inappropriate inherent assumptions. By no means am I rehearsing the arguments about tenured radicals here, nor am I extending such arguments in a liberal fashion in order to maintain some gay ghetto within the institution. On the contrary, I am underlining the fact that the specific phenomena and history of homosexuality, the specific manifestations of homosexuality in the arts, combine to make us necessarily reevaluate our institutionalization of the act of liberation. Moreover, these specific manifestations demand that we reconsider an approach to a study of the subject that may be different from other voices of liberation, such as feminism, African-American studies, and third world literature, that have found some ground in the academy.

Three components in the manifestations of homosexuality compel us to approach the subject in a way that suits its history and characteristics. These components, which will be discussed in turn, are: the general continuity of homosexual *poiesis*, the presence of homosexuality at the heart and beginning of literary and philosophical endeavor, and finally a particular semiotics of invisibility. In order to show what I feel is the difference of homosexual poiesis from other endeavors, I shall be arguing from the phenomena offered throughout history, rather than from the a priori assumption of categorical repression. In so doing, I realize that there have been and continue to be acts of repression directed against public homosexual poiesis. To recognize the direct attempts made to silence this homosexual poiesis, one need go no further than the furor over the funding for the National Endowment for the Arts in the United States or the arrest of the director of the Cincinnati art museum because of an exhibition of photos by Robert Mapplethorpe. The ironic result of one of these attempted acts of "repression," or more exactly "oppression," is that the name of Mapplethorpe is known far more widely in middlebrow circles than it would otherwise have been. It may be ideologically convenient to associate production with the simultaneous rise of oppression of homosexual poiesis, to marry in an unholy *ménage à trois* the words "homosexual," "homophobic," and "heterocratic." History tells a story different from that simultaneity. But that is only a quibble. Despite continued oppression of homosexual poiesis, there are an extraordinary number of artifacts that fall into this category: the oppression of homosexual poiesis has continuously been far more ineffective than comparable acts of censorship on or of other "marginalized" cultures.

First of all, it is less ludicrous than it may appear to say that there have been known or presumed homosexuals throughout history. Specifically, there has been a game of naming and discovery related to the sexual identity of prominent individuals. Long before the self-affirmation phenomenon, the "I'm OK, you're OK" of the seventies, gay men often found solace in a party game of making lists of famous men throughout history who were homosexual or bisexual. This is received knowledge, even folklore, and part of the social structure of the homosexual community throughout the ages. Think about what that means, when such folkloric knowledge is set against the general knowledge about women or African-Americans and especially the general knowledge about women's poiesis or African-American poiesis. If the average educated white heterosexual male may be able to name one or two women or African-American figures of note before the twentieth century, he would certainly be hard pressed to name a woman or African-American artist or philosopher. Perhaps a few names of women writers would come to mind from the nineteenth century: everyone, I suppose, has heard of Jane Austen and Emily Dickinson. The game could not go much further than that. And yet the list of homosexual figures is well known to all, not only to the "in" crowd of homosexuals passing down the lore of their tradition.

On the surface, if there has been more repression of the specific sexual behavior of homosexuals in the real world, there has been less repression of their cultural performances and products. From the evidence, then, regardless of the individual acts of repression and regardless of the number of individual acts of production over the course of history, homosexual poiesis has been far more continuous than any of its counterparts except for male heterosexual poiesis. In fact, even if the continuity of male heterosexual production provides the most detailed (even if exclusive) picture of production over the course of time, the homosexual picture does not lag far behind. And again, even if critical and intellectual endeavor needs to look at what has been repressed and in so doing discovers a secret history, a chartable map of the history of homosexual poiesis is certainly already present.

The course of the various manifestations of homosexual poiesis has been more or less continuous, though it has not always necessarily taken the same form as that of the dominant culture. Hence, rather than a series of dominant acts of culture, we have at times had dominant phenomena, like the presence of homosexuality in the twentieth-century French novel. Alongside such a plethora, there have also been parallel activities essential to an understanding of cultural phenomena, though they are not in themselves the absolutely dominant moment: think of the transvestism on the Elizabethan stage. While an understanding of that phenomenon is important to our understanding of the culture of Elizabethan theater, it may not necessarily provide a dominant meaning for the plays we read.

All in all, we can read a continuity, even if the paths taken are not necessarily always the main roads. In contrast, the history of women's poiesis is filled with long stretches of invisibility; African-American poiesis seems to require massive archival unearthing for anything earlier than the 1920's and the Harlem Renaissance. Yet because in one way or another poiesis always is presumed to reflect on the producer, homosexual poiesis is nevertheless perceived as having a somewhat intermittent continuity different from the organic continuity of other productions. The male homosexual is perceived as being a nonproductive part of society in that his actions are not perceived as working toward its continuation. A woman's production or the production of an African-American are seen too as metonymies of their authors, and as such, they are perceived as being part and parcel of an organic continuity from one act to another. While the history of homosexual poiesis is far more continuous in a global fashion than the production of other minority voices, each individual act—at least until quite recently—has been perceived as an isolated instance of production.

So, from the point of view established by a dominant economy and mode of production, homosexual poiesis is seen as a repeated outcropping from that dominant culture as opposed to being or having a continuity of its own. If the disadvantage in that interpretation is that some sense of identity is denied to homosexual poiesis, the advantage is that homosexual poiesis or at least some homosexual poiesis is considered not as alien to the dominant culture as an oppositional position might have led us to believe. For—and this is the second point—homosexual poiesis is intertwined with heterosexual poiesis from the very beginning. No amount of bowdlerization can expunge every last trace. Although John Addington Symonds, one of the pioneers in the study of homosexuality, maintains that there is no trace of pederasty in the Homeric poems (1), he goes on to say that "the love of Achilles for Patroclus added, in a later age of Greek history, an almost religious sanction to the martial form of paiderastia" (2). Unerasable, incontrovertible, and undeniable are the homoerotic elements in the story of Achilles and Patroclus in the *Iliad* and the birth of modern philosophy with Socrates in the golden age of Athens. To read Western philosophy and literature is to know that their primal scenes include a homosexual component.

On the level of poetics, male homosexuality and heterosexuality are not opposites but interwoven phenomena. It is far easier to oppose women to men or men to women, even as, as Thomas Laqueur has shown, the two appear throughout centuries, to come from one indeterminate pretext. The phenomena are of opposition even if the genealogy is the same. And we should remember that, even as far as behavior is concerned, it is only in the nineteenth century that the "homosexual" was invented as an individual in the West. Before that, there was a series of names for acts that were either accepted, ignored, or punished depending on times and mores, but there was no "homosexual" behind the acts. On the other hand, men were men and women were women.

No complete disimplication of homosexual and heterosexual poiesis can ever occur. If most discrete sexual acts of two individuals in the real world can be labeled as coming under one or the other of the two broad categories, poiesis seems to maintain a necessary ambiguity. Poiesis is not indiscreet, as much as it is indiscrete. While Freud was at great pains to answer the question "Was will das Weib?," it was far less difficult for him to see the organic relation between homosexual and heterosexual behavior, or to presume to understand the homosexual mind, as in his study of Leonardo da Vinci. His reading may be aberrant, but he presumes it can be done. He may have shocked his contemporary readers, but he said something far more understandable in the world of men than any posited description of woman's desire, with the exception of the phallocentric descriptions of women's hysteria. These, of course, were totally believable to his largely male, heterosexual community precisely because of their inherent phallocentrism, which reconfirmed the ideological bias of the readers. As for the well-adjusted woman, however, who knows what she wants? Yet everyone knows what a homosexual wants! At the popular level, in the 1990's, we could translate this into the discourse of an imaginary army recruit who doesn't understand women, can't for the life of him figure out what his girlfriend wants from him, but who, in the same breath, is convinced that fags would be staring at him in the showers if such men were let in the army.

The third distinction has to do with what I have called the semiotics, or the phenomenon, of invisibility. The minority status of the homosexual individual is not as immediately apparent as the status of an African-American or a woman, as defined against the dominant white male heterosexual culture. The measure is important, for within each very broadly defined category, there is a comparable internal semiotics of visibility and invisibility. As Adrienne Rich points out:

> White feminists and lesbians are not, on the whole, immediately identifiable: they have to be pointed out. Women of color are, on the whole, identifiable; but they aren't supposed to be here anyway, so their presence, and whatever we have in common as women, must be erased from the record. (78)

Before the now-famous invention of the "homosexual" in the mid-nineteenth century, this invisibility was even more the case. If it is only the act that defines the individual as homosexual, and the act is carried out in secrecy or privacy, then there is no definite feature that can make someone definitively and overtly a dreaded sodomite. It is only the egregiously obsessional repetition of Gilles de Rais or the nakedness of Astolphe de Custine that brand them for ever and ever as sodomites. And even after the individual appears to be an individual, there is never any sign that definitely makes him homosexual in the eyes of all. Even Oscar Wilde was accused by the Marquess of Queensbury as "posing as a sondomite" [sic]; the most flagrant violation, I suppose, had to be misspelled for the ironies of posterity. One may make assumptions, but the proof, short of catching someone *in flagrante delicto*, is never perfect. So, too, the argument is even stronger where homosexual poiesis is concerned: if we now read a strong homosexual component in Thomas Mann's *Death in Venice* or André Gide's *The Immoralist*, the first readers did not do the same, as they preferred in one case and the other to see some indefinable *Sehnsucht* or *mal de siècle* in the characters of Aschenbach and Michel.

There seems to be a contradiction at hand. I have noted that the continuity in homosexual poiesis is visible, known, and recognized as such. On the other hand, homosexuality can maintain a certain invisibility, as can homosexual poiesis. How can this be? First of all, it is not necessary to draw a direct line between the homosexual and homosexual poiesis: no one forces us to recognize simultaneously Walt Whitman and his poetry as homosexual: this is called rationalization. In other cases, the line is not as simply remarked or denied: consider, for example, Freud's reading of da Vinci. Far more important is the fact that homosexual poiesis plays on this alternation between visibility and invisibility and makes it a prime figure of the poetics. Homosexual poiesis depends on the ludic nature of this figure.

The image of the closet has as its attendant metaphors figures of closure, darkness, and impenetrable secrets. To open the closet door is to let in the light of the truth. With the figure of visibility and invisibility, the heliotropic movement is neither central nor eclipsed, but part of a double trope that plays in light and in shadows, that moves both toward the light and toward the dark. Homosexual poiesis is not marginal as much as it is eccentric: not repressed, not pushed off to the sides, it is there at the heart of things, sometimes seen, sometimes not, sometimes recognized, sometimes not. And its entry into the game recasts the disposition of the playing pieces or the figures: Alcibiades at the door is not retained as a marginal figure but forces the people in the room to recognize his eccentric presence. He is not merely the decorative figure of an arabesque at the margins but a decentering and revivifying figure who inverts center and edge as he bends the lines of sight.

It is not by chance that one of the older slang words used to describe a homosexual man was the word "bent," and that one of the words from the same era has recently been revived as an empowering term: "queer." Those two words, and especially the latter one, are more accurately the otherness of "straight" than is the word "gay." Because, as I write, "queer" sets up more red flags than I think necessary for a discussion of a group of rather mainstream authors, I have used the word "gay" to refer to phenomena of modern homosexuality, and will continue to do so in this book. Yet the poetic dimension of the revived word "queer" adds immeasurably to what is at stake in our understanding. A queer or bent line is one that is not orthogonal, not straight: it does not go directly to its target, or perhaps it finds a target other than the one designed for it. A queer line may, however, tell the right story even in being off the mark, off-center, or offhand in its observations. And, for purposes of equanimity, a straight line can be defined relative to a queer one just as easily as the reverse.

Two visual examples will help clarify a different kind of *apposition* (not opposition) of two terms. Again, for our purposes, the examples are to be considered allegorical; by no means am I implying that either Fred Astaire or Ernie Kovacs was gay. To take examples from gay literature might queer the approach a priori, so I have sought allegorical examples in the straight world. One of the examples is from the movie *The Royal Wedding*; the other, perhaps even more telling, is from Ernie Kovacs's television show from the late 1950's and early 1960's. The famous example of *The Royal Wedding* has Fred Astaire dancing all around the room—literally, around the room: on the floor, of course, but also on the walls and on the ceiling. Everything looks "right" but nothing is right. The dance sequence was shot in a trick set put in a drum that turned as Astaire danced, so that his feet were always on the ground, though that ground at times was the walls or ceiling. At the end of the dance, everything is right again and his feet and gravity are back where they belong. It is a model for the fifties that makes sure, whatever the momentary lapses, that everything is right as rain in the end.

More jarring is a famous scene from Ernie Kovacs's television show. The set consists merely of a man seated at a table. And the man does very simple things, like pouring milk or rolling objects along a flat surface. Nothing seems to work right and the milk we see being poured never gets to the glass at which it is aimed. The trick is simple, as is the truth: the whole set is built at a 15-degree angle and the camera is set parallel to the angled set. So nothing looks "wrong" yet everything goes "queer." As I remember it, Kovacs keeps up the trick until the end of the sketch, and no one comes in to right the image at the end. Kovacs's shows were filled with a host of such images that stayed queer, but after his early, untimely death, television quickly abandoned that format and possibility and straightened things out.

For me, the Kovacs scene is a modern version of Alcibiades at the door: the trick is the truth. The truth is no longer straight but bent, curved, or queer. Moreover, there is no recuperation. Tied in with this queer figure is the notion of *dépense*: the excess in an economy that is never wholly recuperative, the overflow that is more jouissance than recuperable seed. Like the nonreproductive yet intermittently continuous history of homosexual poiesis itself, this excess at every moment signifies the whole process of homosexual poiesis.

Homosexual poiesis participates in a model of production but not one, quite literally, of reproduction: that one needs straight lines and heliotropic movement, and cannot admit any version of the spilled seed of Onan.

There are examples of homosexual poiesis that do not mime heterosexual poiesis. Certainly numerous examples exist among a contemporary post-closet generation of writers in the United States. This is less often the case in France, where the notion of *dépense* has continued to operate and has kept much homosexual poiesis far from the straight and narrow. Throughout the twentieth century, the figures of homosexuality in French literature have stretched the openness of the situation, have reinforced the joy of Alcibiades at the door, and have tended to refuse the categorization foisted upon writers of the Anglo-American tradition. Of course it helps that the single most important French novelist of the first part of the century was Marcel Proust and that André Gide discussed the subject of homosexuality in various parts of his writing over the years, including his plea for a normalization of homosexuality, *Corydon*. It helps, too, that distinct from the Anglo-American tradition, France decriminalized sodomy close to two centuries ago, whereas England kept such laws on the books until 1967, and in 1995, half the states in the United States still have such laws.

Thus, to summarize the story so far, I am making two distinctions. The first is within the history and developing institutional validation of studies in the humanities, other than those of white male heterosexuals. Though sharing some aspects of other nondominant cultural praxes, homosexual poiesis has a singular position in that it has been recognized as necessarily interwoven in the most intimate fashion with the dominant culture for a long time. Hence the model of oppositional repression that may be useful in explaining the status of women's writing or African-American cultural systems does not apply for homosexual poiesis. Second, from a crosscultural perspective, there is a difference between the functions and forms of homosexual poiesis in Anglo-American culture and those appearing in French culture. No matter how strong the social repression of homosexuality in France, the absence of criminal status influenced French versions of homosexual poiesis and produced a comparably freer field of examples.

In starting with the image of Alcibiades at the door, I want to underline the apparent joy and mirth of the character. Still, there is another aspect to the figure. Remember that before the door is opened, the speakers are not at all sure whom they will find outside. And so Alcibiades, even in his joyful dance, continues to occupy a liminal position until the others are sure of who he is. At that point he reorients the dynamics and dances his way into a newly energized situation. It remains nonetheless true that Alcibiades is the mediator par excellence between inside and outside. Were the mixing of the metaphor not so apparent on a sexual level, a deconstructer would make Alcibiades the hymen, the *paroi* between inside and outside. And again, the difference from the heterosexual model is obvious: whereas the hymen is almost nothing in itself, its act of division is everything. Here, with Alcibiades, the separate worlds are themselves far less exciting in the poetics than the figure itself dancing between the two worlds.

And so the focus of this book will be on the sinuous, queer line limned by a figure dancing between the worlds of inside and outside. In each of the chapters I shall focus on the figures that occur between inside and outside in a series of homosexual literary works. And I shall concentrate on difference, on distinctions, on appositions, on irreducibilities. Is it pessimistic to say that homosexuality will never be the same in anyone's eyes as heterosexuality? I do not think so at all. For the sameness posited in a politically correct world may in fact be a denial of a rich and complicated history that cannot forget a past filled with margins, repression, exile, and death. No matter how equal homosexual and heterosexual individuals become in the eyes of the law and in the eyes of society, an equality to be sought and fought for, I, for one, would be disappointed to find *all* differences erased. The world might be a bit calmer, and then again, it might not. Yet, it is even more certain that poiesis, both heterosexual and homosexual, as well as everything in between those two artificially defined poles, would suffer by the institutionalization of in-difference and indifference.

Heterosexual Surrealism
and the Problem of René Crevel

> If there were free exchange, perhaps values would
> finally be established justly.
>
> René Crevel, *Mon corps et moi* (148)

> Queneau: I want to know what Aragon thinks of ped-
> erasty.
> Aragon: I shall answer later.
>
> José Pierre, *Recherches sur la sexualité*

I. The Homosexual Surrealist as Prisoner

Often forgotten today except by a small group of experts interested
in Surrealism, René Crevel participated in both the later part of the
Dadaist movement in 1922–24 and the Surrealist movement thereafter until his death by suicide in 1935 at the age of 35. Crevel was
also openly homosexual and romantically involved for a time with
Eugene MacCown, an American painter living in Paris. Crevel's
most well-known books are *Etes-vous fous?*, which has continued to
have some popularity, *La Mort difficile*, which is partly the fictionalized version of his relationship with MacCown, who is given the
pseudonym of Arthur Bruggle, and *Mon corps et moi*, an intriguing
work sporadically engaging problematics of homosexuality. Crevel
begs for rereading and reconsideration for one cardinal reason, if for
no other: the problematic engendered by the difficulty—for him, for
us, for the Surrealists—in negotiating his open homosexuality in
conjunction with the virulently antihomosexual position espoused by
André Breton as *chef de file* of the Surrealist movement.

Extremely compelling both in Crevel's writing per se and in his
image as part of the Surrealist group is the way in which he seems to
be the site of the contradictions contained in the Surrealist problem
of and with homosexuality. This problem can be stated bluntly: given

the extensive, militant, and continuous cries for liberation that are part and parcel of the Surrealist enterprise, how can Surrealism have been so faithful to a rigid heterosexual model and so critical of homosexuality? In *Saint Genet* (196), Sartre unambiguously criticizes the Surrealists for their continued condemnation of homosexuality as late as the forties and early fifties, when they criticized Genet. For Sartre, the problem in their position is obvious. They continually exempt heterosexuality from their "enterprise of demolition," an exemption that does not make sense within the rhetoric of liberation with which Surrealism girded itself because it perpetuates a model of bourgeois society based on fixed sexual and gender roles.

At the same time, while the Surrealists in general omit heterosexuality from their "enterprise of demolition," they make one overt exception to the blanket condemnation of homosexuality, and that exception is René Crevel. Homosexuality may be damnable to them, but the openly homosexual Crevel is still considered part of the group. Aside from this acceptance of Crevel as an individual, a member of the group, and a writer, André Breton allows three historical exceptions to his general execration of homosexuality: Sade, Rimbaud, and Jean Lorrain, each of whom is a Surrealist hero to him. Still, it may be easier for Breton, nostalgically romanticizing the excesses of each of the three, to rationalize the presence of homosexuality in their writings or even in their lives than it is to deal with the current, actual presence of homosexuality. So in the contemporaneous figurations of homosexuality and Surrealism, the unique exception to Breton's imprecations, on the level of the individual exercising his or her freedom, is René Crevel. If there is but one contemporaneous exception, the aftermath of Surrealism's relation to homosexuality is far more suggestive. Raymond Queneau will flirt with homosexuality in his writing: think of the gender-bending in *Zazie dans le métro*, as one work among many. And Louis Aragon will eventually be seen as having had a whole underground homosexual life. For all that belated revelation and involvement, Crevel remains the only openly homosexual Surrealist, not only living homosexuality but also writing about it.

Crevel's works are crisscrossed with questions relating to homosexuality; he is also, simultaneously, the practical reflection of what Surrealism says and does about homosexuality. Crevel's very presence in the group gives the lie to the adamant exclusion of homosexuality and homosexuals. And while Crevel's presence within the group does not seem to force Breton to rethink his opposition, Crevel's somewhat aberrant presence produces a singular context for his own writing. His work illustrates the struggle for liberation that the very announcement of homosexuality implies at this time and place, as it simultaneously reflects the internalization of the forces surrounding him that inveigh against homosexuality. Reading Crevel in context provides insight into the discursive possibilities for homosexuality, both within Surrealism from the early twenties until Crevel's death in 1935 and in its perpetuation since then. Crevel in context, Crevel and context: this is a privileged moment in our understanding of literature and gender studies, for it is a moment and a textuality that face, at every level, the dualism between inside and outside, between public and private, between fiction or received knowledge and truth. Crevel's writing is the transcription of an extended crisis of that dualism; moreover, the Surrealism that surrounds him as a context and as a means of social construction illustrates the institutionalization of the same dualism through a discourse of power that finds the dualist position effective. Yet a reading of Crevel's work will bring out the challenges to the dualist model; after Crevel, we can no longer be sure what is inside and what is outside, and what closet, if any, might be invoked to frame the matter.

The crisis of René Crevel's writing is everywhere apparent, both inside and outside the individual literary pieces. Crevel is torn between his homosexuality and Surrealism's mandatory heterosexuality. And within that split, the problem becomes even greater, for even if he has freedom, he does not know how to write as a homosexual. Consider the models he may invoke, such as Proust, Gide, and Wilde. Crevel needs to examine each of them himself, for the relation of each to a dominant bourgeois culture must give the Surrealist in him pause. Given Surrealism's extensive opposition to the structures of bourgeois society, the sexual liberation of the individual posited in turn by Wilde, Gide, and Proust fades in comparison with the participation of each of them in bourgeois society and culture. Separate and apart from any condemnation of homosexuality by Breton's group, for a Surrealist, the sexual liberation of such men, representatives of the bourgeoisie, must necessarily remain illusory.

There is an additional point for Crevel, in which he goes far beyond the Surrealist position of criticizing society's institutions to a more radical critique of society's basic structures: similar to Antonin Artaud, who will find the Surrealist revolution a maintenance of the narcissistic subject, as I have shown elsewhere, Crevel finds the critique others offer to be limited because it maintains memory as a heterosexual institution. Not until the very processes of memory are challenged will Crevel's concept of liberation be actualized.

Crevel must also negotiate the transparent fiction of his existence as a public writer: he must write as if there were an absolute split between the subject of action, who is the homosexual character, and the subject of enunciation, decreed by the reading public and the Surrealists alike necessarily to be a heterosexual subject. Because of that difference between expectation and actuality and because of that nonnegotiable split in the subject, Crevel's writing is alienated from itself, from its author, and from its readers. An examination of the discursive quarantine on the question of Surrealism and homosexuality will break the several *cordons sanitaires* around Crevel's work: first, the framing of his work by general Surrealist discourse and subsequently by a literary history that binds him to a generic version of that discourse, and second, the *garde-fou* already in Crevel's own writing to preserve textual sanity.

Almost immediately after René Crevel's death by suicide in June 1935 a certain consecrated reading of Crevel appears. It is structured around Crevel as a vaguely tragic figure, the scapegoat of society, the victim of an unhealthy environment at home and, one presumes, in the workplace known as Surrealism. What I find most interesting here is that this reading of Crevel, which essentially amounts to an interweaving of life and art, and which discovers nothing more than a set of predictable obsessive themes in his work, depends on a stable constellation of pretexts. This word should be taken literally: the pretexts are those "events," "figures," and "meanings" in the life of an author seen retrospectively to have been the raisons d'être of his writing. As Crevel himself puts it in *Mon corps et moi*, there are "pretexts of other bodies, other thoughts" (74). As soon as Crevel is dead, these pretexts are seen as stable and unvarying, and their haunting alterity, now solidified, is supposed to have produced the complexes in the writer and in his art that generate the constant themes of his works.

In Crevel's case, the pretexts are the thumbnail psychological pro-
file of an author with a hateful mother, a father dead by his own
hand, and an obsession with suicide—quite a good formula for producing an unhappy homosexual. With those pretexts, one might re-
assuringly produce a straightforward thematic reading of Crevel's
main works. François Buot's biographical study of Crevel starts with
a chapter entitled "The Fatality of Suicide" (15), and goes on, in
quick succession, to discuss that suicide, the suicide of Crevel's father,
the figure of the mother, each of these discussions moving smoothly
between life and correspondence, life and literary works. Obviously
one could ask how a stable configuration is translated so neatly into
a textual one: for example, does the appearance of suicide in the family of an author necessarily translate as suicide when it comes to con-
structing a text? Freud, for one, would say no: that if there were in
fact such a weighty obsession, if it were truly profound, more likely
than not it would appear masked, displaced, or translated in a literary work, as in a dream.

Let us put that aside, because it appears to me that there is a far
more pressing problem in these readings of Crevel. In a general
sense, what I find difficult to deal with in such a translation of life
and art is the convenient way in which homosexuality is packaged as
a by-product of the family romance, a phrase that becomes the title
of the first chapter of Michel Carassou's full-length study. Again, the
argument is that Crevel's homosexuality is the product of a dominant
mother and an absent father. So be it. Still, we must ask how that homosexuality or, better yet, how homosexuality in general is reflected
in his writing. To force Crevel's textual homosexuality into the figure
of the family novel is to do him a disservice by framing it with the
understanding offered by heterosexual dominance. And beyond that,
why must Crevel's homosexuality be necessarily an aberration, the
product of an unhealthy, dysfunctional environment? Is there something noxious in homosexuality itself, something poisonous that
comes from an unhappy inheritance? Or is it rather that the space allotted to that homosexuality, itself as innocent (or not) as heterosexuality, is perhaps itself a space of dysfunction?

Crevel's dysfunctional family, unhappy life, and martyrdom, all
viewed as being transparently reflected in his writing, do serve a purpose. It has been useful, I think, for some critics to maintain Crevel

in the position of "society's suicide," as Artaud called Van Gogh, for three reasons. First of all, the figure of the writer obsessed with suicide and whose ultimate act of writing is an act of suicide is a long-cherished romantic notion. In a world without heroes, it can be useful to see someone as the Werther or the Chatterton of his generation. By seeing Crevel as a latter-day Chatterton, we can exclude the very modernity that disquietingly churns at the heart of Surrealism. In Crevel's case, we might conclude, Surrealism's clashing modernity is really a mask for Romantic longing, the nostalgia that befits the homosexual seeking an unattainable ideal. Second, the Freudianism with which Surrealism was often a strange bedfellow seems on the surface to provide a convincing, albeit pop, psychological analysis. Renée Linkhorn's comments (80–81) are a case in point: "Certain events of his childhood created complexes in the young Crevel which were to mark him forever." That, of course, could be said about anyone. She goes on to discuss the "Orestes complex," Crevel's own term in "Le Clavecin de Diderot" (*ECR* 223–26). The Orestes complex, a "reversal of the Oedipus complex," is a "factor that may have had its influence on the sexual orientation of the young man." Third, the picture is completed with the story of Crevel's traumatic circumcision at the age of three: it is offered up in the third paragraph of Carassou's study (24–25). One wonders whether Crevel's Oedipally timed circumcision is meant to explain his writing. Is this foreskin brandished as a sign of lack for the world of heterosexual readers? Also, maintaining these pretexts precludes engaging the question of homosexuality on its own merits. The pretexts preserve the standard mythology of the unhappy homosexual: unable to negotiate a fulfilling life in this world, he dramatically kills himself as a challenge to society as a whole and as a tacit admission of the not unmerited victory of society and its structures. These pretexts maintain homosexuality as an aberration, a dysfunction, a misreading of life's correct paths; they continue to foster what we would currently call heterosexism. But most important, these pretexts prevent a reading of Crevel that tries to engage the figures of homosexuality itself on its own terms.

Much of the received criticism of Crevel, which has been extensively documented by Myrna Bell Rochester (131–73), focuses on the obsession with suicide, as it provides a neat psychoanalytical framing of his homosexuality as "something" whose borders are defined by a dominant heterosexuality. Fabienne Cabelguenne (102) puts Crevel's supposed raison d'être as an adult and as an author quite pithily:

A permanent confrontation with death can be read throughout the works, an image of Crevel's obsession, marked as he was at fourteen by his father's suicide. This event would have [*aura*] such a deep influence on him as to become the center of his life and the center of his work.[1]

But can a work in fact have a center and could that center be something outside the literary work, like the suicide of another? One need not have recourse to an orthodox deconstructive model, such as that posited in Derrida's critique of structuralism in "Structure, Sign, and Play in the Human Sciences" (*Ecriture* 409-28), to put the notion of a textual center into question. Seeing a center means deproblematizing writing, taking away writing's effect and difference, reducing writing to some shorthand that merely transcribes a previously existing structure, be it the suicide of a father or the subject's own homosexuality. If this is true as a general statement, it is a fortiori true for a writer such as Crevel, whose Dadaist and Surrealist iconoclasm admits no possibility of a center. Still, I do not want to fall into the trap of intentionality by taking Crevel's writing as a function of his own iconoclastic beliefs. We should at least try to determine where Crevel might be in order to know what the center might look like if we ever were to find it. Contextually, then, I would like to examine some aspects of a greater socially constructed textuality in which the possibilities for Crevel's acts of enunciation may be found.

In an era known as a period of "gay" liberation both in Paris and Berlin, in an era marked in London by a game of bisexual musical chairs in Bloomsbury, French Surrealism remained steadfastly negative about homosexuality. At first glance, one would have expected the Surrealists' attitude toward homosexuality to be far different

---

1. Using not so much the language of psychoanalysis but Crevel's own anti-Bergsonian expression, Louis Morin writes of Crevel's "*élan mortel*" (959; quoting *MCM* 95). At the end of this article, one reads the following: "Editor's note: Two days after having brought us the preceding article, Louis Morin killed himself; he was 28. A professor for several years in the United States, he had worked on a thesis on René Crevel" (961). Thus is the drama visited on Crevel by the insistence of the family novel extended to Crevel's critics as well.

from the antipathy recorded by literary history, a hatred and prejudice fueled in large part by André Breton's rabid opinions on the subject. As the apostles of the liberation of the unconscious, the Surrealists might have been expected not only to understand the differences of sexual identity or preference, but also to be militant apostles for a liberation of the individual from the constraints that bourgeois morality visited on that sexual identity. Even in adopting a Freudian position, they might already have questioned the construction of the bourgeois subject (in the family romance, for example) as a distinct, determined individual; they might also have adopted Freud's position of tolerance and understanding. Yet what occurred is far different.

Led by Breton, the Surrealist movement was virulently antihomosexual, despite its admiration for certain figures like Rimbaud and Sade, despite the presence within its group of one openly homosexual individual, René Crevel, and despite the presence of others, like Louis Aragon, whose strict heterosexuality was already in question in the twenties. Even more puzzling than the position of the Surrealists on the subject is the way in which literary history seems blithely to have accepted the enunciation of that position. There is something jarring in that received knowledge: the simple fact that after all the studies of Surrealism and Surrealists, and in spite of the challenges posed to our understanding of the question by the work of and about such related figures as Georges Bataille, Artaud, and the young Jacques Lacan, the same three stories are repeated over and over in a litany. One story concerns a polemical position, one concerns an insult, and one concerns a homosexual.

If I take time with these three stories it is to show how Crevel has become imprisoned in the web of repeated stories and to sketch out the need for a new examination of the question of homosexuality in Surrealism. The first story, concerning the polemical position of the Surrealists against homosexuality, is found in every detailed history of Surrealism. In "Recherches sur la sexualité," published in 1928 in *La Révolution surréaliste*, Breton rails against homosexuality; he is vehemently opposed to *any* acceptance of homosexuality: "I accuse pederasts of proposing for human tolerance a mental and moral defect that tends toward its own institutionalization and that paralyzes every undertaking I respect" (*Rech* 39). Pederasts are the most depraved beings that Breton can imagine, insidious by nature and in their unholy intentions. In fact, Breton is even outraged that the subject comes up; such matters are so revolting that they should remain taboo. He introduces a vocabulary tinged with the ethics of church and state: the terms "moral defect" and "respect" seem hardly compatible with the Surrealist revolution, and even with the symposium on sexuality of which his outrage is a part. Breton does not believe in discussing male homosexuality and is prepared to call the whole discussion of sexuality off if the members of the group continue to engage in a discussion of that most vile subject. Breton generously and briefly makes two exceptions: the Marquis de Sade and Jean Lorrain. In the first case, as Breton points out, Sade is a man for whom everything is permitted "by definition" (40); in the second, Jean Lorrain is an exception because he had true conviction. The third individual exempt from Breton's imprecations is Rimbaud, who does not appear in this discussion but is deemed a Surrealist "in the practice of life and elsewhere" in the *First Surrealist Manifesto* (329). Why Crevel or Aragon or Breton himself could not also be individuals for whom everything is permitted "by definition" is not clear.

Given the liberation of the self that is one of the basic foundations of Breton's discourse and the "absolute *non-conformism*" on which the *First Surrealist Manifesto* closes (346), one is forced to conclude that homosexuality is as much of a danger for Breton as the bourgeois society itself against which he is railing. For Breton, the danger of pederasts seems to be the threat they pose to Surrealism itself. Though each individual action is absolutely nonconformist, the banality of the action of homosexual activity makes these individual actions all too conformist to one another. Perhaps homosexuality is too much like heterosexuality, with enough of a difference to force the necessary but impossible reexamination of the categories of sexual preference. There is, one suspects, something singularly underhanded about the seduction of homosexuality in Breton's eyes. The danger of homosexuality is that it may mimetically infect another individual and thereby introduce a representation that prevents the liberation of the psyche and the necessary absolute nonconformism. Like the image of an insidious vampire miming human existence, pederasty puts liberation at risk because it is all too close to the heterosexual institutions of which it seems merely to be a copy with a twist.

Absent from the discussion in name as well as in body is René Crevel, who would seem to be one of the damned. His presence might have considerably altered the discussion but in his absence the forces for and against pederasty are lined up quite clearly. In Breton's camp are Benjamin Péret, who voices "protestations," the exact content of which remains unrecorded, and Pierre Unik, who seems to go even further than Breton in his disgust at the thought of two males copulating: "pederasty disgusts me as much as excrement" (39). While Yves Tanguy is more or less indifferent, Raymond Queneau, Jacques Prévert, and Man Ray, among others, disagree with Breton, as many, including Carassou, in "Mère . . . putain" (23–26), and Xavière Gauthier (230–40) amply document. Not only does Queneau have no moral objection, but he also says pointedly that "there is a singular prejudice among the Surrealists against pederasty" (39). Louis Aragon, whose comments might also have tempered Breton's outrage and Unik's disgust, is absent for the first round table, but is there for the second one four days later: "Pederasty seems to me a sexual practice just like other sexual practices" (67). A dry remark at best; Aragon finds pederasty to be singularly unremarkable. This second discussion brings out a new aspect: rather than restricting the condemnation to moral grounds, several of the discussants, including Georges Duhamel, condemn the effeminacy and extravagant gestures of pederasts. Jacques-A. Boiffard insists on a nuance and notes that not all pederasts are that mannered: for him, in fact, there are women whose gestures are "more ridiculous and annoying" than those of pederasts (67). Thus antihomosexual rhetoric is outflanked by misogyny.

Finally, despite Aragon's presence, Breton can take no more of this outrageous discussion. He threatens to end the debate if the topic does not change from the one he finds so odious to a more acceptable subject of inquiry. With a single statement, Breton becomes an extravagant dictator: "I am absolutely opposed to the discussion continuing on this subject. If [the discussion] starts touting pederasty [*la réclame pédérastique*], I shall immediately abandon it. . . . I want to be an obscurantist in such an area" (68). One should not think, for all that, that Breton is a prude; not for a moment should we think him closed-minded on the matter of "perversion." He is quite glad to support every sexual perversion other than the one "that we have just spoken of for too long" (68). Even naming it, Breton seems to fear, may cause mimetic infection.

History has let Breton's view dominate and has neglected the weight of the opposition; the received knowledge of literary history is that Surrealism was opposed to male homosexuality. In their study of homosexuality in Paris in the twenties, Gilles Barbedette and Michel Carassou repeat the same story: "When several, Queneau, Prévert, Man Ray, and especially Aragon, expressed a more tolerant position and refused to make a moral judgment, Breton wanted to end the session" (Barbedette and Carassou 129). Aside from the facts that the authors seem to have condensed the two sessions into one and that the word "especially" does not seem to apply to what Aragon says any more than to what anyone else says, we need to delve further into the contradictions between discourse and practice in the Surrealist group.

Though literary history seems to mark Crevel as *the* example of *the* homosexual Surrealist, there are at least two challenges to this position. As the years have gone by, the apparently monolithic heterosexuality and heterocracy of the Surrealists have been shaken. Gauthier (230–32) notices this reflected in certain Surrealist figures of the period, such as Aragon and Queneau. And while Daniel Guérin goes over the familiar territory of Crevel being the only open homosexual in the group, he fans the flames, so to speak, with a new rumor. As Guérin writes, "André Breton's first wife told me that Breton was a latent, repressed homosexual. . . . He had a sort of physical horror for the practice of homosexuality" (quoted in Barbedette and Carassou, 53). Although an accusation of latent homosexuality may be suspect from an ex-spouse, it is as plausible an explanation as any offered heretofore for Breton's strident opposition to homosexuality.

Finally, along the lines of these biographical remarks, one should remember that during the first night of the discussion "Recherches sur la sexualité," a number of the authors list their favorite sexual positions. Queneau, Breton, and Péret all give a list of three positions. In each case, there is some variant of heterosexual intercourse ("en levrette," "la femme assise de face," "à la paresseuse"); the other two favorite positions are not some other variants of heterosexual genital intercourse, but sodomy (anal intercourse) and "69" (mutual oral sex), which Breton (436) will qualify elsewhere as his favorite sexual position. Is it an accident that these positions are often more closely associated with homosexuality than with heterosexuality?

A rumor about Breton's latent homosexuality is problematic because of the psychoanalytical bent of its language: Breton has to have been a latent homosexual because it is in a way a requirement for belief in the version of psychoanalysis of the era. So, whereas that latency certainly helps explain the violent reaction of Breton to a discussion of homosexuality, it does not wholly explain it. Reducing Breton's acute response to the discussion of homosexuality to a manifestation of his own latent homosexuality—that is, homophobia, heterocracy, and the like—is tantamount to reducing Crevel's figures of homosexuality in his own work to an Oedipal or Orestean triangle. More interesting by far than such reductive schemes is the structuring of gender and sex in Breton's writing from the same period. This does not fall into the rigid dichotomy that one might have predicted from his remarks in the discussion group.

A reading of Breton's *dispositif* of the sexes could be extremely fruitful for understanding his attitude. Briefly put, and surely astonishing to some, Breton seems to accept the tacit possibility of bisexuality, *even in himself.* In *Poisson soluble* (1924), Breton revives a catachresis as he moves from the eye color hazel [*noisette*] to hazelnut flowers [*fleurs de noisetier*]. He explains that his eyes are hazelnut flowers, "the right eye, the male flower, the left, the female" (381). Of course, birch trees, of which the hazel is a species, are monoecious, that is to say, hermaphroditic: each plant has both pistils and stamens. Reviving the metaphor means accepting that bisexuality as both a ground for the metaphor and a consequence of it. For those not versed in botany, a more obvious sexual ambiguity is found earlier in the same book:

The two men were then walking in the park, and smoking long cigars that, while partially consumed, still measured one meter ten and one meter thirty-five respectively. Explain that if you can when I tell you that he had lit them at the same time [*ils les avaient allumés en même temps*]. The younger, whose ash was a blonde woman he saw clearly when he lowered his eyes, and who produced an unheard-of exaltation, gave his arm to the second, whose ash, a brown-haired woman, had already fallen. (371)

Phallic symbols stuck out in front, the two men get excited [*allumés*] at the same time. Linked arm in arm, the two men get off together, and though their phalluses produce women as a supplement, as an afterthought, and as a by-product of pleasure, they go off homoerotically arm in arm. In no other spot in Breton's writing of this period is the woman seen so blatantly as a tangential object when compared to a homoerotic couple. Yet in one other short passage, Breton even manages to do without the woman entirely: "in the museum of the home-town of all poets, the ancient statues are made of sugar candy. But the poets do not have fun sucking the phalluses of sugar candy" (447). Not amused, perhaps; disdainful, perhaps; homoerotic nonetheless.

As suggestive as they are, these examples are few and far between in the corpus; I would venture to say that the element of homoeroticism subsequently disappears or is successfully repressed in most of Breton's work in favor of Breton's capacious image of the "woman" who in fact occupies the same locus as that of the homoerotic sign in the constellation of signifiers and meanings. The early references to homoeroticism are replaced, as it were, by a translation into an acceptable vocabulary of heterosexual desire as Breton creates the image of the Surrealist woman, the object of desire that is herself never self-reflective and that reflects only male, phallic, heterosexual desire. For Breton, the woman is both an immediacy of presence and the eternal deferral of death and the meaning of the sign in a heterosexual and phallocentric universe. Breton's vision of the woman's desire is, crudely put, that she wants to be fucked; her desire is not hers, but a reflection of, or a complement to, the desire of the man. And thus her desire, the desire of the other, does not need representation as a vehicle for its free expression. Meaningless in herself except as the reflection of the liberation of desire for the heterosexual man, the woman also conveniently ensures the perpetuation of the parts of the system that Breton does not wish to challenge. Hence we can understand a criticism of the Surrealist revolution by someone like Artaud, who says that he is not "masculine affirmative" but "neuter expulsive" (15:195), and who cannot possibly accept the continued materialist repetitive definition of the sexes that Surrealism seems tacitly to accept.

On the other hand, in Breton's definitions of sexual identity and the Surrealist enterprise, the homosexual is dangerous because he enters into a game of mimetic behavior and heterogeneous representation. The homosexual implies that there is a desire at the locus of the other, separate and apart from the reflection of the liberty of the desiring Surrealist subject: two desires, possibly opposed to one another, possibly not, do not produce liberation but constraint. Like the Surrealist woman, the homosexual may in fact just want to be fucked, but that desire is not dependent on the Surrealist act of liberation of the self; that desire is independent. And perhaps the other wants to commit active sodomy, which would bring him into conflict with the desiring subject who acts out his liberation through active sex. Finally, homosexual behavior brings the Surrealist enterprise into question for Breton because it constantly intimates that desire is a product of representation as opposed to being just a liberation of the struggling unconscious.

Homosexual desire poses a threat to the Surrealist enterprise because it requires representation to be expressed. In a mirror game, the Surrealist can point to the transcendent immediacy of the woman's desire as the proof of the man's liberation of his own unconscious; his need to represent his desire seems to disappear when she is magically there. It is not so with homosexual men: the homosexual man must make his desire manifest, and there is no figure that glosses over this act of representation. Oddly enough, then, given the Surrealist understanding of sex and sexuality, the homosexual is a prisoner of the models of representation that his egregious behavior, shriekingly decried by Breton, would lead us to believe he has forgotten. It is perhaps better to remove the homosexual from the playing field, for he constantly reminds us to what extent desire needs representation as its vehicle.

How can the unconscious be truly freed if it is subject to the imposition of representation? It is not the least of Surrealist ironies that it was Crevel himself, as Breton generously notes (276), who introduced spirit writing to the Surrealist group, a writing whose virtue is its immediacy and openness to a greater unconscious. Even in that irony lies another: these Surrealist anecdotes, like those of Bloomsbury and of any other literary circle in which art and desire are both ambiguously given (in the Maussian sense) or exchanged (in the Lévi-Straussian sense), often are the differential vehicles for the revelation of what is at stake. In this first attempt at the generalized Surrealist practice of spirit writing, we find that another name is exchanged. In Breton's interrogation of Crevel during the latter's first trance, Crevel writes one name: Nazimova, a well-known lesbian actress and director (and reputedly the lover of Rudolph Valentino's wife, Natasha Rambova), who in 1923 produced a version of Oscar Wilde's *Salome*, supposedly with an all-gay cast. Deep within the telling of the tale lie layer upon layer of (homosexual) representation: How could this liberate desire?

Paths cross, and the intertwining of Breton and Nazimova in an odd story about the discovery of spirit writing brings us, in an awkward segue, to the second story, which deals with the encounter between Breton and another Soviet citizen, Ilya Ehrenburg. Again, it is significant to the extent that literary history has made it a story to be passed down as part of the orthodoxy about the sexualities of Surrealism. Ehrenburg called Surrealism a pederastic enterprise (as Claudel had already done). He was in Paris in 1935. Breton ran into him on the street and slapped him for having insulted the group. The take on the story is interesting, for while one eminent critic leaves out the specific nature of the insult, others, while telling the story, ensure that the direction is political. No one seems to take the insult at face value. Anna Balakian's version of the story is purged of the homosexual content: she says that Ehrenburg "had insulted the Surrealists by treating them as loafers and suggesting that they had squandered their wives' dowries" (227n). In his biography of Crevel, Carassou (9–10) sets the story of Breton slapping Ehrenburg in the context of Ehrenburg's visit to Paris for the international congress of antifascist intellectuals. Is the specificity of Ehrenburg's remark insignificant? Is it one of those insults whose contents are less important than the sign that it is an insult? Or is it perhaps a version of the truth, as we have already indicated: the figures of homosexuality eschewed by Surrealism as anathema seem, not coincidentally, to be the threat to the Surrealist enterprise that most clearly and most blatantly puts the entire endeavor into question.

Having looked at these two episodes from literary history, we can turn to the third story, which concerns René Crevel in particular. As I have indicated, his niche in the history books is that of the only openly homosexual Surrealist. That act of inclusion, which seems to be a token gesture, helps assure the safety of the heterosexuals in the group by having homosexuality restricted to one individual. It also helps diminish the apparent virulence of Breton's terroristic antipathy toward male homosexuality: if Breton were truly as opposed to homosexuality as he seems to be, he would never allow Crevel into the circle. So while the exclusion of homosexuality makes sense for Breton's understanding of desire as a heterosexual male phenomenon and makes sense as well because of the perceived dangers that the concept of homosexual desire might provoke, the inclusion of a token homosexual helps mitigate the anger perceived in his stance. Yet these two reasons seem to cover some other, less clear-cut matters. For example, the outside world did not seem to know that Aragon's own leanings toward homosexuality were probably somewhat of an open secret in certain circles, a fact that allowed Sartre, in *L'Enfance d'un chef*, and Drieu la Rochelle, in *Gilles*, to make allusions understandable to the cognoscenti. Aragon survived the stories by maintaining a public position of heterosexuality insured by his long marriage. To take one more example, for all of Salvador Dalí's heterosexual bravado as the last of the red-hot heterosexual Surrealists, there is enough sexual ambiguity in his work and his life to fill several monographs; one need go no further than the gender-bending involved in using his wife Gala, the ex–Mrs. Eluard, as his model for Jesus. Dalí, who would be the subject of one of Crevel's late works, retreated behind a myth of self-proclaimed divinity while talking about homoerotic "ass-kissing," be it literal or figural (Bosquet 24). Elsewhere, Dalí denies having had sex with Lorca while seeming to be aware of the physiological side of such an activity, when he says that Lorca "was homosexual, as everyone knows, and madly in love with me. He tried to screw me twice. . . . I was extremely annoyed, because I wasn't homosexual, and I wasn't interested in giving in. Besides it hurts" (Bosquet 36). Dalí's famous paranoid-critical method may, after all, have been the best name for a level of homoeroticism Dalí still entertained late in life as the last living Surrealist. In fact, just to round out the circle of anecdotes, I would quote another marginal story that Andy Warhol tells. It is about Dalí and a transsexual who still had her male genitalia: "At Studio 54 later, I asked Potassa if she'd ever had sex with Dali, and she said, 'no, he just picked my cock up once and kissed it.' . . . She said when Dali kissed her cock he said, '*Magnifico!*' " (188).

One would think that this long-lived set of anecdotes would be enough to put into question the whole articulation of the Surrealist enterprise, not as it relates to sexuality in general—though this is certainly a plausible critique—but simply as it relates to homosexuality in particular. And still, we find Crevel's case patly sewn up. Labeling Crevel as the Surrealist homosexual or the homosexual Surrealist seems to be sufficient for most critics. The inscription of the epithet is resoundingly repetitive, again, as if we had nothing to learn about that situation but the very fact of its existence. Gilles Barbedette and Michel Carassou (129) note: "The only recognized homosexual, tolerated as such, was René Crevel." In his article on Crevel, Carassou says that Crevel "was the only recognized and accepted homosexual. He refused to adopt the solution of disguising himself, and condemned the hypocrisy of writers who, like Proust changing Albert into Albertine, disguise the men they desire as women" (24). In her chapter on homosexuality in Surrealism, Xavière Gauthier says much the same thing:

The only admitted and recognized homosexual in the Surrealist group was René Crevel. He never hid it and, on the contrary, complained of the hypocrisy of homosexual writers who, in their writing, transform the men they desire into women—Proust, in particular, in whose work Albert becomes Albertine. (234)

In telling their tale, critics seem content to "recognize" Crevel as a homosexual, thereby reinscribing him in a category that depends on external signs for internal proof. And then, to seal the bargain, they seem to insist on aligning Crevel with Gide and against Proust. Crevel is automatically set in the framework of homosexual writers, a move that distances him from the other Surrealists, allows the reader to pigeonhole Crevel merely because of that author's sexual preference, and fits him into the appropriate subcategory of liberated homosexual writer. Against that, I would maintain that the figure of homosexuality is problematic in Crevel's writing and that the categorization of him in the appropriate pigeonhole assigned by literary history clouds our understanding of his work. Understanding Crevel's intermittent depiction of homosexuality in a work like *Mon corps et moi* depends on seeing how the figure works in the literary work, not by marking the individual.

Still there is something to be learned, though not merely from contrasting the writing of Crevel directly with that of Gide or Proust, for the oeuvres show little in common. It would be a useful enterprise to compare on the one hand the vision of the Surrealistic act described by Breton and Aragon and the Gidean enterprise of self-liberation; it would also be useful to see the relation between a certain sexualized discourse in Proust and a similar discourse among the mainline Surrealists, far closer to Proust in their metaphors than any of them might care to acknowledge. While Crevel's oeuvre is not essentially comparable to that of either Gide or Proust, Crevel's comments on Proust and Gide, as well as those on the third member of the unholy triumvirate of homosexual writers, Oscar Wilde, are an important factor in Crevel's vision of his own writing.

Gide and Proust figure in Crevel's universe as subjects of commentary. What might be called Gide's manly homosexuality which heads toward noble Greek pederasty contrasts with Proust's taste for inversion, sham, and hypocrisy. At least, the critics seem to be saying, Crevel inveighs against that hypocritical behavior, whereby the sex of a being in the real world is changed when "he" becomes a "she" in the world of fiction. Certainly, at one level Crevel's criticism of Proust is an early version of a critique that has since become standard: Crevel disparages the game of switching sexes in which Proust indulges in *La Prisonnière* and *Albertine disparue*:

The fact that Proust, for example, made Albert into Albertine is what leads me to suspect the whole work and to deny certain discoveries presented to me along the way. . . . If we can affirm that Albertine was a boy, the identity of the other sexes [*l'identité des autres sexes*], from this very fact, no longer appears certain. (*MCM* 65)

Crevel is not so easy to pin down, for the critics seem to be confusing an aspect of literary criticism with Proust or Crevel themselves as homosexual individuals. Crevel's remark is related to the very problem of recognition that the critics seem to take for granted: if we realize from signs external to the novel that Proust has changed the characters' sexuality, we do not know what we can believe.

Crevel's position is both nuanced and ambiguous, and not the least of the problems is the plural phrase "the other sexes." How many sexes are there for Crevel? The answer is not clear, but presumably there are at least two others, and, one would assume as a minimum, there are men who are heterosexual and women who are heterosexual. So the problem is not merely one of a sex change to bow to the "rules of puerile and honest civility" (*MCM* 65); it is also one of identity. Despite the fact that Proust seems to flout convention—Crevel says that Proust "cares little for the rules of propriety" and that he is "free of conventional blocks"—Proust makes us lose confidence because he brings identity into question in an uncomfortable way. As understood by Crevel, Proust's world is one in which phrases like "men are men" and "women are women" have no currency, for among "men" one might classify Swann (a heterosexual), Charlus (a homosexual who has been married and who was a homosexual—Montesquiou—in the "real" world), and Albertine (a man—Agostinelli—in the "real" world).

Proust complicates matters far more than Crevel can allow. And though Crevel will come down on the side of frankness against such subterfuge, he does not solve the problem of this ambiguity: why keep Montesquiou/Charlus homosexual, while changing Albert to Albertine? Answers can easily be found, but none is a response to the questions of the ontological identity of the homosexual—is he a man or a woman?—and the epistemological identity of homosexual writing. Among such answers are the wealth of metaphoric and intertextual possibilities Proust can explore in a heterosexual relationship and the propriety of having a heterosexual narrator who is also the nominally heterosexual protagonist. More important, the structure of the *Recherche* depends on the narrator's mimetic repetition of Swann, and not Charlus. Moreover, the coming to knowledge of the narrator that is the central theme of the *Recherche* depends to a great extent on the readers' knowledge of "Marcel's" ignorance and subsequent enlightenment about homosexuality.

Gide, then, would seem to be a more propitious model for Crevel, someone on whom to write and whom he can emulate, for one could set Gide's frankness against Proust's ambiguity. Again, as with Proust, there is a difference between the explicit discussion of homosexuality and the implicit extension of arguments about liberty to the area of sexual preference. For Crevel certainly, as for most readers today, Gide scores a greater success in the latter category than he does in the former. Gide's apologetics for homosexuality in the contemporaneous *Corydon* are not as persuasive as the Gidean *disponibilité* and the *acte gratuit*, exemplified by Lafcadio in Gide's earlier work *Les Caves du Vatican*, which dates from 1914.[2] And Gide's version of the *acte gratuit* will be taken up verbatim—in a version that is somewhat more violent because it involves a weapon—both by Sartre in "Erostrate," one of the stories in *Le Mur*, and by Breton in the *Second Surrealist Manifesto*: "The simplest Surrealist act consists of going down to the street, revolvers in hand, and shooting haphazardly as much as possible into the crowd" (782–83).

Crevel refers specifically to Lafcadio in "L'Esprit contre la raison," as he mentions the *acte gratuit* (*ECR* 44), but it is in a later work, *Le Clavecin de Diderot* (1932), that Crevel seizes what is of fundamental importance to him in Gide's creation, Lafcadio's unbridled and ambiguous eroticism: "But Gide did not ignore how and to what extent Lafcadio's charm would make male and female readers, consciously or unconsciously swoon from love" (*ECR* 230). Significantly, Crevel refuses the Proustian sex change while accepting the Gidean version of (am)bivalent sex appeal. The difference between Albertine and Lafcadio is that Albertine can appeal only to heterosexual men and homosexual women; Lafcadio, a protean Narcissus-like autoeroticist, can appeal to everybody, men and women, gay and straight alike. Lafcadio does not force us to choose, for all we have to do is emulate his own autoerotic desire. In playing that game we allow Lafcadio to collapse into his own reflection; Lafcadio has no difference. Albert/Albertine is difference, as outside and inside contrast. The definition of this outside begins to weigh on Crevel's work in *Mon corps et moi*: it is not only the outside of textuality, such as behavior in the real, nonnovelistic world, but also the perception of an individual from the outside, that is, Crevel's being "recognized" as a homosexual. Finally, what weighs most heavily is the ultimate dualism of any individual, the very skin and sense organs that link and separate outside to and from inside for Crevel. To get at the truth,

2. The avatars of a work are not always clear-cut and the publication history of *Corydon* is a bit problematic. It was originally published in 1911, that is, before *Les Caves du Vatican*, in a small, privately circulated edition of about a dozen copies. The expanded edition was published in 1920, again privately, in an edition of about 21 copies. Finally, it was published by Gallimard in 1924, the date I am considering when I say *Corydon* is contemporaneous with Crevel's work. On Proust's "theme" of homosexuality and on *Corydon* in context, I refer the reader to my book *The Shock of Men*. See also the discussion of Gide below.

Crevel believes that one has to shed the skin forced into place by an outside world, to become, as he says admiringly of Freudianism, *"more than nude"* ("Freud" *MCM* 240).

The third figure in the triumvirate of homosexual writers belonging to a previous generation for Crevel (though Gide was still active) is Oscar Wilde. Significantly, Oscar Wilde's appearance occurs when Crevel is forsaking the establishment of his homosexual discourse, at the moment of his own textual self-castration:

> As long as third parties believe in a vice, as long as they await well-prepared spectacles, or even a shower of gestures that they pride themselves on judging as guilty and as rare as Oscar Wilde's orchids, there is respectful interest. But let suffering come revealed by no antics, inflated neither by social persecution nor prison, nor the paraphernalia of the worst aestheticism, let wordless, silently gnawing suffering come; those who had awaited curious decors, salty stories, scandalous chronicles, do not forgive passion its too simple pain. (*MD* 174)

Wilde's social persecution, his imprisonment, and his ignominy are burdens imposed from without that do not get to the heart of the matter. What they tell about is the crime of sodomy, yet what, if anything, do these really have to do with Wilde's subjective perception of his own homosexuality? And Wilde's eternal defense of aestheticism, that of the perennial poseur, is not a solution either. Wildean aestheticism focuses entirely on the surface: no outside or inside, no opposition, no contradiction, but merely the infinitely thin and infinitely supple surface that Wilde endlessly uses as a mask for no describable underlying reality. Wilde's freedom, which means his freedom to be outrageous, and his very superficiality are neither the revolutionary act or polymorphous perversity of a Lafcadio, which engages the inner and outer selves, nor the imbricated restructuring of the real world in the Proustian construct of art. Yet as foreign as he may be to Crevel's grappling with the writing of homosexuality, even Wilde will be brought back in service to the revolution in "Individu et Société": "Wilde undoubtedly went through Lafcadio's train" (*RC* 143). At this point, a sad commentary on Crevel's failure to find the solution he sought, Wilde appears as the figure of the other homosexual: the homosexual as other, summary and object of the world's opprobrium. That abject state may in fact be useful in a final revolutionary act. Though to the Crevel of 1935 Wilde seems to have been a revolutionary by the challenge he offered society, we remember nonetheless that Wilde was a victim. In the end, the ambiguity about Wilde remains: for Crevel, will Wilde have been another Lafcadio or just another hapless victim thrown off that train?

Crevel seeks a homosexual writing as free as the figure of Lafcadio himself, as free as automatic writing or the Surrealist act, as free as the *accepted* heterosexual discourses of his own Surrealist contemporaries. For Crevel, the pure *acte gratuit* is not, for all its power as an image, the defenestration of a bourgeois parasite, but something far more revolutionary from his point of view: the unveiling and parading about of an erect penis. This figure, seemingly the most conservative and heterocratic, becomes for Crevel the sign of the *acte gratuit* because the penis becomes the sign for all and any male sexuality. In seeming contradiction, this is the sign of a dephallicized sexuality of Barthesian jouissance and general excitement, whose sign is no more than a catachresis of the power system from which it is wrenched: the revolution is the parading of a penis as nothing more than an organ of pleasure, and not as an organ of power. As Crevel remarks in his 1932 piece, "Le Clavecin de Diderot," "The power [*poids*] of Lafcadio, of his charm, and of his influence is a sexual power. He is the standard weight of a measuring system whose fundamental unit is a member, his own member in the state of erection" (*ECR* 231). The homosexual position appropriates the phallus of male heterosexual domination for its own pleasure and allows the homosexual subject to function as an independent subject. No longer doubly subjected to the "Oedipal" or "Orestean" complex, that is, subject to the woman/mother who is subject in turn to the phallic father, the homosexual male in this vision of Lafcadio has a sign of pleasure completely separated from the subjection to abusive power.

As ideal an image as this Lafcadio may be, Crevel fails to find him in *Mon corps et moi*, where he struggles with the impossibility of reconciling internal visions and external forces, and in which the discussions of homosexuality are symptomatic of that struggle. Faced with that failure, Crevel takes a turn in his work. Later, Lafcadio is belatedly remembered in Crevel's last writing, "Individu et société," the speech that Crevel was supposed to give at the international anti-Fascist writers' conference in 1935; it is a speech he never gave, since he committed suicide the night before. By this time, all hope and all humor are lost. In this last work, Lafcadio is no longer playing Alcibiades disrupting the prepared discourses of the *Symposium*. In his stead, there is a rather sexless, ruthless revolutionary Lafcadio who "not only throws a bunch of the bourgeoisie out the door, but also throws down the gauntlet to this bourgeoisie, the dominant class" (*RC* 143).

In his last writings, Crevel translates the dynamics of Lafcadio's action, his sensuality, and its attendant martyrology; he turns Gide's latter-day, eroticized Saint Sebastian, the master of autoeroticism and omnisexual attraction, into a socialist—perhaps even a Stalinist—revolutionary. Unable to negotiate the lingering traces of the contradiction of being a homosexual Surrealist that dog his every action and every moment of his being, Crevel's last writing denies the possibility of an individual ever being united except in his own death. Suicide is the answer, not because he has been haunted by the suicide of his father, but because in killing himself he can finally collapse the unbridgeable distance between "mon corps" and "moi." Suicide is the solution to Zeno's paradox; the arrow finally reaches its mark, which is the body of this new, socialist, disenchanted, and Surrealist Saint Sebastian, Crevel himself.

We have begun to look at Crevel through the eyes of literary history by examining the points of received knowledge that have marked out the contours of his portrait for posterity. All of this works into the figure of Crevel as *the homosexual Surrealist*, portrayed as troubled, even fundamentally distraught, by a series of remarks that participate in the rhetoric of familial dysfunctionality, the received knowledge of psychoanalysis, and the general tenor of a literary history that blurs the line between author and work. Yet, blatantly, the fundamental despair, existential in nature, that is Crevel's theme in *Mon corps et moi* foresees the misreading, and obviously the double bind of recognizing the truth of that misreading. Crevel knows that he will always be misread, and that knowledge is a correct reading of the situation. For Crevel reading himself or having others read him, there is a process of misreading that insists on dualism, that prevents the emergence of the truth of oneself to oneself, that may even force a suicide. Yet that dualism, interchangeable sign of the ambiguity of misreading, is ineluctable: the moment of truth to oneself, the moment at which one has gone through the skin that protects and separates in order finally to unite, the singular moment of correct meaning, is the moment at which the self disappears. We have read Crevel, if we have read him at all, imprisoned in a discourse that he himself predicted as the natural consequence of his own structuring of language and desire.

II. The Confused Negation of the Homosexual Body

Instead of accepting the versions of Crevel that include him as suicide, as father-lover, as mother-hater, and especially as "homosexual," all of which seem to crave teleological readings, I would like to explore what Gertrude Stein (227) pithily called Crevel's "confused negation." Stein's remark is as insightful as it is succinct: it marks Crevel as being caught in an undecidable flow, a difference from the norm to be sure, a discourse written against context. Perhaps it had to be Stein, living her homosexuality, who alone could see the conflicts in Crevel's life and work, conflicts between an active process of defining the self through writing, though in a language wholly unsuited to that self, and the pigeonholing discourse of a social context that categorizes the individual as homosexual, and in so doing, seems for many to have said all that needs to be said.

Homosexuality is a key element in *Mon corps et moi*, which dates from 1925; for Crevel, homosexuality is part of a larger problematic that is tantamount to an interrogation of the orders of sexuality in general. Hesitatingly, sporadically, and incompletely, Crevel develops a renewed ordering of sexuality, but because he is always prey to the social constructs into which he is foisted by his unique situation, he does not go completely to the end of this vision. Still, the restructured concept of sexuality underlying the work forms a new *dispositif* predicated on the development of a homosexual discourse as a nonoppositional alternative both to heterosexual discourse and to heterocratic order. In particular, *Mon corps et moi* is the story of a separation from a dominant heterocratic structure that imposes the values and signs of heterosexuality, including the constant demand of the system to be reproduced. Freedom is sought through embracing a different discourse that unproblematically includes homosexuality, that separates the pleasures of the flesh from models of reproduction, and that refuses the institutional channeling and regularizing of desire.

It could be said then that for Crevel every act of ordering desire, even if that desire is labeled "homosexual," is a sign of the heterocratic order: not for him is the homosexual underworld of bars and secret assignations. In *Mon corps et moi*, Crevel seeks a way out of the doubling and duplicity of both that general situation and that situation as defined by the contradictory logic of liberation and heterosexuality of Surrealism. In other words, he seeks release from Surrealism's double bind that paradoxically orders him to be free. He attempts to solve the problem of a dualism imposed by the conjunction of homosexuality and Surrealism. The question in this work is simple: How and where can "I" write? Allegiance to a Surrealist aesthetic that promotes engaging the unconscious means opening up the literary work to homosexuality, but homosexuality has no space within Surrealism in which to be articulated, if we understand Breton's virulent opposition in 1928 to be symptomatic of his longstanding opposition to homosexuality.

The development of a nonoppositional structure and its concomitant discourse is incomplete, and that will to nonoppositionality is never smooth sailing. In fact, the strategy of nonoppositional homosexuality never resolves the doubling, division, dualism, and difference at the heart of the book. In that sense, the work can be seen as a failure. On the other hand, in its attempts to posit alternative means of approaching and overcoming dualist oppositions that Surrealism itself could never fully negotiate, the book could be counted as a qualified success. Crevel goes further than many of his literary contemporaries in trying to solve problems of inside and outside and self and other and in seeking a resolution between what we might today call the social constructs that force a position for the self and the struggles of the self to appear as an independent singularity.

Mon corps et moi illustrates the failure to integrate the subject of enunciation and the subject of action. The family novel that depends generically on the constitution of the heterosexual subject as a reference point is not sufficient for explaining a work like *Mon corps et moi*, which, like most of Crevel's work, is both the antithesis of the family novel or the bildungsroman and the idealized nonoppositional other of those consecrated forms. This uncomfortable marriage between opposition and difference makes *Mon corps et moi* anything but an integrated literary piece. Rather than being a sign of mere opposition or obsession, the fragmentation should be understood as the reflection of the impossibility of constituting a homosexual Surrealist writing subject within the literary work.[3] With *La Mort difficile*, for example, Crevel retreats from the open exposure of *Mon corps et moi*, which is tantamount to a public display of self-flensing. In *La Mort difficile*, the subject of enunciation returns to a vision of homosexuality distinct from that of the subject of action. The power of the subject of enunciation to write according to a homosexual consciousness and unconsciousness is undercut by the rape of the figure: the subject becomes one who does not speak for himself but who is subject to a sodomizing by the text of others, as if he were in the last analysis an unwilling heterosexual victim.

The complex constitution and dissociation of the homosexual discourse in *Mon corps et moi* must be seen as a reaction to the more standard discourse on the position of homosexuality in *Détours*, published the year before. Though disparate in its commentaries, *Détours* constructs homosexuality as an abstraction culled from a predominantly heterosexual discourse. Homosexuality is a lack, a failure, an absence, something disdained by a bourgeois who undoubtedly cannot negotiate this sexuality with himself: "But to get mushy over a biblical king; in the bars, all the Davids are natives of Asnières, all the Saint Sebastians from the provinces" (*D* 49). Homosexuals are posturers, self-absorbed narcissists enchanted with their own beauty or taken with their own seductive powers. Moreover, they are pitiful lower-class individuals from the provinces or the suburbs. The overt reference to homosexuality in *Détours* is equally deprecating, for it associates homosexuality with a set of weaknesses that are the stereotypical objects of derision of a phallocentric and Eurocentric discourse: "Both psychologists and the Larousse dictionary explain homosexuality in the East in terms of women's intellectual inferiority" (*D* 58). Even if a certain nobility in male-male relations is the validation of homosexuality, this validation comes at the expense of

---

3. The problem is not unique to Crevel: Surrealism's subject is almost uniquely male and heterosexual. Chénieux-Gendron's comment (178) about "the insufficiency of the suggestions of Surrealism" about love and sexuality seen from the woman's point of view is extraordinarily cogent.

women and non-Westerners. For Crevel writing *Détours*, the figure of the homosexual is one of derision; he has not yet risen above the *bienséances* of a bourgeois discourse. He has also not yet struggled against the mandatory heterosexuality of Surrealism.

Everything changes in *Mon corps et moi*: Crevel faces the question head on, accepts no preconceived notions, and uses homosexuality as the motive force that produces the texture of the work. *Mon corps et moi* goes beyond a thematics of homosexuality, a thematics that cannot ever fully occur because it is impossible for him to bring closure to the subject, just as it is impossible to solve the contradiction between public and private selves. When limiting himself to a thematics of homosexuality, Crevel chooses to see the subject from the outside: thematizing homosexuality means implicitly subjecting it to a controlling system or discourse external to it. As I have shown in *The Shock of Men* when I critiqued discussions of homosexuality's thematics in Proust, the idea of the theme continues to enforce the dominant structures of heterosexuality as if they were transparent givens for any reading. When an author questions the transparency, however—as Renaud Camus remarks, the words "heterosexual film" are meaningless (177)—or develops his or her own clearly homosexual hermeneutic, the thematics once tacitly accepted begin to crumble. Crevel is at the point of rejecting thematics only in *Mon corps et moi*. In *Détours* and in *La Mort difficile*, he buys into that thematics and thereby reinforces the power of the dualistic model. On the other hand, in *Mon corps et moi* he fully expresses the goal of getting beyond dualistic oppositions and, despite his failure to attain that ideal, homosexuality still becomes an open, productive figure for him.

Dualism is the mode of knowledge that risks opposing self and other, homosexual and heterosexual, Surrealist and Surrealist, and, most important, self and self. Discourse is produced through recognizing the opposition between one's self-reflective concept of the self and the vision of the self absorbed as a phenomenon from the outside and internalized along with the truthful "more than nude" (*MCM* 240) image from within. Discourse happens in *Mon corps et moi* as Crevel puts everything into question, as he goes beyond the certainty of Cartesian doubt to a place in which the doubt casts a shadow on the doubter. Crevel undoes Cartesian certainty, the same thing as Cartesian doubt, not with reason, but with irony. The process starts with the possibilities of asserting a fact and of being certain about it: "And certainly [*certes*], when it is a question of the spoken or written word, the affirmation is less the proof of a certainty [*certitude*] than the desire for certainty born from some fundamental doubt" (*MCM* 52). Statements of certainty of knowledge are now open to doubt. The doubt that was the founding moment of knowledge for Descartes becomes yet another indication of not-knowing and of not being sure for Crevel. At stake are the epistemology based on the certainty of a doubt and a basic ontology whereby what something "is" is subject to the same divisive scrutiny. Thus with one sweeping movement ironized by the "*certes*" of uncertainty, Crevel dissociates himself from the images imposed by the other, which now include, by implication, the tautological reinforcement of the self that comes from the coalescence of heterosexuality and heterocracy.

Neither the doubt of certainty nor the certainty of a doubt is enough, because in and of themselves they do not engage the particularities of the baggage that the individual self has carried to that point. Crevel needs to dissociate himself from what the world has visited on him, but must find a way to do so that gets at the heart of the process of learning those images and not simply understanding the rules by which are produced. Intimately bound up with the refusal of the others' figures is a desire to reduce the most dangerous influence of all, the memory that remembers for you as if you were another. In remembering, one is one's own worst enemy, for memory insists that the subjects of enunciation and action are different. It is not enough to castigate oneself, here and now, for an involuntary action: "today, it is no longer I from whom I pretend to escape" (*MCM* 29). Involuntary memory is linked to the production of the structure of heterosexual dominance in which he endlessly finds himself. Undoing the impositions of involuntary memory does not, for all that, mean undoing the imposed images that resurface now and again, but rather it means learning to understand the rules by which those images were imposed. The images still remain.

In order to gain a measure of control, Crevel feels that he must act to reunite the subjects of action and enunciation to make his action and his words coincide in their parameters, effectiveness, and result. The way to produce the dissociation of the self from the images of the other thus does not depend on a remembering for oneself, be-

cause the model of that remembering is the same, preexisting dualistic one. Rather, the means of effecting the dissociation depends on
a will to forget, even if it means expunging memory: he hopes that
"it would be possible for me to get rid of memory itself [*il me serait
possible de me débarasser du souvenir même*]" (*MCM* 31). Remembering,
either for oneself or because of another, means continually maintaining oneself in the thrall of a dominant ideology that maintains
the individual as a simulacrum (23), an empty, vain copy of himself
or herself, dressed up for others. At least initially, in order to "get
bliss from thought [*jouir avec des pensées*]" (23), the individual must be
alone, stripped of his or her false images, copies, and simulacra. And
through solitude, "it is possible for man to get rid of memory itself
[*il est possible à l'homme de se débarasser du souvenir même*]" (34). The
same phrase was used three pages earlier, but with a different form
of the verb: the hypothesis implied by the use of the conditional has
been replaced with the certainty of the present tense. But it is more
than the images of the other that must be discarded; why does Crevel go so far as to want to expunge memory itself?

   Far from being the Romantic figure of *Erinnerung* that remembers through a reinternalization of the past, memory is a theatrical
travesty of flour and greasepaint; indeed, memories are personified
as "strange wig-makers, those of you who have written, painted, or
sculpted" (58). Quite bluntly, memory is false because it is heterosexual. The choice of image seems at first aberrant to the images of
heterosexuality, but it is not at all so: it is only the heterosexual that
confuses the travesty with the homosexual, that confuses a false hair-
piece with the internal self of an other who is not *intrinsically* opposed to the dominant mode. Heterosexuality makes the false homosexual, parading as if the only mode were to camp, dressing up as
if the only way to be homosexual were to internalize the images of
the other.

   But we already know this from the criticism of Crevel: the reader
will recall that if Crevel is remembered at all it is as the homosexual
Surrealist, and thus he is remembered from within the structures of
heterosexuality that name "homosexual" as the different or other; no
one would call Breton a "heterosexual Surrealist." What Crevel is
making clear about memory is that memory is structured according
to the meaningful systems that the heterosexual world provides.

While this may be balm to the self-defined heterosexual because his/her images seem to coincide with the externally imposed ones, it is torture to Crevel. Yet the images are as false in one case as in the other: it is the perception of that falseness that becomes acute for the homosexual, while the heterosexual may more easily choose to ignore the matter.

For Crevel, then, memory is the falsification of the self because it is entirely constructed of figures generated by the other. No amount of self-generated memory can ever eradicate the final traces of the images of a heterosexual world. Society forces certain structures on its victim, and it is as a victim that Crevel sees the unfortunate subject. In every case, the victim is the "*moi*" dissociated from "*mon corps*"; the victim/subject is the fragmented individual who can expect no whole image of himself or herself. No different from other Surrealists on this matter, Crevel holds that there is an enemy within, who exists beyond and before the impositions of the laws of the socius. Where Crevel goes beyond the position of other Surrealists, and where, in a "rational" way, he parallels Artaud's explorations, is that Crevel believes, as the very title of his chapter indicates, that the enemy is memory itself. Whereas other Surrealists believe in the possibility of complete liberation, Crevel seems always to harbor a doubt: for him, the desire for that liberation and the image of that liberation are imposed, internalized as his own, and remembered as déjà vu. But that desire and that image are *not his*.

The very idea of liberation, along with the constructs of memory, is resolutely heterosexual. Memory can take purity and subject it to the internalized laws that restrict the freedom of the individual to act and to be. Occasionally, away from the fixed gaze of society that forces the gazed-upon individual back into a *caleçon* or a straitjacket, an individual can attain momentary freedom in an act blissfully occurring in the moment of lethean presence: "When a person eats a peach, does he worry whether the fruit is male or female? I believe that, in bed, he hardly thinks more about the gender of the sex on which he is getting drunk" (66). Dividing the objects of desire into male and female is a tiresome heterosexual activity that repeats, Crevel seems to be saying, the elemental, primitive dichotomies of totem and taboo. One is therefore not surprised to find recurring bisexual images in the work, not as some rationalization of homosexual behavior, but as a refusal of the classifications of heterosexual memory and structures: "a woman's hand and a man's hand divide my ten fingers between them" (39).

At the moment of jouissance, when a person hardly thinks about "the gender of the sex on which he is getting drunk," there is no dualism, no separation of body and ego; action is as one with whatever concomitant discourses are present. As soon as distance appears, however, as soon as there is a transformation from the presence to oneself into a past of remembering, the censorious voice of the other seems inevitably to reappear:

Once the work of love is done, when it is a question of memory, if he gives false proofs, false names, false details about a chest or about what is ordinarily found between the legs, he will delight in his own hypocrisy and call the little well-wrapped [*empapilloté*] lie perversity. (66)

This, then, is the necessary outcome of a work, like Proust's *Recherche*, that depends on the figures of memory for its impetus. Hence the criticism Crevel has leveled at Proust a page earlier is nuanced here with a delight that Crevel cannot refuse the author of the *Recherche*. The work is hypocritical, perhaps, but not necessarily as blindly dualistic as the unvarnished memory. At least in the rewriting of memory, there is a consciousness of its artificiality, of the lack of unity in the subject, and the subject, while remaining disparate, can realize the fictionality of his own position through a dialectical reversal. Proust has his little hypocritical game and Crevel has his own, in his remembering and refiguring not the sex of the other but the otherness of sex itself. Frankly, it is the otherness of the other: short of remaining the prisoner of a silent onanism, Crevel must introduce the other into his own discourse, must do to the other what he fears doing to himself, and must therefore recognize and engage the hypocrisy, sham, and loathing in his own writing, an engagement that necessarily falsifies the subject of the other as well.

Crevel cannot structure his own memory system without the imposing presence of the other. The introduction of radical doubt allows for stripping away the accreted structures of the dominant discourse. Having done this, he finds not the certainty of the self, but the locus in which the self can come to stand. The simple division of the world into two sexes is questioned because the nature of sex and of gender is no longer knowable. The rejection of the means of knowledge as well as the constitution of the object that those means imply leads to a doubt about the very constitution of nature and its division into male and female. This doubt now simultaneously moves to create text. In fact, this sexual agnosticism is the motive force behind the construction of the subject of enunciation, now constituted from within the discourse that he himself tentatively creates:

Suddenly a virility rises up right in the middle of a Greek courtesan's dress. Men, women. One no longer knows.

There are houses where these galas occur more than twice a year. Nocturnal boys in tunics reign there, tutus, and crinolines [*paniers*]; only a few years before they had been little buggers, feet planted firmly in their big shoes. (*MCM* 59)

The confusion of sexuality is what is currently known as "gender-bending," wherein the outward signs of socially constructed gender do or do not correspond to some inner, "essential" sexuality and where, conversely, the "essential" sexuality is not bound by the trappings of the dominant social order. In that separation of sex and gender and in that willful confusion lies a freedom to be and to participate in actions that cast off the social structures imposed on the individual. The mask donned with full cognizance of the masquerade can be doffed with the same gesture. Thus a young hoodlum (*voyou*) comes just to "see" and has turned tricks just for fun (*rigoler*) (*MCM* 61); another is "*coquette*" (62) and has shaved armpits. Though he proffers gender-bending as a possibility, Crevel cannot accept the easy solutions offered by that possibility, which lies so close to the acts of the wig-makers, because those solutions, all superficial for him, never engage the essence, heart, or being of sexuality. Every mask, in its artificiality, is a death mask because it kills the appearance of the truth. Death is already found in that celebration: this very same *coquette* is a "suburban lady of the camellias" (62); and this Camille is already a martyr, "a young neighborhood Saint Sebastian" (63), who recalls the earlier Saint Sebastian from the provinces (*D* 49). Crevel's glimmer of hope seems to fade, for he can never be certain that the mask is entirely off, or that the role chosen was actually chosen by the subject.

A doubt always remains as to whether the role one hypocritically and perversely chooses to play may somehow have been chosen *for* the subject instead of *by* the subject. The imposition of a role means that the obvious difference between what is inside and what is outside the subject returns to the fore. Like the other roles imposed by society on the individual, an imposed sexual role falsifies what one is and who one is. Time and again in Crevel's work, as well as in that of other writers considered in this study, the same problem arises: there is a repeated doubt that the external, behavioral signs associated with homosexual freedom are actually signs of the individual's homosexuality. For those signs may be no more than the powerful, yet untrue, signs forced on the individual to structure his or her desire, and especially to channel the semiotics of the phenomena and the manifestations of that desire into the spaces allotted them by the dominant heterosexual classificatory schemes.

Crevel's work alternates between a celebratory discourse of freedom and a restraining discourse that brings the homosexual individual back toward the restrictions imposed on him or her by society. Alienating and reductive, this second discourse perpetuates the duality in which the homosexual constantly recognizes himself or herself. Even in those moments when the homosexual is free to be homosexual, his or her freedom is limited to a few acceptable stereotypically homosexual actions. In society this opposition appears when, in the supposed freedom of a homosexual subculture, the ego realizes its limitations: "I went down the staircase that led to the bright underground bar. I drank and I danced. I lost feeling in my flesh. I kissed every mouth to be quite sure that I no longer had desire or disgust" (*MCM* 96). The limits on the individual appear most readily when he or she is forced to decide to which society to belong. The individual's will is castrated; his or her freedom is limited; his or her voice is disguised behind the mask of the safer voice of another. Such a strategy is an act of closure to freedom that, while allowing him to participate in the Surrealist group safely, keeps Crevel from writing a singular discourse of the ego according to the acts of freedom to which he often aspires. Being the openly homosexual Surrealist thus comes at a price, which is the freedom to write as he will. For him, homosexual writing is only a hypothetical act ready to occur when the last traces of the preexisting system have been wiped away: "With the point of a knife I'd like to make designs all over his body" (*MCM* 88). Remaining in the realm of the impossible, true homosexual writing has not gotten past the violence with which it is marked by imposed constraints.

Within the homosexual subculture, still bound part and parcel to a dominant heterosexuality, Crevel seems to posit a mute figure who is incapable of writing. It is a black man, undoubtedly not long out of Africa, who symbolizes both the ridicule to which colonialism subjects its victims and the stereotypical purity and phallic power associated with the West's myths of Africa: "He is nude. His skin is the color of black pearls. A small pair of white underpants stretches from thigh to thigh under the burden of African genitals. . . . He wants to cry. The underpants make him ashamed" (64). Later the author will equate clothing and illness (81) and, ultimately, the shame of the veil will become Crevel's own: "I am ashamed of what remains of my clothing" (118). Like the black man, he is wearing the clothes he is forced to don by straight white society. Through an act of posturing that is a self-congratulatory, Gidean act of freedom, Crevel reveals himself, but that unveiling is itself still part of the dominant structure. The move toward freedom must occur within the structures provided by the other: "I cover a skin of which I am ashamed, of which I am right to feel ashamed, for sensuality, true sensuality would not be so fussy" (121). My own skin may lie to me about who and what I am. Since the dominant role of the skin is to falsify, Crevel begins to wonder whether or not a subject can believe the images he perceives that arise from the skin of another. Images are projected onto a skin that absorbs them to make the activity of veiling seem to be natural, but Crevel knows that the role of the skin is to restructure, reform, and falsify desire. Crevel says that he is "unable to get absorbed in a pleasure for which several pieces of skin are the starting point" (*MCM* 127).

The more radical one's position becomes in requiring honesty with oneself and self-identity, the more tempting solitude becomes, along with the idea of ultimate union with one's own solitude: "being haunted by suicide will undoubtedly remain for me the best and the worst guarantee against suicide" (*MCM* 102). So if that suicide is created for him out of the memory imposed by heterosexuality, his own suicide appears to be constructed from his own doubts and struggles with the sense of sexual identity and with the *genre*—both the gender and the form—of his writing. That haunting possibility of suicide is not so much the obsessive return to the Oedipal model but rather what remains of a shattered dream of being alone, united with oneself. At the beginning of the book this dream is rejected as he notes that he no longer thinks solitude possible (22). Now it would appear that this solitude is in fact possible, but that that possibility comes at a price. One can guess the price from *Mon corps et moi*, and I have already indicated that in Crevel's later books there is a turn away from the overt homosexuality explored in that book. So it will come as no surprise, as we have already seen in Crevel's allusions to the figure of Gide's Lafcadio, that the possibility of solitude, which for him means the total escape from the other, eventually means complete desexualization. If the homosexual is not free to be himself or herself, he or she is not free at all; but there is, ultimately, no freedom for the homosexual from the social constructs that he or she is thrust into. He or she can choose: not to remember the difference from heterosexuality, but to forget his or her sexuality entirely and thereby push his or her otherness into oblivion.

The radical requestioning of the truth has begun with the questioning of certitude, but Crevel realizes that a simple statement of position is not sufficient for stripping away all the layers that have been imposed on him. The only possible position of freedom available in society is the one that cannot communicate for itself: it is the unsigned, unmarked position. Quite obviously, it is also the freedom of the penis to be itself, and not even a symbolic phallus that has to be hidden from view because of its deadly or destructive power. Such freedom is but glimpsed, for the black man, on the verge of one sort of freedom in his nudity, has to become a "you" for a powerful "I." When he talks we remember that he too is imprisoned in that nudity, just as he is imprisoned in the white system that demands his nudity. He must answer when addressed, must babble "Me beautiful Lola" (64). Speaking means speaking to someone and repeating that one is engaged in a social, linguistic, and sexual hierarchy. Moreover, it means having been spoken to by someone else and having one's words come after those of another: "White hoodlums, obscene little Negro, the audacity of your gestures, their exhibitionism of order means neither frankness nor truth" (64). In the long run, being in society and being commanded mean being subject to the voice and power of another and, for Crevel, this means not being able to write.

To be reborn as a homosexual with his own discourse depends on a gradual dismantling of what has already occurred, so as to produce a naked being, true to himself. In the liberation afforded by this initial truth, he is like an embryo freed from the laws of ontogeny; he can determine his own gestation, order, and structure. Neither father nor mother will come into play in this autostructuring of the self. The flensing process is not without its temptations; the resurgence of the other is possible at every turn. At the same time, even the momentary absence of the structures of the other produces a chaos, the only solution to which would be order, but that order does not exist. It is the perfect, classical description of schizophrenia:

> Besides, our sexual research can itself be quite believably explained by the axiom: "Pleasure [volupté] is a function of pain." But, because our bodies and souls cannot control these states of bliss [jouissances], which, allowing them to forget previous states, permitting them a few seconds of a life that is finally disdainful of memory, because we lack substance and measure, constrained to perpetual overbidding, we are brought, depending on our temperament, to want sleep or death, and by dint of ardor, we wish for the minute that will free us from an existence to which we cannot give order. (100–101)

Giving free rein to the joys of his body, the homosexual individual finds himself or herself caught in that freedom as in a trap. For the state of forgetting is still, as Dalí would entitle his most famous painting, "the persistence of memory." And as we know for Crevel, memory is still one of the prime constructs and forces of heterosexuality. To be disdainful of memory is merely to distance it. By no stretch of the imagination is it a means of finding a site free of memory, or of filling the locus of heterosexual memory with some homosexual mnemotechnics. For the homosexual, then, even more than for the heterosexual, the *petite mort* becomes a sign of a totally chaotic universe. Rather than being a sign of pleasure, the bliss that precedes that postorgasmic depression is a reminder of the chaos into which every homosexual is thrust as soon as heterosexuality is distanced. For Crevel, the tragedy of the imprisonment of the homosexual in heterosexual structures is that the homosexual individual has no comparable structures to replace the ones from which he or she has tried to free himself or herself. For Crevel, even the structures of the Freudian psyche remain resolutely heterosexual, not because they are intrinsically or genetically so, but because they have always been addressed and remembered that way. The homosexual individual is thus perpetually at sea, and his or her bliss and *petite mort* become the signs of a will-to-death instead of a lust for life.

The obvious imposition of the rules of the other produces a disgust and a focusing on the self as image in an autoeroticism that is an escape from the power of the dominant discourse: "The mirror of a nasty armoire reflected the image of a young naked boy, crouched next to a sloven [*maritorne*]" (*MCM* 124). Focusing directly on the self amounts to refusing the shackles of the other in the equivalent of a Surrealist revolt. Yet such a direct assault has as its greatest effect the reintroduction of the festering, insistent images of heterosexual otherness. They are reminders of the extent to which the other has penetrated even to the subconscious of the self. If, as Lacan would have it, the unconscious is structured like a language, for Crevel, it is structured like a heterosexual language in which, for example, male figures have to be referred to with masculine pronouns.

For Crevel, the depths of the unconscious, the locus of the libido, are as limited by the imposed structures of the other as the conscious and outer selves and the masks worn to protect oneself are. A person is not even free in dreams to be one single united self:

Everyone for himself, it had to be repeated again, everyone for himself, and it was this sort of onanism that we had believed the somewhat shameful sign of childhood, but although one's early youth had passed, it continued to look for pretexts in other bodies and other thoughts. (74)

The other is the source of external pretexts as well as of objects of positive or negative desire imposed on the self to structure it according to dominant laws. These very same pretexts have worked their way into the heart of the self. Pure autoeroticism or sexual autism is not possible, for at every turn the phantasm of the other appears as a weight, deviance, or deviation that mutes or detours the pleasure of the individual. The autoerotic impulse is not constitutive of a good sexuality for the ego; in fact, the ego ultimately sits in opposition to masturbatory self-indulgence, which after all is still guided by images of the other. In a piece dating from 1929, "Réponse à une enquête sur l'amour," Crevel notes that the constant self-indulgent feeding of the self through autoeroticism will not end with the constitution of an independent self:

> In other times, undoubtedly, I would have preferred not to look like a reconstituted ruby, but, today, love has made me so superbly egotistical that I no longer think of myself. This is the opposite of innumerable masturbators—of which I admit I was one—who spend half their time putting character in doubt, and the other half writing books that inexorably start with "I." (*Baby* 222)

In *Mon corps et moi*, he continues to put his character in doubt. Still to be found is the way in which this love will effect the change that moves from an internalized "*moi*," the product of the other, to a new position, that of the "*je*," a subject independent of the external forces that once controlled the "*moi*." How can Crevel desire in a way that is not according to the desire of the other? How can Crevel escape Hegel? How can he be, as Claude Courtot (23) puts it, a "subject without an object"?

One solution, hardly valid in the long run, is to choose objects within the realm of the fully prohibited. If homosexuality is condemned by the superegoizing forces of the Surrealist circle, so be it. For a variety of reasons, it is still somehow tolerated and therefore still a part of their structures; if for no other reason, the mimetic nature of homosexuality makes it all too similar to heterosexuality and therefore dangerous. Breton's attempt to exclude homosexuality depends on an exclusion of the known and the similar, not the taboo. Yet other vices are not so easily subsumed into the law of the other. So, for example, there is bestiality: "I've heard that animals lend themselves willingly to man's sexual curiosity. And undoubtedly, both groups usually enjoy it, since no religion omitted outlawing it" (116). The seeming excess notwithstanding, bestiality is ultimately just indifference for Crevel: "I concluded that a dog's tongue, as deftly as a human one, could lick in me what I like to have licked" (129). And while pederasty was an abomination for Breton to be combated at all costs, bestiality for him (*Rech* 41) is merely a joke (*une plaisanterie*) that is not worthy of serious consideration. Moreover, for Crevel, bestiality seems to have its followers, and he cannot be alone in it, to revel in it as his.

For Crevel, so conscious of the structuring of the world by the other, if others are violating the taboo, that very multiplicity makes it less alien and less forbidden. So bestiality too can bring about the same sadness of recognizing that one's desire is structured by the other: "Even if you have fornicated quite a bit with both sexes of your own species and even with several dogs, just to test the waters, you can find yourself a teenager again, ready to drown his memory in the eyes of a nanny" (*PP* 179). If bestiality is not sufficiently perverse, one can always choose cannibalism, for that seems to be a desire that no one can countenance: "Thus we are looking for *clear and insufficient* feelings capable of recreating a *vague and sufficient* state. I dream of the taste of human flesh (neither caressed nor bitten, but eaten)" (*MCM* 114). And later, there is always coprophagia (*PP* 206).

Though the evocation of these "perverse" sexualities may be momentarily liberating, that very evocation brings about a reactivation of memory that interferes with the self-identity of the sexual act. The lack of self-identity, the inability to recognize the act as one's own, and the realization that one is never *fons et origo* of one's own desire are the signs of eternal alienation for Crevel. Because it can never fully identify the individual's desire and the individual life, sexuality seems constantly to invoke death, not in its synecdoche, "*la petite mort,*" but rather the "*grande mort*" of death itself:

Distraught over what the Larousse dictionary, in its professional school diploma–like severity, baptizes *solitary vice*, I would tell myself that my teeth, knocking against other teeth, strangers' teeth, would wind up believing, at least for a few moments, in the reciprocal intimacy of skeletons. (*MCM* 129)

The second attempt at constituting a sexuality different from one imposed by the other involves a fragmentation of the body, as if the body were nothing more than a heterogeneous collection of desiring machines. The fragmentation of the body occurs within a fantasy; at this point, the other has no determined sex. Using the standard narrative tenses of the *passé simple* and the imperfect to recount a grotesque heterosexual experience with an obese woman, whose flesh he wishes would just melt once and for all (124), the narrator envisions two bodies that are a collection of sensate parts: "I want only to see this mouth, a humid lichen, which closes softly, a docile ring, on the carnal tree" (127). The bodies are fingers, cells—he speaks of "the joy of his epithelium"—mouths, and genitalia: in short, a heterogeneous mixture of "papillae of pleasure [*papilles à jouir*]" (30, 145, 154, 155). If these parts are the focus of the attention of the already fragmented self, there is no need to invoke lack of wholeness of the self or the purported wholeness and implicit heterosexuality of the other. Papillae of pleasure calling to others need no structure of wholeness and domination in which to operate.

Still, this atomizing of the body is organized by the rules of the other. This time, it is not a question of the rules of order, but rather, the "rules of the game": "Twenty years ago, from what I've heard, love was a sport. To replace the *pushingball*, a little bag of human flesh with various secondary accessories: breasts, hair, ears, soles, hands, buttocks, mouth, etc." (135–36). He has turned the image of the sexual being into a collection of papillae whose express purpose is to provide and/or receive pleasure. Yet even if that collection does not need to be predicated on the structures of the whole, he feels in the end that he can never fully escape from the Cartesianism that forces logic to decide, divide, and then reconstitute the self according to a set of rules that are altrilocal in origin and heterocratic in nature. The desiring machine of the papillae of pleasure is the cause of some self-centered egotism that cannot rightly take place because there is no center; the ego thus constituted is still a product of alterity. The ego can willingly dissolve the last bit of glue holding it together, in which case, completely atomized into a heterogeneous collection of desiring machines, it is completely annihilated: "A body lent me, I make a machine of it. Egotism, they will say. But if I accept being an altruist, it is I who will become a machine" (*MCM* 146).

This, then, is Crevel's act of self-liberation, the complete destruction of every remaining bit of the self as social construct. We could ask if it is a matter of burning down the barn to get rid of the rats. Certainly, it is a means of disengaging oneself from all the posturing and masquerades associated with the falsifying orders imposed by heterosexuality. Toward the end of the book, Crevel writes of "today's false order, the taste for inversion, for example, pushing homosexuals to become heterosexuals, for if, in times of apparent uniformity, everyone seems to accept the same rule, everyone has but one desire, to free himself from the rule" (*MCM* 148).[4] The complete destruction of the organizing ideology of the other comes at a price, which is the inability to constitute any self from the atomized fragments. If the desire is to see oneself "more than nude" ("Freud," in *MCM* 240), there is no optic so fine, no tool available that is so selfless as to be able to produce a completely unalienated individual from the shattered remains. Thus the seeming off-handedness or *désinvolture* of the Crevel-like character in *La Mort difficile* when it is a question of homosexuality relates more to a deconstitution of the self than it does to a nonheterocratic order. A liberation from heterocracy has occurred, but without the self coming into being as an independent individual; he or it exists as an altruistic machine. After *Mon corps et moi*, Crevel may still have his "papillae of pleasure" but they are always wearing protection, as are his words, a protection that he had wanted so desperately to avoid.

In one of the late works, "Dali ou l'anti-obscurantisme," Crevel writes in hope, but it is a hope that will never be accomplished: "The right to think of paranoia, whatever our Mussolinis of mental health might say, is the same as that of an erect penis, an ejaculating penis. No more slipcovers [*housses*] on objects or rubbers on ideas. They stiffen and break the condoms, battleships against pleasure [*volupté*], spiders' webs against risks" (*ECR* 125). Summum of Crevel's image of the papillae of pleasure, the erect penis at the moment of ejaculation might, but will not, be the sign of total bliss, full liberation, and the complete overthrow of the dominance and discipline of a heterosexual system. Crevel's remaining writings, however, will continue to wear the condoms quickly donned after *Mon corps et moi*, for that book does not or cannot resolve the problems of discourse for the only "openly homosexual Surrealist."

Crevel's next book after *Mon corps et moi* is *La Mort difficile*, which escapes from the deep questions related to the problem of homosexuality by turning it into an *ad hominem* question. The book is a somewhat transparent autobiographical work in which a sizable portion of

4. In "Freud, de l'alchimiste à l'hygiène," a short text that dates from several months earlier, Crevel says more or less the same thing: "today's false order, homosexuals making themselves heterosexuals out of a taste for inversion, for if everyone rallies under one rule, everyone wants to free himself from it" (in *MCM* 240).

the plot is a thinly veiled version of Crevel's love affair with Eugene MacCown; the two fictionalized in the characters of Pierre Dufour and Arthur Bruggle. Here, homosexuality is a social or psychological problem, but it is no longer a textual or philosophical one. Even if the book eerily predicts, once again, Crevel's own suicide in that of the protagonist (*MD* 227–28), homosexuality basically has a thematic that relates to plurality and public face. Thus homosexuality deals with a question of jealousy (*MD* 96–97) or with a question of the courage it takes to "come out": "He'll have the courage of his tastes. It has been decided. The courage of his tastes" (*MD* 121). In *La Mort difficile*, homosexuality has a public face. The book returns to the outside, to what is beyond the skin and to the dishonesty of the world at large: "the friendship of two men [would] go so far as to become what hypocrites and the ignorant believe possible only between individuals of different sexes" (*MD* 173).

So the recurring problems of writing in a discourse that engages homosexuality in *Mon corps et moi* seem to have disappeared in *La Mort difficile* in favor of the more easily asked and answered questions of public behavior. *Mon corps et moi* does not resolve questions; the answers are endlessly deferred because what answers there are seem too dangerous to pursue: the price of freedom and truth is solitude. After *La Mort difficile*, homosexuality is marginalized, treated lightly, and made banal, if not to say downright silly: "In the spirit of simultaneous, reciprocal fellations, he leaves for the land of the fellahin" (*PP* 285). In *Babylone* (1927), there is an occasional hint of eroticism reminiscent of an early piece like *Détours*. In *Babylone*, however, homosexuality is primarily a commercial venture, an affair of socially disenfranchised gigolos: "Each of the men walking around the old port, with his sideways glance, promises, for fifty francs, a knowing, robust virility, a fresh chest, a hard stomach, things that, unaware of the hypocrisy of underwear, make the slightly rough fabric smell good" (*Baby* 166). Though it is difficult to believe that in three short years Crevel could have changed so much, it is nonetheless the case that after his initial writing culminating in *Détours* in 1924, Crevel engages the question of homosexuality in *Mon corps et moi* (1925), disengages himself from its problematics in *La Mort difficile* (1926), and then takes a completely different course in *Babylone* (1927) and the writings that follow. In general, the tone has changed: the works are not without interest, but the reader wonders why Crevel never deals with the unanswered question and thus why his later work does not fulfill the promise, in this sense, of some of his earlier writing.

Two acute contemporary readers and acquaintances of René Crevel, Gertrude Stein and Georges Bataille, both find clues in his writing to the problems of the author and the man as an individual. Stein (227) says that Surrealism provided a clarification for Crevel. Thus, one might assume that the materialist approach of Surrealism to which he gradually turns in the thirties is a means of not grappling with the spiritual or metaphysical questions that are the focus of *Mon corps et moi*. He does not therefore have to resolve the question of liberation and heterocracy if he makes revolution out to be basically a materialist process. In a book review of *Le Clavecin de Diderot*, Bataille says that having ridiculously quoted Marx, Engels, and Lenin, the bulwarks of a certain engaged Surrealist discourse, Crevel used their principles "to castrate himself" (1:326). So for Bataille too, Crevel refuses to follow the path set out in *Mon corps et moi*. As Bataille pursues his spiritual quest in the thirties, Crevel seems to remain behind with what is, at least for Bataille, the overly Marxist turn of Surrealism's revolution. Perhaps, then, in an engagement and assumption of the Surrealist discourse, Crevel silences a certain specific part of his own voice, the voice that says for him what it means to be homosexual. And with that castration, silence, repression, reordering, or simultaneous dimming and clarification necessarily comes, as was predicted, the author's suicide.

Though Crevel ultimately performs the gesture of Origen, sign of a permanent *petite mort* and preview of a self-inflicted *grande mort* to come, the knife was provided by Surrealism. For Surrealism could not negotiate the conflict it engendered by its adamant refusal of male homosexuality. To welcome Crevel and to deny his sexuality is a contradiction that could not be overcome when the stated rhetoric of Surrealism was one of liberation, a liberation that seems to be militantly sought except in this one, singular instance. The cogent remark of Gilles Deleuze and Félix Guattari about Breton and Artaud could be applied to Crevel as well: "There will always be a Breton opposed to Artaud . . . to superegoize [*surmoïser*] literature" (*Anti-Oedipe* 159). Yet what weapon or superego does Surrealism give to or force on Crevel; what punishment does he readily accept?

To say the least, Surrealism's discourses and actions relative to homosexuality were problematic, if not to say openly hostile. Crevel meets and engages these discourses and tries to resolve the questions through a logomachy in *Mon corps et moi*. Unable to win the battle, he no longer uses homosexuality as an active, productive matrix for engaging discourse. After the discursively chaste work of *La Mort difficile*, Crevel turns away from the problem in his writing, having failed to reconcile the irreconcilable network of oppositions: the preaching of liberty versus the prohibition of homosexuality among the Surrealists, especially Breton, and the very same prohibition of homosexuality versus the acceptance of Crevel as an openly homosexual individual.

Needing to continue to belong to the Surrealist group and finding in it one set of answers to the problems of sexual liberation, Crevel decides that it is perhaps better to be completely free of the need to veil. Significantly, the clearest announcement of these new positions comes in a piece on Dalí. This artist seems to offer a cure for the despondency to which Crevel feels brought by the paths taken in his own work. Moreover, Dalí is one of the rare individuals to live his crisis instead of succumbing to it; Dalí gets beyond mummification and what Crevel believes to be the naive opposition between introspection and the objective (*ECR* 117). Crevel perceives a failure in the relation of art to Surrealism, as he notes that even the liberation of the senses promised by Surrealism finally leads, despite the continued promises, to sclerosis and paralysis and to the incapacity to produce movement and a freedom of hypotheses (*ECR* 322). Now if the violence of the revolution extends even to the sex organs themselves, there is no need for a fig leaf. Ironically enough, the thorough accomplishment of the revolution returns sexuality to a state of nonexistence; the revolution will repeat bourgeois respectability: "The only thing that is correct, chic, and distinguished is what has previously been desexed" (*ECR* 228). Liberation from sex means liberation from its last vestiges in symbols and signs; the whole symbology associated with sex becomes nothing more than a "phallic nostalgia" (*ECR* 218).

Ironically for a Crevel seeking freedom from the oppression of the other, the closer he draws to the Surrealists in the thirties, the more his own lingering sexual fixations return to the fore. The more he is supposed to conform to a role defined for him by the other, the more he becomes obsessed by the figures of homosexuality that, in *Mon corps et moi*, he would have seen imposed on him by a hostile world. In *Le Clavecin de Diderot*, his own fixation on circumcision (*ECR* 222) is revived, he posits the diabolical nature of sex (*ECR* 222), and he even brings the old demon of castration anxiety to the fore as he notes a dream of having his penis falling from his body (*ECR* 250). All of these appear in the image of a jack-in-the-box, which follows shortly after a mention of castration:

It is, moreover, completely clear that the devil symbolizes an erection and vice versa. To dispel all doubt, I need do no more than recall the jack-in-the-box [*diable-qui-sort-d'une-boîte*], a toy from my childhood. A hairy, cylindrical character on springs lifts up his cover with one push. The red cotton [*andrinople*] with which he was dressed, when he had extended it, made him look like a horse's penis outside its foreskin. (*ECR* 222)

This obsessive return needs to be checked, for every such involuntary memory brings about a return to complicated sexuality, a fear of castration, and a fear of rejection. Yet perhaps the most horrible part is that even trying to get beyond castration anxiety to assume the controlling role of the castrator forces even the dominating individual into the same straitjacket of programmed behaviors.

For example, of William Tell, who as late as 1931 in "Dali ou l'anti-obscurantisme" is depicted as a Christlike figure, Crevel writes not two years later in his return to Dalí that the role is taken on "in order to pierce the aforementioned apple with an arrow, as if the child was to be castrated, sodomized, and eaten all at once" (*ECR* 328). Sacrificed in an earlier version, William Tell here is forced by another; his behavior too, seemingly powerful, is reduced to a sexual game in which he too is "bristling with erections." Ultimately, there is no escape outside the final, self-uniting act of a suicide that kills the homosexual difference as it kills the body. In the end, Crevel is neither William Tell nor his son, both William Tell and his son. With his final actions, Crevel becomes Saint Sebastian and turns his desiring papillae into the bristling arrows that ecstatically penetrate and fulfill the papillae just as they end the differences between inside and outside, between self and other, and between his body and his self.

Sartre as Midwife

> Should we believe the absurd legend according to
> which Rollebon would have had to disguise himself as
> a midwife to get to the palace?
>
> Jean-Paul Sartre, *La Nausée*

I. Figuring Out Homosexuality

Complex and multiple in its formulations, the figure of male homosexuality in the writings of Jean-Paul Sartre is a fascinating one, as difficult to seize as it is involved to study. Even when understood thematically, and therefore necessarily circumscribed by a fiction of literary closure and by a metaphysics astride idealist categories and positivist categorization, Sartre's depiction of homosexuality still manages to resist interpretation. Even if one has digested the entirety of the oeuvre, impediments appear that block the reader's easy access to something that should be, one might think, rather transparently readable in Sartre's universe. First of all, the delineation of homosexuality seems to change as the oeuvre develops. Starting as something tangential, even accidental, it looms large and occupies center stage in later works. Second, one cannot be certain that there is a relation between the more marginal depictions of homosexuality in *La Nausée* or even *L'Etre et le néant* and the fleshed-out development of *Les Chemins de la liberté* or *Saint Genet*. The pederasty of the Autodidact is readable as an excuse for a plot development in *La Nausée* and the passing references to homosexuality in *L'Etre et le néant* could be nothing more than examples. Such instances, which could be reduced to cases of blindness to oneself, seem to have little to do with the depiction and situation of Sartre's three major homosexual characters, all of whom are painfully aware of their situation, often to the point of self-loathing: Daniel Sereno, in *Les Chemins de la liberté*, Inès Serrano, in *Huis-Clos*, and Genet, in Sartre's massive introduction to Genet's works.

The third initial resistance is generic: the context in which homosexuality is found varies along with the genres of Sartre's writing. One should not initially presume that the consequences of the representation of homosexuality in a philosophical tract are necessarily the same as in a fiction. In a philosophical text, for example, an example of homosexuality may be nothing more than an excuse for a discussion of contingency, freedom, or existence. Or it may be taken "merely" as an illustration of one kind of bad faith or another kind of engagement. On the other hand, given the social context in which Sartre places his fictional beings, for an individual character condemned to his or her freedom, the nature of that homosexuality is all-important, and is not just one contingency among others.

The last initial impediment to reading homosexuality in Sartre is that an interest in homosexuality can operate as a double bind. Even as late as *Saint Genet*, Sartre gets caught in such a situation. Let us consider what Sartre says about projection in the Freudian sense. Sartre says: "I would bet that for those who condemn Genet the most severely, homosexuality is a constant temptation that is constantly denied" (*SG* 40). Yet in the very next sentence, Sartre takes the denial that he has just ascribed to others and enacts it himself: "And I don't mean, of course, that this constantly refused pederasty appears to them as some inclination of their own nature" (*SG* 40). Nowadays, often shying away from the kind of Freudian vocabulary that some would find condemnatory in itself, we have renamed one specific kind of projection "homophobia." Is Sartre focusing on and denying his own homophobia, illustrating it all the while?

This is perhaps one of the clearest problems in dealing with homosexuality: if one talks about it, one is *parti pris* and perhaps a closet case; if one is hostile toward it or does not talk about it, one is perhaps latent. Though perhaps without intending to, Sartre illustrates how our inherited conceptions of homosexuality "infect" the text: homosexuality, it comes as no surprise to the reader, may be unconsciously considered to be a communicable disease. No sooner does Sartre mention a Freudian denial than he himself repeats that denial for his own writing: "I don't mean" means, perhaps, "I do mean," but that would put Sartre in a relation to homosexuality that he does not wish to aver. Beyond some simple game of naming homophobia, Sartre shows how the very concept of homosexuality that we all have been handed informs the possible reactions to it; we have all been infected with the idea that homosexuality can be spread like a virulent disease. Again, no one "reacts" to heterosexuality, for it is never seen as a strain of a disease, a toxin, or an allergen. In that unholy dyad that seems to define gender for the West, it is only homosexuality, serving as other, that has the capacity to produce the anaphylactic shock of homophobia in others.

At the same time, the characterization of homosexuality as something "always already" submitted to a medical discourse makes us aware of how ambiguous any reaction must be. Sartre is no exception here. In fact, there is almost a virtue in his depictions of unsolvable, incurable ambiguities, for he never takes the easy way of merely welcoming the murkily defined "other" that is homosexuality for him. Of course that "other" is not completely different or alien; his sympathy as well as his own somewhat viscous depictions of homosexuality do signify a deeper personal relation to homosexuality than that offered by some distant *moraliste*. And without going so far as to say that Sartre was a latent homosexual (which is not far at all because it is so easy), I would allow that Sartre's continued interest is a sign of a complicated, intricate approach and relation to homosexuality, to heterosexuality, to masculinity, and to femininity both in the author's life and in his work.

The signs are everywhere, whether it is in the "ontological androgyny" and the "erosion of masculinity" in *L'Age de raison* that Robert Harvey (110–18) brilliantly discusses in *Search for a Father*, or in the "bisexuality of the book" noted by Josette Pacaly (84). A psychoanalytic reading of Sartre would develop these threads of negation, denial, ambiguity, and insistence that are the hallmarks of the Freudian model; an exemplary reading along those lines is Pacaly's excellent study *Sartre au miroir*, a close psychoanalytical reading of Sartre's autobiographical and critical works. As far as homosexuality in particular is concerned, Pacaly is not so much interested in the subject itself as she is in the repetition of the seduction scene from book to book, the attraction and rejection of the roles assigned to master and disciple, and the fascination with male-male relationships (96). She believes that Sartre's study of Genet makes the former face his own latent homosexuality and his anal fixation (217). If Sartre was a latent homosexual, so be it; even with that understanding, we do not get at the heart of the problematic of homosexuality in his writing. Pacaly's study is certainly a tour de force; yet I want to move away from a psychoanalytical reading to pick up some of the strands of this book. Bearing in mind those initial resistances to interpretation, I would focus on understanding how homosexuality may or may not operate as a theme in Sartre's various works, on how it is a shifter between inside and outside, and on how Sartre reads and "unreads" his own figures of homosexuality. The resistances are a sign of something deeper—not only a purported latency but also a complex of textual ambiguity that operates at many levels of Sartre's writing.

For a theme that one would think so easy to describe or circumscribe within what we now understand as the existentialist project, male homosexuality is uncomfortably categorized and recategorized. The depiction of male homosexuality returns with great frequency as a subject in Sartre's writing, yet each time the problem seems to resurface with the ends even looser than before. While I am not suggesting that Sartre might have ignored homosexuality, I am suggesting that if the matter were just another situation for him to describe, he might much more easily have dealt with it. And moreover, if it were just another situation for him, he would not have returned so obsessively to it. So it is not the subject itself that gives us pause; it is rather the frequency with which it occurs throughout the oeuvre that challenges the reader to rethink what "homosexuality" or "pederasty" might mean for Sartre.

Although it is not so easy to define, we can at least make some initial distinctions. In the earlier works, the figure of male-male eroticism falls more into the category of pederasty, or more exactly, into "ephebophilia," love and/or sex between an adult and a postpubescent young man. This is essentially the model of Greek love to which Sartre, as we shall see, is not indifferent. Works engaging this aspect of the subject include a story entitled "L'Enfance d'un chef," in Le Mur, in which there is a brief fling between an older man, Achille

Berger, and an adolescent, Lucien Fleurier. The same sort of homosexuality is the basis for one of the central dramatic events in *La
Nausée*, where the Autodidact molests a young man in the library.[1] Of
course in this case there is neither love nor sex, only a clumsy, failed
act of molestation. It is the perception of that failure that spurs
Roquentin to act. Like Proust's Queen of Naples offering her arm to
Charlus to lead him out of the disastrous soirée he has organized
(3:825), Roquentin offers the Autodidact safe passage.

In the forties, Sartre seems to change stances as his depictions of
ephebophilia give way to a more general definition and portrayal of
homosexuality. Though an age difference still characterizes male-
male couples portrayed during this era, that difference has receded
as the singular defining factor of such relationships, and Sartre
broadens his perspective to portray the male-male couple in general.
One of the three examples he gives, male homosexuality is an important part of the discussion of bad faith that is a cornerstone of
L'Etre et le néant, and male homosexuality continues to be an opera-
tive reference throughout the rest of that treatise. A similar widen-
ing of scope can be seen in his fiction of the same decade. One of the
main characters in *Les Chemins de la liberté*, Daniel Sereno, is homosexual. He is arguably one of the most complex characters in the trilogy, as he is placed in situations that show a wide variety of interac-
tions and engagements. He starts out evincing selfishness, even self-
centeredness, and a self-loathing in *L'Age de raison*. As Philip Wood
(122) rightly notes,

Daniel is a homosexual in an age and a society where homosexuality is necessarily almost always clandestine outside of rare and tiny coteries or marginal groupings. Which means that he has inevitably internalized the
loathing of homosexuality of the homophobic society in which he lives. To
be a product of this society, and homosexual, is unwittingly to install one's
tormentors in one's own mind.

Yet despite that "internalized homophobia," things do change, and
Daniel develops as a character and, dare we say, as a real homosexual
individual, as opposed to a stereotype of such an individual, even despite some temptations on Sartre's part to create stereotypical situa-

---

1. For reasons that will become clear below, I am keeping the name of "Autodidact" instead of using the more common English version of the "Self-Taught Man."

tions and reactions. In *L'Age de raison*, Daniel seems to be both the continuation and the final chapter in Sartre's somewhat predictable depictions of the homosexual figure in the early works. The immeasurability of the war and its change from a *"drôle de guerre"* to a worldwide catastrophe crystallize Sartre's concept both of the individual and of the group. As the trilogy and the war progress, Daniel assumes responsibility beyond the cares and needs of his individual self defined by petit-bourgeois logic and ideology. Daniel embodies the existentialist belief in the individual's capacity to change radically. For example, he symbolically accepts responsibility for the future as he marries the pregnant Marcelle: even if the original motivation for that marriage and for the concomitant refusal of homosexuality comes from self-loathing, the result is an engagement and the acceptance of the consequences of that self-loathing. Daniel begins to assume his freedom. Daniel's homosexuality becomes part of him, part of a *pour soi*, and not the end-all *en soi* that Sartre seemed to imply in *L'Age de raison*. The change is not absolute, and what we now currently call the "internalized homophobia" of *L'Age de Raison* lingers.

In the second and third volumes, moments of self-loathing are still present and from time to time the weight of freedom is soundly rejected. This burden of freedom is not easily shouldered by any Sartrean character of the era, be he or she homosexual or heterosexual: "To be what I am, *to be* a pederast, a meanie, a coward, finally to be that garbage [*immondice*] that does not even manage to exist" (*S* 850). Just as often, especially in the last volume, there is a recognition of the possibility of action, freedom, and responsibility. Daniel's illustrations of a renewed concept of *Mitsein* in his relations to the AWOL soldier Philippe in *La Mort dans l'âme* (1256–73; 1284–89) raise Daniel's homosexuality to a level of responsible action that exceeds any stereotyped behavior that Sartre may inflict on his character.

As Christina Howells says in her study of freedom in Sartre: "The early Sartre (for convenience, up to the mid-1950's) is concerned primarily with the individual, his situation and his facticity; the later Sartre with society, 'pre-destination' and the 'practico-inert' " (1). So the concept of both the individual and the group change after the war and culminate in the reign of the practico-inert described in the *Critique de la raison dialectique*. It is less and less clear that an individual can function as such by living the freedom to which Sartre once felt that individual was condemned. After the war, Sartre's greatest homosexual protagonist of all appears in Genet, who is also his most abject figure. Sartre's Genet is Daniel Sereno endlessly condemned to relive the bad faith from which he eventually escapes; Sartre's Genet is Inès Serrano in drag and forced by society to love Garcin. Canonized as the saint of the abject, Sartre's Genet lives an enforced martyrdom aswim in a sea of bad faith, as he is predestined to his condemnation by society.

After the two-edged sword that is the hagiography of *Saint Genet*, Sartre turns back and revives an earlier concept of homosexuality in the first volume of the antihagiographic study of Flaubert. And yet perhaps the two books are both hagiographies, one about a saint, one about an idiot; the difference is not as great as one might think. If Sartre wonders how one can be an individual in the world of the practico-inert, a world that is quintessentially bourgeois, he also wonders where that realm arose. Why not return to the epitome of petty-bourgeois mentality, Gustave Flaubert, whose final project was a catalog of the discursive versions of the practico-inert? In part, Sartre's shift after the war years could explain the choice of subjects. At the same time, Sartre's return to the nineteenth century may relate to a lingering, nostalgic belief in the possibility of the individual; writing about Flaubert may be seen as a pulling back from the monstrosity he himself created in his depiction of Genet as the example of perfect bad faith.

The return also revives an unresolved notion of how to view homosexuality and how to write about it. It is no coincidence that this return occurs just as Sartre is once again asking how to write about an author and how to view an artistic work. In that final chapter of Sartre's engagement with the question of homosexuality, the study of Flaubert embroiders on Flaubert's travels in North Africa. Now just as the question of homosexuality occupies very little space in the study of Baudelaire (though there, too, the references are quite significant), references to homosexuality are few in number in the massive Flaubert study. Still, I would like to beg my readers' indulgence relative to those few remarks and just indicate for now that the study of Flaubert will come back from time to time in these pages, despite the relatively minor role homosexuality plays in it.

In a way, *L'Idiot* is the most contemporary of Sartre's late projects, for in it he seeks the total of what one can know about what deter-mines an individual. Significantly it is the history of Gustave Flaubert before *Madame Bovary*, thus before Flaubert becomes "Flaubert" for the world at large. But *L'Idiot* is also the most impossible and most *retro* of Sartre's works, for he stubbornly returns to an insistence on his powers of observation, as if his singular gaze were exempt from the reign of the practico-inert. And specifically, in *L'Idiot*, Sartre re-turns to a view of homosexuality related to his earlier work, where knowledge of homosexuality depends on its absolute visibility and provability. Whereas most of Sartre's other concepts change quite radically between the relations of the freedom of the individual and the realm of the socially constructed practico-inert, the role given homosexuality in *L'Idiot* anachronistically returns to earlier incarna-tions.

While Flaubert's comments on every aspect of dysfunctionality engage Sartre throughout *L'Idiot*, and while Sartre generally shows great interest in questions of marginality and dysfunction and in signs of railing against family and state, in this case Sartre takes great pains to deny what Flaubert is saying. Quite simply, Sartre refuses to believe Flaubert. Sartre does not believe the homosexual act is a real part of his subject, since he, Sartre, cannot know it. And although Sartre has never needed the Berkeleyan vision of presence for proof of anything else, in the case of Flaubertian homosexuality he remains steadfast. By maintaining his nonknowledge, Sartre returns Flaubert's "homosexuality" to the realm of the fictional. There, in a world of authorial determination of freedom, a world that is a veri-similar *mélange* of Sartre's and Flaubert's Normandy of the mind, Sartre can decide on the import of the episode while simultaneously eliding reality.

In these pages, I shall focus on those works of Sartre in which ho-mosexuality is presented as an episode, as a discontinuity, and as something less than a full-fledged subject for investigation. The chiaroscuro figure of homosexuality and of the male homosexual limned within a larger context of textual development shows the most basic textual functions of the figure. In *La Mort dans l'âme*, for example, the narrative and novelistic exigencies of the work in which a protagonist is homosexual may weigh on the development of the figure. This *écart* between reality and its fictional mistranscription, as

Denis Hollier (123–26) has shown, is also at work in *La Nausée*. In that book, however, this gap does not impinge on the construction of the homosexual character as much as it does on the heterosexual relationship between Roquentin and Anny. Constraints on the writing, whether generic, verisimilar (the war), or biographical (Genet), often involve the figure of homosexuality in a context that may hide some of the aspects of the Sartrean conception of the figure. And certainly in *Les Chemins de la liberté*, Sartre's changing concerns tend to dedramatize Daniel as "the" homosexual of the novel, in order to integrate homosexuality into a broader perspective of *Mitsein*. Thus, ironically, the more freedom the homosexual character has to act and to take responsibility in a situation, the less freedom Sartre has to make homosexuality something singular. The less "realistic" the character, the more freedom the author has to weave the threads of his poetic or philosophical figure. Even more than the bloodied Genet, Flaubert, apotheosis of realism for the bourgeois culture he so hated, will then become for Sartre the most unrealistic and fictional of his creations.

As Daniel approaches his own freedom as an individual and not as a homosexual *en soi*, he becomes Sartre's own vicar in the novel. He can manipulate stories of homosexuality and he even invents a use for homosexuals: they can get married, get involved in the war, and assume responsibility. This is a sea-change from early Sartrean fiction, where there is revulsion, or even nausea, at the manipulation of the homosexual anecdote: "Lucien was conscientiously trying to understand, but lots of things escaped him and he was shocked because Rimbaud was a pederast" ("EC" 346). Daniel has no such problem, as he has become as good as Sartre at reinventing the anecdote and at using it as currency: "So you understand what I mean: methodological doubt, eh? the systematic disordering of Rimbaud" (*MA* 1273). Rimbaud, the fellow traveler, has become as useful in a homosexual seduction as Descartes himself is in a philosophical enterprise.

II. The Art of Midwifery

Early in *La Nausée*, we read the following question about the Marquis de Rollebon, Roquentin's biographical subject: "Should we believe the absurd legend according to which Rollebon would have had to disguise himself as a midwife to get to the palace?" (*N* 22). To get to the seat of established power, the palace that is both the center of meaning and a safe haven, one has no need for disguise, and certainly one has no need to pretend that one is a woman. What would it mean for a man to be a midwife or for a man to dress as a midwife? What would it mean for a story about such a pretense to be true or false? The profession is not just one among many, for it is enshrined as a noble profession at a critical moment, the beginning of philosophy in the golden age of Greece.

Midwifery is a profession exercised in the real world by dedicated, wise women (as the French would have it) and in philosophy by Socrates himself. Standing at an intersection where philosophical truth encounters a pederastic ethos and a maieutic method, Socrates brings new ideas into the world through a birthing process. In the *Theaetetus* (149a), Socrates says that he is a midwife like his mother. Yet Socrates is different: he practices on men, not women (*to te andras alla me gynaikas maieuesthai*) (150b); moreover, he tends to the souls of these men, not to their bodies. He coaxes forth genuine offspring from the young men he tends, but not without pain, for he puts them to the test and tortures them (*basanizein*). No one should think this midwifery business easy: it is a painstaking, difficult task, especially when the goal is giving birth to the truth. Moreover, no one should think that this midwifery is without power, for included in it is both the power to torture and the power to coax. And though Socrates first says that he practices on men in general (*te andras*), from one sentence to the next, he shifts from this general opposition between men and women to looking for a real or false image from the mind "of the young man" (*tou neou*).

False images, false clothing: Sartre will have none of that. He must seek out the truth, dig it out from the tenacious thrall of the pretenses of bad faith, the abrasions of the practico-inert, the viscosity of everyday lies. Ever wary, Sartre will, in the third version of bad faith discussed in *L'Etre et le néant*, show that a discourse purporting to be direct truth is itself a pretense: the so-called frankness and understanding of the friend of the homosexual are actually, for Sartre, a means of insisting on the bad faith of both individuals. In *La Nausée*, though, perhaps less subtly than in the philosophical study of bad faith, Sartre launches a frontal attack on pretense, masquerade, and the persona of the mask, that is to say, the role already determined and played out ahead of time (*SG* 75). For Sartre, the pretense of midwifery is absurd: the truth should be visible. One should not need a midwife to coax it out through a difficult birth. This is not the place for a disquisition on Sartre's concept of truth, appearance, and visibility. I would simply remind the reader that in a work like *Vérité et existence*, Sartre maintains the truth of the visible, at least on the potential level: "In other words, in the couple 'appearance-reality' (a false couple invented out of necessity), appearance is always true, error is found at the level of reality. Appearance is always the revelation of being, reality may or may not be the revelation of being" (16).

This means, in philosophical terms, that there is no need to pretend that one is like one's mother or to pretend that one is a male midwife coaxing or torturing ideas out of the mouths of born philosophers, in this case, Roquentin himself. At the same time, by not pretending one is a woman, one is implicitly identifying with power. It is as if the individual, through an act of self-revelation of what is already visible and present, could show the truth of appearance, that is, the revelation of being. Moreover, the masquerade is elsewhere. If Rollebon does not need to get dressed as a midwife, it must mean that he is already disguised. The power in question has no transcendental validity: absolutist power is itself a travesty, a miscarriage of justice and reason; it is the deification of a mere mortal and the transformation of his minions into the transcendental power of the absolutist state. We already know this: we can see it in the very trappings in which Rollebon is always simultaneously disguised and not disguised. The clothes that sign him as a noble also reveal the hollowness and falsity of that position. No midwife is needed in such a case; the naked truth will serve just as well. Faced with this tyranny disguised as law, a travesty is redundant. The travesty is even more obvious for someone seeking safe haven while pretending to help engender the truth. Rollebon is always in travesty, for he is a man passing for his station, an individual who thinks he is "a marquis," just as the famous waiter of *L'Etre et le néant* will think (or not think) that he is a waiter, and just as every pederast Sartre invents will think, to a greater or lesser extent, that he is a "pederast," that monstrosity described by the other, supported by superior power and station.

There is thus reason to dismiss Rollebon's disguise as useless and the tale of that disguise nothing less than *absurd*, the very word used by Sartre. What does "absurd" mean here? Meaningless, ridiculous, unprovable, or unphilosophical? Or is it the reverse? Is it the absurdity called forth as a basic tenet of what will be Existentialism: meaningful because it is meaningless, central because it is ridiculous, philosophical to its very core of contingency? In *La Nausée*, the story of a travesty is denied by being labeled absurd, and we think we understand it for philosophical or ironic literary reasons: a travesty cannot re-travesty itself. And ironically, the truth is there, undisguised, as plain as a shock of red hair or a chestnut-tree root. One is always in travesty, one is always the feminized other to some corrupt power lording its truth; one is always being screwed by the powers that be, and taking no pleasure in it, except the vicarious one of bringing some image, be it false or true, to light.

Many years later, Sartre will repeat the same story, though with a different protagonist, and subject the story to the same denial. Only this time it is not Roquentin who cries absurdity relative to some imaginary "petit marquis," but Jean-Paul Sartre himself. And this time, it is not some pathetic lieutenant of the ancien régime, but Gustave Flaubert himself, self-described "bourgeoisophobe" and confessed pederast. Nevertheless, Sartre is firm: he cannot, will not believe as "true" that a man, capable of choice and decision, able to act, will take a role other than that of a heterosexual male. Sartre recounts the scene in Flaubert's memoirs in which the latter talks about his homosexual experience in a Near Eastern bathhouse. For a whole variety of reasons, Sartre is doubtful about the veracity of the story. Yes, Flaubert probably went to the hammam, but no, Flaubert was not a "consumer" in the situation. It does not even matter that Flaubert might have remained the active partner. Sartre says point blank, "I do not believe him about that [*je ne l'en crois point*]": the information is too sketchy, Flaubert finds it amusing, the boy is not attractive, the description is too picturesque and typical (*IF* 1:691). Flaubert may talk a good game, but he certainly did not have that homosexual experience of which he writes; to think that, dear reader, would be absurd. Flaubert is an armchair tourist in the realm of practical pederasty. Flaubert might have invented the scene, for Flaubert is a writer, but he certainly did not have homosexual sex.

To ensure that we do not believe Flaubert, Sartre adds one more warning, as he goes beyond the specific scene of Flaubert in the bathhouse. Sartre makes sure that he puts the male gender of Flaubert's other into question: "it is not the man he is looking for, but domination by the other [*de l'autre*]—who could also be a dominatrix" (693). Obviously the "de" of the French is ambiguous, for it could imply domination of the other or by the other. What is clear is that Sartre cannot accept that the other remain an undefined neutral term or a purely masculine one: he must introduce the female dominatrix as a possibility. In other words, Sartre implicitly defines homosexuality as a very narrowly framed physical situation of anal penetration, travestied variant of heterosexual coupling, and makes every other sexual act between two men implicitly or at least potentially a sign of heterosexuality.

These are not the only cases in Sartre's writing in which he refuses to believe in the homosexuality of the other. And we should note that the reality of that homosexuality has nothing to do with the case, that is to say, even if the individual himself says that he is homosexual or has participated in a homosexual act, that does not matter for Sartre. Think of his version of Genet: not content with Genet's own admissions, Sartre has to invent Genet as the homosexual and thief par excellence. In the study of Baudelaire, we find a variant of the same situation. Here the rumor of Baudelaire's schoolboy pederasty must be quashed. It is a rumor that Baudelaire himself indicates he started. How then to explain Sartre's vehement use of the word "perfidious"? Sartre says that "he is undoubtedly at the origin of the perfidious and unfounded echo recorded by Charles Cousin according to which he had been expelled from the Lycée Louis-le-Grand for homosexuality." Perhaps it is because Sartre could not find a story that he, Sartre, could ascertain, prove, or disprove: perhaps it is Baudelaire who betrays not himself, but his reader in Sartre. Sartre's exculpatory remarks (Pacaly 203) about Baudelaire's femininity and dandyism are, as might be expected, framed with the denial of a homosexuality that he, Jean-Paul Sartre, has not invented: "But a man-woman is not necessarily a homosexual" (194); "what the myth of dandyism covers is not homosexuality, but exhibitionism" (195). Again, just as Flaubert's other might be a dominatrix and not a homosexual, Baudelaire's other is also not necessarily a homosexual.

In all these cases, there are refusals to believe that events took place, denials that there might be a blurring of genders or a challenge to a certain order of sexuality. There are questionings of what heterosexuality—not even homosexuality—might mean. In the cases of Rollebon, Flaubert, and the spurious tale of Baudelaire's pederasty, Sartre is talking about an aberrant episode in what would be considered a typical heterosexual existence. Genet's case is somewhat different: there is no heterosexuality to fall back on. For Genet, Sartre invents Genet's homosexuality as an incarnation of bad faith against an imaginary background of heterosexuality, out of which comes Genet the fallen angel. Now since it would be ridiculous to charge Sartre with some sort of heterosexual bowdlerization of the universe, we have to look elsewhere.

What these snippets of stories have in common is that they are received knowledge, tales told by someone else as history's anecdotes. It seems to matter little whether the history is a real or a fictional one. Sartre just cannot believe anyone when he hears that someone is homosexual. Even in the case of Genet, having heard the confession from the horse's mouth, as it were, having read the fantastic confessional novels written by one Jean Genet, Sartre cannot believe him either. Sartre reinvents a homosexual Jean Genet, not the *pour soi* that Genet might be, but some *en soi* homosexual in perpetual bad faith because he has assumed "that" as his identity. It is no wonder that the first volume of Genet's complete works was written by Sartre. It is no wonder that it has passed into the common lore of literary criticism that Sartre "killed" Genet, a murder often discussed in the critical literature (Bauer, "Pretexts" 89–99; Mehlman 167–86; Sichère; Cohen-Solal 412–15). Sartre announces Genet's death from the very beginning: "Genet is nothing other than a dead man" (*SG* 10). Through his own writing, Sartre presides over the liberated author's martyrization, beatification, and sanctification. Sartre's book is the simulacrum of Jean Genet as *en soi* homosexual: *Saint Genet* replaces Genet. Sartre puts Genet to the test and tortures him to see if there is a real homosexual inside or a "mere image, an imposture" (*Thea.* 150c). Genet is weighed by a midwife named Jean-Paul Sartre (who denies his midwifery) and is found wanting. And in the process no one seems to notice that Sartre, like Socrates before him, predictably revealing the true homosexual or the true heterosexual every time, is wearing a midwife's outfit. Like Belshazzar himself, Genet has seen the writing on the wall and comes up short; failing to live up to the total model of bad faith that Sartre has created in Saint Genet, homosexual, Genet is stilled henceforth as a narrative fiction writer. More narrative fiction would mean changing, evolving, erasing, and rewriting. It is better to go to the theater to see oneself, specularly and spectacularly fixed on stage wearing a more and more unremovable mask.

Wrapped up in this revelation, Sartre cannot himself come up short or be found wanting: he cannot become his own Daniel, Genet, Flaubert, or Roquentin. The further he goes, the more he writes, the longer the projects get, the more there is to publish or to abandon. He will not reveal that he is his own midwife, or better yet, he will be the disguised midwife to everyone but Jean-Paul Sartre, for fear of finding either the spurious image or the true one. It is all right to invent homosexuals: Ogier P., the Autodidact in *La Nausée* who molests young boys; Daniel Sereno in *Les Chemins de la liberté*, who is filled with self-loathing; Inès Serrano in *Huis-Clos*, who believes in her own lesbianism; and Jean Genet, who is not only an actor and martyr but also a national treasure and hater of bourgeois hypocrisy. All of that is acceptable, safe, and the surest of disguises.

On the other hand, it is not acceptable to let others invent homosexuals for you. Sartre cannot accept that another invents a homosexual for him, because he must, in that case, reveal himself as midwife. If Flaubert recounts a scene of himself involved in a pederastic experiment, Sartre must deny it; he cannot allow himself merely to be the midwife of Flaubert's self-revelation. It is better to deny every homosexual invented by others. In that way the truth, which is thus the truth of Sartre's own writing that pretends not to have a midwife, reveals itself at every turn. Moreover, if there is the slightest risk of homosexuals being out there, one needs to push away the figures that threaten to invade:

These attitudes-foundations can stay veiled, like a skeleton by the surrounding flesh: in fact, that is what usually happens; the contingency of bodies, the structure of the original project that I am, the history that I historialize can determine the sexual attitude to remain ordinarily implicit within more complex conducts: in particular it is not frequent that one explicitly desires Others "of the same sex." But behind moral prohibitions and societal taboos, the original structure of desire remains, at least in the particular form of trouble named sexual disgust. And this permanence of the sexual project should not be understood as if it had to remain "in us" in an unconscious state. (*EN* 458)

It is difficult to understand the motivation for this disgust that surges up in the middle of a paragraph. Who is disgusted and by what? Everything seems to be clear until Sartre mentions homosexuality and a knee-jerk reaction of sexual disgust immediately ensues. Surging up, perhaps as an example, perhaps not, arising perhaps as an anomaly and perhaps not, homosexuality troubles the order of things. Certainly it is safer to invent it at the appropriate moment before it produces a disgust in the observer or before it overturns the project of order and logic that is now at stake.

Such homosexual desire is infrequent in Sartre's vision of reality: "it is not frequent that one explicitly desires Others 'of the same sex.'" And, one might add, given Sartre's penchant for restricting homosexual behavior to what he wants it to mean, that "explicit desire" is probably even more infrequent. Yet, despite his own acknowledgment of the rarity of the situation, Sartre seems stubbornly to insist on using homosexuality emblematically in his writing. Constrained by the presence of homoeroticism at the origin of philosophy, Sartre simultaneously proffers it and denies it, as he contains it with disgust. Seeking to free philosophy and even action itself from this binding matrix, Sartre marginalizes homosexuality by calling it infrequent. And yet he returns to it over and over again as an example of the developing figure of freedom in his work. Again, the explicitness of the desire poses a problem: Sartre simply cannot believe that anyone is homosexual unless he, Jean-Paul Sartre, has invented that homosexuality for that person. Sartre's concept of infrequency is perhaps correct for the real world, where the percentage of homosexuals is of the order of 1 to 10 percent of the general population, and homosexual desire is certainly less frequent than its heterosexual counterpart. In his writing, however, this supposed infrequency is contradicted by the recurring figures of the homosexual characters, and even if the percentage of homosexual figures in his work is as minimal as that single-digit percentage in the real world, he takes the artistic (or philosophic) license to give those characters great, even pivotal, importance. Already, in *La Nausée*, the Autodidact is a pivotal figure in the plot: it is his singular action of molesting a young man in the library that provokes Roquentin finally to choose an action of his own. If Roquentin's relations with Anny or with the Patronne are more or less floppy, accidental, contingent, thoughtless, or viscously unconscious, here with the Autodidact, homosexuality provides the raison d'être for Roquentin's only act of caring, kindness, involvement, or sympathy. Again, in *Les Chemins de la liberté*, even if Daniel's willingness to marry Marcelle is born of bad faith, it leads to an action that Sartre goes on to accept as being both valid and responsible. And of the three canonic examples given for bad faith in the early pages of *L'Etre et le néant*, the third, which, as we shall see, is extremely problematic, is devoted to the problem of "the homosexual." The percentages have certainly changed.

Are we to assume, then, that there is no exemplarity involved and that these and further examples of homosexual characters in key works, such as Genet, are merely representative of one phenomenon among others in the human comedy? This hardly seems fair, given Sartre's studied choice of detail, never clearer nor more emblematic than in a work like *Huis-Clos*, where every detail has a didactic purpose, down to the Barbedienne bust and the letter opener. As with the three examples of bad faith, once again the percentages are up to one in three. Here as elsewhere, Sartre's characters are less condemned to freedom than they are condemned to choice relative to a given set of details, characteristics, and complexes of elements. In Sartre's work, a character is not homosexual by chance. So what can we make of this exemplarity, and specifically, can we make a leap that seems necessary but that has not yet been justified: what relation is there between the philosophical statement, the literary statement, and the critical statement? Can we make some sort of an adequation between the description of the bad faith of the homosexual in *L'Etre et le néant*, the character of Daniel in *Les Chemins de la liberté*, and the reading given Flaubert's experience in Egypt in *L'Idiot de la famille*?

I have already red-flagged the idea of automatically equating the depiction of the "same" subject in various genres. While the Autodidact and Daniel have a lot in common, do Daniel and Genet? Or the Autodidact and the homosexual in the third example of bad faith? Certainly the argument against that adequation seems at first glance to be the stronger: there is no necessary reason to make an adequation between a philosophical remark, discussion, or development and a literary one (to choose just two, for now). And even if there were some perceptible relation between the two, it is not necessarily a direct one. One could assume, for example, that there is a possible philosophical reading of *La Nausée* or a literary one of *L'Etre et le néant*; the former would involve a discussion of freedom, the latter, a comment about poor character development. As Descombes (31–46) has shown in his discussions of Proust, there are at least two approaches to such a philosophical reading: one takes the philosophical statements of the work as a sketch of the philosophical position at hand, the other takes the stories and draws philosophical conclusions from them.

And yet, to my mind, the holistic approach to the depiction of homosexuality is justified not because the three kinds of statements are the same, but because the attendant structuring of discourse is "oddly" the same. Throughout Sartre's work, whatever the genre, and whatever the stage in his life, homosexuality is presented as *unheimlich*: strange, yet strangely familiar. Sartre's refusal to accept hearsay versions of homosexual behavior even extends to the word itself; it is a word that cannot be believed:

> Will we speak of homosexuality? Perhaps. But not without taking precautions. For this reason, first, that our nominalist framework [*notre parti pris de nominalisme*] forbids us from classifying: sexual drives must be understood— as must all projects—by starting from a complex situation that is irreducible to the sum of its elements, which makes them by its very complexity in the moment that they go beyond it toward their end. (*IF* 1:686)

Here, the *Aufhebung* of the original elements, the basic sexual building blocks that feed into other, more complex behaviors, is the same one Sartre discerns in his earlier approach to the matter in *L'Etre et le néant*. And the sexual elements forming part of the larger behavioral situation come up in the same context as a mention of homosexuality (*EN* 458). Lust, the pleasures of the flesh, and even the famous polite sexual congress between Roquentin and the Patronne admirably discussed by Hollier (203–8) are all in need of phenomenological analysis in and of themselves. The reported stories of homosexuality are dissolved into a larger context and are part of a behavioral pattern that cannot be reduced to its constituent parts.

Unique among phenomena, homosexuality may not be able to be subjected to phenomenological analysis. For once, appearance does not reveal anything.

Like a good investigative journalist, Sartre will not believe any previous story of homosexuality unless he has probed it himself, unless he has proven it himself, and unless he has (re)written it himself. Early on in the study of Genet, Sartre says that "we will be very close to deciphering Genet's secret: his passive pederasty" (*SG* 94). Yet as might be expected, Sartre chooses to reorganize Genet, even when he, Sartre, has done this deciphering of the invisible secret. As Sartre notes, Genet says that he was a pederast before he was a thief and that the latter was only a consequence of the former. Still, even when Sartre has done this deciphering, he says that "we cannot follow him along that line [*nous ne pouvons le suivre dans cette voie*]" (*SG* 94). Again we are reminded of the denials of Rollebon's travesty and Flaubert's and Baudelaire's homosexual encounters. That passive pederasty, Genet's deep dark secret, nevertheless becomes the insistent truth that Sartre resurrects not two pages later, as Sartre repeats the action: "Genet, sexually, is first of all a raped child. This first rape was the gaze of the other, who surprised him, penetrated him, transformed him forever into an object. Let me make myself clear [*Qu'on m'entende*]: I am not saying that his original crisis *resembles* a rape, I am saying that it *is* a rape" (*SG* 96).

If we think back to Sartre's insistent denial of homosexuality, Sartre is saying that the original crisis also *does* resemble a rape. Genet's original crisis both *is* a rape and *resembles* a rape. Only in a world of insistent bivalent logic does such a remark appear facetious. Within the context of Sartrean phenomenology, it makes eminent sense; and within the context of the construct I am proposing of Sartre's concept of homosexuality it makes even more sense. Let us briefly see how it works within a Sartrean phenomenology: Sartre is endlessly insisting in *Saint Genet* that Genet is the apotheosis of bad faith. As such Genet founds his own concept of his self, as a being in bad faith, on the dispositions and constraints of the other. The rape of Genet is such a founding moment: just as the waiter is a waiter or the homosexual is a homosexual in *L'Etre et le néant*, this rape is a rape, and that means, for Sartre's Genet, that his body is a "that." Like the hand of the woman in the same chapter of *L'Etre et le néant*, Genet's anus is a thing, not part of him. Genet goes on to found the bad faith of his being on that anus as *en soi*. At the same time, the action resembles a rape: it is a theft of Genet's very capability of defining himself through his own actions. Like a rape, this resemblance violates him to the core of his phenomenological being as well.

Finally, what also is provocative about this remark is the statement of disbelief: "we cannot follow him here." In saying that, Sartre takes the final steps in his path of disbelief, vision, and invention. Sartre is caught in the same game of Freudian denial in which he simultaneously tells the truth: Sartre is not following Genet, because that would mean to some that Sartre too is homosexual. Sartre is not following Genet, because he, Sartre, can never accept that a homosexual is there before Sartre himself has had a chance to establish the individual's homosexuality. Yet in a manner of speaking, he does follow Genet: with his eyes, here and elsewhere, with his pen, Sartre rapes Genet to make him the homosexual Sartre has always wanted Genet to be.

Unless Sartre sees it, unless Sartre writes it, homosexuality does not exist. It is no problem, then, when he writes it, even if he has not seen it in action: he can invent homosexual characters and create the most stereotypical situations, including many of those in which Daniel is thrust in *Les Chemins de la liberté*, whether it is the scene in a homosexual bar or Daniel's meditation on the invading blond warrior-gods, a description that is almost too good to be true:

[Daniel thought] "our conquerors" and he was enveloped with pleasure. He boldly returned their gaze, he filled himself with that blond hair, those tanned faces in which the eyes seemed to be glacial lakes, those thin waists, those incredibly long, muscular thighs. He murmured, "How handsome they are!" (*MA* 1218–19)

If elsewhere, following Descartes, following Sartre himself, we doubt, here we must not follow Sartre's doubting example. He has doubted the existence of homosexuality for us and reinvented it so we take his word as the truth. Whereas for Crevel, it is memory that is insistently and jarringly heterosexual, for Sartre, denying Socrates as midwife, it is truth itself that is resolutely, obstreperously heterosexual.

Sartre's act of invention is the same in the fiction, the philosophy, and the criticism: having doubted, and lacking the proof he needs, Sartre decides to tell a story of a homosexual. In all three areas, Sartre invents stories of homosexuals. So even in a philosophical tract like *L'Etre et le néant*, a homosexual is and is not taken as part of a philosophical argument. Since such situations are so infrequent (*EN* 458), they are singularities that could not possibly be used to found a philosophical argument; they are well-nigh worthless in their exemplarity. And yet one of Sartre's greatest homosexual stories appears as the third example of bad faith, one nonexemplary example along with two exemplary ones, a story for the less-than-philosophical reader. Thus there can never be any phenomenology of homosexuality for one more reason: homosexuality is "always already" subject to narrative. It does not exist except as invented discourse.

The "always" is clear: for Sartre, the only way of introducing homosexuality is with his own narrative. Homosexuality does not exist "out there" in a way that he can believe. The "already," however, is less clear. For Sartre, homosexuality occupies a special position in the world of phenomena, because unlike all others it is completely resistant to the gaze (*le regard*) that will be a focus of *L'Etre et le néant*. Alain Buisine notes that in the Sartrean universe, what the homosexual desires is "to extinguish the interior gaze to coincide with the image that others make of him" (102). The Sartrean figure of homosexuality goes beyond a phenomenology of the internalized other to a resistance to phenomenology itself. Homosexuality is invisible. No amount of external signs of it can be perceived as anything but accidental, contingent, and perhaps even misleading.

Take the case of Daniel in *Les Chemins de la liberté*. His presence at a hangout for homosexuals (*AR* 530) can be as contingent to his homosexuality as is his eventual marriage with Marcelle: in neither case do the facts of the situation actually indicate that Daniel is (a) homosexual. No, for Sartre the only thing that a gaze can espy is the act of anal penetration that for him is the key act of homosexuality—and that act is invisible. Flaubert is not homosexual because what he really desires is to have his penis manipulated by the mouth or hand of another individual. In that Flaubert is not the active sexual partner, for "active" is defined as the one moving (and not possessing) the phallus, Flaubert is not really homosexual (*IF* 696ff).

This redefinition of active and passive may be significant. Ordinarily, one would define the active partner in a homosexual relation as the one actively penetrating the passive partner, who is the one being anally penetrated. And as we know, this dyad has often been viewed in a lopsided manner, with the penetrator not always being considered homosexual. Sartre, however, takes "active" and "passive" literally: the active partner is the one who moves, the one who acts. Thus for Sartre one can actively be homosexual (or heterosexual, for that matter) or one can be condemned to the Sartrean limbo of in-activity. As Toril Moi shows in her reading of the scene of bad faith in the cafe, Sartre denies a project to the woman; her only possibili-ties involve reactions to the project of the man (Fourny and Mina-hen). Condemned to a Sartrean hell of bad faith, the passive homo-sexual is also denied a project. And the active homosexual seems to have a project because Sartre has invented one for him. In Sartre's world it may be impossible for there to be another project when a straight white male already has one.

As to a move away from the somewhat mechanical model of anal penetration, we have a curious remark by Sartre in *Saint Genet* (148), where he says that fellatio, which is "the job of the passive pederast," is particularly "ignominious [*infamante*]." Now, this would seem to be a clear-cut case of *discours indirect libre*, in which Sartre is speaking for Genet's fictional characters. Yet Sartre adds a note that puts everything in question: Sartre explains that this fellatio is not igno-minious "in itself," but is so here "because it is without reciprocity" (*SG* 148n). It is no longer clear that Sartre is referring to Genet's own writing: Genet's stylized, role-oriented personae have been em-phasized from the beginning of Sartre's study. One would not expect to find any sexual reciprocity either in Genet or in Sartre's version of Genet. But neither do we find reciprocity in the scene between the man and the woman in the cafe, so his action or her action must be ignominious as well. Within the context of Genet's world as de-scribed by Sartre, the alternative to the situation of reciprocity, which I would assume to be mutual fellatio or "69," is the one-way nature of anal penetration. So one wonders why this intrusion of the igno-minious occurs, though it is perhaps that Sartre considers this act of fellatio either not a truly homosexual act, that being uniquely anal penetration, or a travesty of that act. Certainly, Sartre's concept of oral sex is ambiguous; elsewhere in *Saint Genet*, Sartre once again seems to be changing his previous position that mechanically and strictly defined activity and passivity:

He penetrates his lovers only rarely, and he never speaks of such intercourse with the pomp and lyricism he keeps to celebrate sex in which he played the passive role. On the contrary, he practices *fellatio* frequently, and with casual partners, and often does only that. It is that fellatio is considered by inverts [*invertis*] to be the female's job: one gives the indolent male his pleasure. But at the same time, the passivity of the sucker is not complete: he *caresses*, he *acts*. Thus he can present it as the whim of a man even when it is lived by him as the submission of a woman. (*SG* 463)

Sartre adds in a note: "Some prideful women, far from considering *fellatio* as a sign of subjection to the male, see it as a way of equaling the male. To them it seems that they possess him and they prefer it to letting themselves be penetrated" (*SG* 463n).

This ambivalence about oral sex does finally show a loosening up about roles, genders, behaviors, and sexes. By *L'Idiot de la famille*, there has been one significant fulfillment of the Sartrean model of action: the acceptance of freedom and acting upon that freedom have been extended, not to sexual orientation, which for Sartre precedes the ability to act, but to sexual preference. Amid all the discussions of bad faith and all the indications of Sartre's own literal and figurative eye-rape of Genet, from time to time in *Saint Genet* one can attest to the construction of a homosexual subject. As if by miracle, in one of the last chapters of *Saint Genet*, entitled "Please Use Genet Correctly [*Prière pour le bon usage de Genet*]," Sartre says quite bluntly that Genet "invents the pederastic *subject*" (*SG* 649). Sartre relates this remark to a reference to J. Vuillemin on Shakespeare, wherein the spectators "participate instead of seeing." Finally, then, at the end of *Saint Genet*, there will be no penetrating vision that insists on seeing or on inventing what must be seen. Is this too dangerous, too problematic for Sartre? Does it shake up too many of his phenomenological presuppositions? I do not know, but I do know that the study of Flaubert returns to an older model to insist on the vision of the other as the constitution of that other.

Since homosexuality cannot be seen, because it is knowable only through what is revealed in narrative, it is always already parading about in the veiled garb of fiction. And any look, any gaze, no matter how penetrating, is in error. For Sartre, the voyeur (undoubtedly always a masculine position) never sees what he sets out to see:

It can be said that I can discover that I made a mistake: here I am, hunched over the keyhole; suddenly I hear steps. I am traversed [*parcouru*] through and through by a shudder of shame: someone saw me. I stand up, I run my eyes over the deserted corridor. It was a false alarm. (*EN* 324)

If there are other telltale signs of heterosexuality, that is, visible anatomical difference, no such signs are present for homosexuality, and without difference, one can never be sure. Looking through a keyhole, the voyeur cannot even then see homosexuality outside of himself, for at that very moment he is penetrater and penetrated, homosexual and, *horresco referens*, pederast. As Sartre says in the study of Baudelaire, "And the one who watches, anyone can test this, forgets that he can be watched" (*Baud* 188–89). This double vision and double homosexuality in the voyeur become a more precise homoerotic scopophilia in *L'Idiot de la famille*: "[Alfred] would like to be seen by Gustave as he has an orgasm, swooning, and knowing that the spectacle of this abandon gives the voyeur an erection despite himself" (*IF* 1:1048). Since Sartre seems to insist on seeing, since therefore his position would be that of the doubly homosexual voyeur, and since that insistence is impossible to accept, when all is said and done, it is safer to avoid being made homosexual by just telling the story oneself.

Male homosexuality must remain invisible for everyone to remain imprisoned in his or her own heterosexual freedom. Yet this invisibility should not be equated with absence. Paradoxically, like the famed Freudian castration scenario, absence or lack is all too palpable. When there is an absence, the situation is far clearer than this twilight world of male homosexuality for Sartre. Lesbianism is visible, not as the interiority of the woman, but as the exteriority of two phallusless males: difference is posited against the internalized image of the male self. As Simone de Beauvoir points out in *The Second Sex*, the lesbian "obviously remains deprived of a male member; she can deflower her friend [*amie*] with her hand or use an artificial penis to imitate possession; she is no less a castrato" (1:493). The lesbian is visibly *en manque*; Sartre would not disagree. The problem with the male homosexual is that there is no distinguishing exterior sign; his difference is within and is repeated at every sexual congress by a repetition of the innerness, and thus the invisibility, of his behavior.

As Oreste Pucciani (639) points out, one can make an analogy between the "becoming homosexual" that Sartre wants to demonstrate in Genet's case and Simone de Beauvoir's famous line that one is not born a woman but becomes one. Sartre himself makes a parallel between Genet's conception of himself as an object for others and Simone de Beauvoir's discussion of the structuring of female sexuality through the perception of the woman as object (*SG* 48). As Pucciani (642) notes, Sartre himself says of Genet that one is not born a homosexual; ostensibly, then, Genet becomes a homosexual as others become women. The opposition in Sartre is not the same as Simone de Beauvoir's opposition of man and woman, however, for Sartre opposes "homosexual" and "normal." Even though, according to Sartre, any individual becomes "one or the other according to the accidents of one's history and one's reaction to these accidents," normalcy gets no more than a passing nod. Normalcy seems to be the irony here, not homosexuality, for what is normal here if not male and heterosexual? Because of the unremarkable, nomothetic nature of his categories, the male heterosexual easily identifies with "The Male Heterosexual," which is the *en soi* to end all *en sois* and simultaneously the founding myth that the society maintains for itself.

So perhaps it is not the woman being courted, nor the petty-bourgeois worker who elevates his oppression into a profession as he becomes "A Waiter," nor even the homosexual who is in bad faith, but ultimately the male heterosexual who has assumed his normalcy without question. Sartre's exploration of the bad faith of others screens a refusal to explore his own bad faith as he himself defines it. It is a way of avoiding the putting into question of either the purported normalcy of the *en soi* of "male heterosexuality" or the purported normalcy of any male heterosexual, in this case Jean-Paul Sartre, who identifies with that transparent, normal, clear, and ever-present *en soi* that moves the world in which we live.

III. Hermaphroditic Hotels

As Sartre's own reading of Flaubert shows us, reading the work of an author written before he or she becomes the author we know, the author of his or her first mature works, is not the simplest task. One hypothesis to use in approaching such works is that in these works the distance between "individual" and "author" is minimal. It is not that the works are somehow transparently biographical, but rather that the tricks the author will discover to both become and create the project of his own writing, which always involve degrees of camouflage, *escamotage*, and detours, will not yet have occurred.

In the writings before Sartre was "Sartre," the opposition between heterosexuality and homosexuality is not polarized, as it was to become in *La Nausée* and *Le Mur*. In Sartre's early writings, there is talk, for example, of "hermaphroditic hotels" (*EJ* 44). More notably, friendship is described in one piece as being "stormier than a passion" (*EJ* 140), with the narrator admitting his jealousy, like that of a "maniacal lover." Comparing a friendship and a love affair brings both into a continuous spectrum of human relations which neither the phenomenology of Sartrean love nor the distancing of the authorial self from the homosexual character will fully shake. Even in *L'Etre et le néant*, Sartre continues to make parallels between the two situations, though he will manifestly not draw the same conclusions. For this phenomenological Sartre, these two situations are two forms of constitutive structures, still similar in that capacity of making a "we": "the coexistence that appears in my friendship with Pierre or in the couple that I form with Annie. What should be shown is that 'being with Pierre' or 'being with Annie' is a constitutive structure of my concrete being" (*EN* 293).

It is only when Sartre *sees* the other that he establishes the distinction between love and friendship, the difference between homoerotic/homosexual behavior and heterosexual behavior. Sartre was certainly correct in entitling the memoir of his childhood *The Words*; it is a childhood of sound and language that is clearly reflected in his youthful writings. As he becomes the mature author with works such as *La Nausée*, he shifts from the presence of the aural and the oral first to a representation of that presence and then to the realm of the visual and the visible, necessary for action to occur. *La Nausée* is a record of that change, with the primacy of sound already having retreated into the record that produces a mechanical sound from a jukebox. With sound receding, it is the surface of the object that becomes visibly present: the moving hand of the Autodidact, the root of the chestnut tree, visible spurs to action and engagement.

Yet for the earlier Sartre, the structures of friendship and love are not merely two different varieties of what he would later call constitutive structures, because they seem to bleed into one another to become indistinguishable in some cases. In a piece ostensibly based on the friendship between Richard Wagner and Friedrich Nietzsche, the chapter in which the two meet is entitled "Les lèvres d'Organte" (*EJ* 201, 224). From the very first, Sartre values the oral and the aural: the lips that speak and the lips that kiss are the same lips. In the realm of the oral, no distinction is drawn between homosexuality and heterosexuality. In these early works written before the emphasis on visibility and on the problematic nature of invisibility associated with the Sartrean "vision" of homosexuality, the other senses are recognized. The tactility and coenesthesia alluded to in "Les lèvres d'Organte" bring proximity and homoerotic sensibility into the same sphere: "He was more sensitive to movement: movement in a face showed him the eyes, but he could not have said what color his eyes were. He thought, 'He blinked his eyes as if . . . ' " (*EJ* 224). "*Quos ego*," one might say, since there is no follow-up to the "as if," but, on the next page, there is a hand placed "familiarly on his knee" and the joyful feeling that the older man has at those "young eyes attached to him." Further along, there is a singular description of the two men as having the same "incontinent" facility to generalize, and yet another analogy between friendship and love:

From that moment until the end of their conversation, he constantly felt the strong temptation to ask Organte: "Do you want to be my master?" In the same way, when he had had his first mistress, a hooker in the Latin Quarter, more fresh and more tender than the others, he had been obsessed by the crazy desire to ask her, "Do you want to marry me?" (*EJ* 230)

Immediacy and the illusion of the indivisible ideality of the universe are maintained, a whole in which one does not completely distinguish between heterosexual love and same-sex friendship, and in which the latter has thus more than a tinge of homoeroticism. Significantly, when there is separation, when both men are forced to read at a distance, as Organte reads Frédéric's manuscript and writes him a letter, Frédéric realizes that "I was your toy. . . . You have no love" (*EJ* 285). Reading and vision at a distance are the irrefutable proof of the impossibility of the ideal of hermaphroditic hotels and indistinguishable relations.

It is not merely that some youthful idealism disappears in *La Nausée*; it is more that the reliance on visibility as the cornerstone of Sartre's developing phenomenology comes to the fore and brings with it a distinction of sexualities. Since that visibility is in direct contradiction to what Sartre believes to be the invisibility of homosexuality, the system threatens to collapse unless there is an escape from the imprisonment of vision. Thus, still invisible, homosexuality becomes an insistent phantom: something that cannot be seen, but about which one must endlessly speak, as if in so doing one might make it appear. But how, in fact, might one make homosexuality appear through discourse?

One way of considering it is to see it as a phenomenon analogous to the nausea that surges up, unnamed, at various moments in *La Nausée*. Discourse, Sartre seems to believe, may make homosexuality appear; at the same time he knows that any appearance is subject to that discourse and therefore always distant from it, always a case of falsification. Consider the example of the Autodidact, named, or not named, "Ogier P***" (*N* 8n). In "Sartre's Homo/Textuality," George Bauer points to the pun in the first name, "*O chier*—the eye that eats the excremental text-object" (in Stambolian and Marks 312). Other readings of this allusion-pregnant name come to mind as well. One might read the punning name in another way, as "Oh shit, p . . . ": excrete what makes you a pederast, force that phallus out that you have been hiding, show that you are involved in anal intercourse instead of hiding what is happening from the world. Or, alternatively, "Oh, j'y ai p": "Oh, I have some pederast," like the Voltairean "Mangeons du jésuite." Like Roquentin's nausea, homosexuality is an excess that explodes categories and overturns the order of discourse.

So perhaps the simplest reading of the name is the best: the alphabetic sequence of the initials of the first and last names, O-P, the fact that the last name is not a name but an initial, less the conventional sign for some modest anonymity than the unspeakable or unwritable sign of the "Pederast" he is. This character can be called the Autodidact because he has gotten through the A's in the library and has thus read the reflection in discourse of that part of himself. He cannot yet have a last name, for he has not gotten as far as the P's in his reading. From his point of view, someday, "some of these days" perhaps, he will reach the part of the library in which he reads of himself, in which he knows how to be a pederast, and in which the written signs of pederasty will suddenly become visible to him. Until then, prisoner of the invisible, the Autodidact can show only signs and displacements that may or may not be true. In *La Nausée*, such a point is in a hypothetical future, never to be reached by the Autodidact who will thus never successfully read himself. The moment of self-definition through language is reached in works like *Les Chemins de la liberté* and *L'Etre et le néant*, yet Sartre will still insist on its difference from the truth: written signs will not coincide with being or nature. Daniel must be in bad faith, as must the frank homosexual admitting his homosexuality in the third example of bad faith. For Sartre, the interpretation of signs happens in an uncertain future: in *Huis-Clos*, Garcin can never be sure of his readership and Inès can never be sure who will read the letters she handles. Like the existential Dasein, signs are thrown into the world of uncertainty. Sartre's project, however, involves interpreting signs backwards: reading the truth behind Flaubert, behind Genet, behind being itself. Sartre will continue to invent the nature behind the signs. It is Sartre alone, not Genet, not Flaubert, not Daniel, not the Autodidact, who can be in good faith when speaking of homosexuality. The position is his and his alone.

Since the homosexual as such is invisible in his truth, what is visible can only be thought of as being stereotypical. Thus the Autodidact's "eyelids are lowered and I can leisurely contemplate his beautiful curly eyelashes—women's eyelashes" (*N* 38–39), and later on, the Autodidact "blushed and his hips swayed gracefully" (*N* 91). Ignorance abounds and dissolves in a sea of bad faith: the Autodidact has not reached the letter P in his reading, so he cannot know who he is; Roquentin does not yet know that the Autodidact is what others will call a "queer [*pédé*]." Thus before the screaming assault of the guard in the library, the Autodidact is not yet a *pédé* for other characters in the novel. And even though the reader has figured out that the Autodidact belongs in the category of homosexual males, the character only presumably becomes a *pédé* for us when he has been called that. As Sartre notes in his study of Genet, there is an incisiveness of the act of naming when it comes to homosexuals; he says that every pederast has been "treated as a *pédé* at least once in his life and the name remained engraved in his flesh" (*SG* 53n). Along with

Roquentin, along with the Autodidact himself, we are witness to this act of engraving, as the Autodidact-as-*pédé* is written into existence as a pederast.

Before that naming, the Autodidact is not a friend, not a woman, not a suitable object of desire for anyone; he is seen as a caricature, even a travesty, of a woman. He seems to have her eyes and hips, yet he has no definite or indicative signs. And then again, in that he spurs Roquentin to some action, that is, the offer of a helping hand immediately refused, the Autodidact is ironically that midwife, a loathsome one to be sure, who brings forth ideas and action. As Rhiannon Goldthorpe justly notes, the explicit act of writing at the end of *La Nausée* is Roquentin's account of the scene in the library. As she notes, "the validity of narrative is not questioned" (44). So this scene of molestation has complex results. It is the scene of self-discovery for the Autodidact; he does not discover a homosexual male living his freedom, but a loathsome *pédé*, an abject creature scorned by society. This is as it must be in Sartre's world, however: without Sartre, the individual's recognition of his or her own homosexuality is always an alienated recognition of someone who has internalized the hateful words and has turned them on himself or herself in a painful act of self-mutilating tattooing. For the homosexual to be homosexual, as *pour soi*, he or she needs Sartre or Sartre's vicar, in this case Roquentin, to write, describe, and finally invent that homosexuality from a dispassionate position. Only then can the individual be free as homosexual. And yet there is one final irony: Sartre or Roquentin needs the self-loathing, the bad faith, the other defined as *pédé* in order to write and to separate false ideas from true. Roquentin's action and his act of witnessing through writing invent the Autodidact anew, and after the fact, as a homosexual. Roquentin needs the Autodidact to have been called "*pédé*," Sartre needs Genet to have called himself the same thing, Sartre needs Flaubert to have admitted having had a homosexual encounter, Sartre needs Baudelaire to have spread rumors about his sexual preference. In all these cases, Sartre needs the spurious discourse of the other as his midwife just as he, as if in a mirror, serves as midwife to them, and separates what he believes to be true from false images: the list of who is and who is not gay. Complicitous with Sartre in this invention through writing, we have helped write the Sartrean homosexual into existence.

Disguised as a pederast and in travesty as a scholar, the Autodidact is never what he seems because he cannot seem to be anything known or knowable in this world: "And the Autodidact's hand; I had taken it and shaken it one day at the Library and I had the impression that it was not completely a hand. I had thought of a big white worm, but it wasn't that either" (*N* 154). Transparently, the hand is and is not a metaphoric penis, the same hand that will eventually be used as a sexual organ as the Autodidact caresses the young man's hand, an interplay between hands and sex organs that continues in *L'Etre et le néant* (Hollier 195–200). Visible organ metonymically substituting for an invisible penis, the hand is a "big white worm," a metaphor for the absent organ. Not wholly absent, not subject to the castration of a Freudian reading, not the always castrated other who will figure in *Le Deuxième sexe*, the Autodidact remains some viscous human floundering around between presence and absence and between the thrownness of existential freedom and the budding bad faith of those who refuse their freedom. Disgusting travesty who is a poor excuse for a midwife, the Autodidact elicits perhaps nothing more than the viscous afterbirth for a stillbirth.

For the Autodidact can never be free. He is a slave to the alphabetized world of what has already been written, the practico-inert world wherein he would find himself. He is destined to remain a slave, and an ignorant one at that. He will never get to the P's in the library; he will never find out what the basest, vilest definition of a pederast is. A poor excuse for a midwife, he is rather a back-street abortionist who cannot even aspire to being in bad faith. Later, clad in clothes that can never be removed, dead in a Second Empire drawing room, the Autodidact will not become Inès, the lesbian, but Estelle, the infant-killer.

Now, Sartre will not let the Autodidact freely use his penis; even if the author were to permit that freedom, the organ in question would immediately disappear behind a shroud or sheath that makes it invisible. This is not at all the castration scenario of some Freudian phantasm of heterosexual lovemaking, the image with which all children are supposedly scarred at one point or another. Given the biographical data, we know that Sartre did not espy his parents in the act. Believers in this scenario, including Sartre's own version of Freud in the proposed movie script, well-discussed by Rhiannon

Goldthorpe (Fourny and Minahen), might hypothesize that it is that very absence of the phantasm he knows *must* be there that controls Sartre's depiction of the problem of invisibility: Sartre is *en manque de fantasme*.

In heterosexuality, Sartre is always sure that the other is just what *she* is, though Simone de Beauvoir will obviously take great pains to disagree, since for her, the woman is decidedly *not* what *she* is. Sartre does not waver in his understanding of the heterosexual couple, act, or relation. Undergoing a Husserlian *epoche* on the carnal level, the male member can be bracketed as invisible in heterosexuality, for the woman, *there* as desire's phantasmatic Dasein, object of the male project, is herself always proof enough. She incarnates the desire by the male; she is the metonymy and metaphor for his penis and we do not need to see it to believe it. Her very presence ensures the viability of the model and the phenomenology of heterosexuality, founded on the woman as *en soi*. With homosexuality, no proof is ever adequate, nothing can serve as a metaphor or metonymy for the male member.

In these early writings, Sartre structures homosexual desire as a scene of pederastic power. The scenes in *La Nausée* and in *Le Mur* are recounted from differing points of view, the first relative to the actions of the Autodidact, the second relative to those of Lucien, the high school student who has a homosexual experience with an older individual, Achille Bergère, and cast by that name under the Gidean sign of the pastoral. In both cases, an older individual, the pederast as such, successfully (*Le Mur*) or unsuccessfully (*La Nausée*) attempts a seduction of a supposedly innocent young man. Of course we can never know if the youth is "innocent," for we can see nothing. And we know that no midwife will be allowed to determine the rules of the game for the young man. Moreover, for Sartre, a power differential is always displayed in the homosexual seduction. In these works, homosexuality is placed under the rubric of pederasty, but it is a reversal of the Gidean model illustrated in works such as *Si le grain ne meurt*. As shall be seen below, even if in Gide's argument for the naturalness of pederasty he places it under the double sign of the pastoral and the educational in *Corydon*, in works such as *Si le grain ne meurt* the younger man, the natural Maghrebin male, has the power of innocence and nature on his side. It is only after the initial act of liberation that the pederastic model comes into play. Such an idyllic view of nature scarcely exists in the Sartrean universe, where it is the older man who has knowledge and experience, even if, as is the case of the Autodidact, that knowledge is considered perverse or parasitic. It is no wonder, then, that in his eulogy for Gide, "Gide vivant," Sartre reproduces his attraction and rejection of Gide, just as he both internalizes and reverses the model of Gidean pederasty in his writings of the thirties: "every movement of the mind brought us closer or distanced us *as well* from Gide" (*S4* 85).

Sartre cannot yet allow a homosexual relation to assume the amplitude of a heterosexual relation, nor can it have the freedom and equality he ostensibly associates with his own relationship to his peer, Simone de Beauvoir. Perhaps the concept of homosexuality developed in these works is itself a travesty, a disguised heterosexuality in which the young man plays the role of the innocent young girl caught in an unequal situation in which the male dominates, in which the man decides everything, but in which, at the same time, the man takes responsibility for nothing. Certainly, this dissociation of power and responsibility will carry over into *Les Chemins de la liberté*, in which the concept of homo- and heterosexual relations has shifted noticeably, especially in regard to the problematics of freedom, bad faith, and responsibility outlined in *L'Etre et le néant*. In the trilogy, characters seem to have internalized the Sartrean concepts of freedom and bad faith at the same time; there is no Gidean *disponibilité*, no idyll, no utopian sexual act. In the trilogy, the heterosexual Mathieu will ultimately refuse to take responsibility for having fathered a child, and the homosexual Daniel, despite his chicanery about money in the first volume, will eventually accept being the father of the same child, his own homosexuality notwithstanding. So by this point, Sartre can at least project the idea of a homosexual who is not wholly in bad faith and who is at least partially *engagé*.

Now the initial model of homosexuality in Sartre's writing is not without its continuing effect, for the question of visibility and invisibility continues to work long after Sartre has abandoned that model in favor of the engaged model of the trilogy or the model of absolute bad faith, the obverse of the same coin, in *Saint Genet*. In *La Nausée* and *Le Mur*, the structure of unequal power that forms the homosexual relationship also interiorizes the invisibility Sartre associates with homosexuality. For Sartre in the thirties, homosexuality is the unhappy marriage of Victorian heterosexuality and invisibility. The invisibility is present on both sides of the structuring of pederasty, but Sartre underlines the relation between this invisibility and the point of view. Invisibility is turned into blindness: homosexuality is not wholly invisible, but the agent, whose point of view we are following, cannot see. Thus the Autodidact, who continues to read poorly, refuses to see the egregious nature of his own behavior in caressing the hand of the young man in the library: the Autodidact cannot see that he is a *pédé*. Caught within a binary structure from which the world has disappeared, the Autodidact blindly pursues his action as if he were free to do so, as if he were a character in a work by Gide.

Sartre is not stressing the antisocial or immoral nature of this behavior, for the same scene exists in a more positive light in "L'Enfance d'un chef." This time there is completion of the action, a homosexual episode in a life that seems to be, if somewhat epicene, less determined by homosexuality than by power. On a thematic level, this story is about overcoming weakness: when Lucien is initially described as a girl ("EC" 324), this feminine nature is more the stereotypical sign of weakness than the indication of some hidden sexual orientation. Still, there is a wealth of oral imagery in this little scene, a figural node that will come to stand in Sartre's work for a blurring or ambiguity in sexual stance, as George Bauer has shown in "Eating the Other." Mme Portier tells Lucien's mother that he is cute enough "to eat" (*croquer*) and M. Bouffardier, whose name is a sign of food (*bouffe*), caresses Lucien's arms as he feminizes him. And once again, this will appear as late as *L'Idiot de la famille*; the moment of oral incorporation will be projected backward out of the present into some original past of textuality: "To taste man, that is what is the best; love devours; to kiss is to eat—Hegel said it first" (*IF* 1:708n).

Still, like the Autodidact blind to his actions, Lucien is equally oblivious. He does not consider himself homosexual even though he has taken part in homosexual activity: "It's not so bad, he thought, I can still save myself. He took advantage of my confusion, but I am not *really* [*vraiment*] a pederast" ("EC" 357). Perhaps, as the German expression goes, for Lucien "*einmal ist keinmal*": once is never. A childhood experiment, a chance occurrence, something with no consequences, we would undoubtedly think in real life. But narrative consequences are different, and Sartre's construction of the story gives us a model for the bad faith that he will name as such in his philosophical writings. So the chance event in narrative has consequences, not the least of which is the construction of a sentence of bad faith: Lucien is a pederast to the extent that he believes he is not a pederast. Yet phenomenologically, Lucien is willfully blind and, since he cannot see himself as a *pédé*, he is therefore *not* one. Moreover, the Sartrean *pédé* occupies only one role: from Sartre's point of view, the pederast is the active older man. Even as late as the study of Flaubert, Sartre still believes in this rather narrow definition of the pederast. It is as if, once again, only the adult male can have a project, in this case the project of being a pederast; what will be denied to the woman in the cafe is also denied to Lucien. As he grounds the consumption of human flesh in a homoeroticism one hardly suspected in Hegel, Sartre will eventually spell out what he means by pederasty. In the world he constructs for Gustave Flaubert, Gidean before the fact, the description of pederasty makes the innocence of the younger other very clear. It also erases pederasty as a homosexual act:

[P]ederasty (in the narrowest sense of the term) seems to him somehow the noble part of homosexuality: one *takes*; the lad [*giton*], with his smooth skin, is the simple *ersatz* of a woman: as Genet says, the male who submits sexually to another male takes him for a supermale. (*IF* 1:704)

Over the course of a career, Sartre has returned to his original position only to wipe it out. The pederasty that he sees and describes in the thirties, the pederasty that he invents for us to see, will be in the final analysis just a poor man's version of heterosexuality. The boy is not a boy but a substitute woman. And Sartre ironically supports this contention with a reference to Genet, who sees male and supermale, and who, perhaps through his own bad faith, sees the submitting male as feminized. But Sartre makes the jump to a completely different position from the one he ascribes to Genet. Sartre translates effeminate or feminized into "woman" and thereby erases sexual difference by insisting on a simplistic reading of sexual difference: a woman is he or she who gets fucked. For Sartre, the dominated other is always female, and the dominator, the one with the project, is male. As for the dominatrix who appears in the study of Flaubert as an explanation of Flaubert's necessary heterosexuality, does she now become a travesty of herself, a male to whom the female Flaubert is submitted? Perhaps; but in any event the situation remains, in Sartre's mind, a heterosexual one.

For Sartre, homosexuals exist in the abstract but homosexuality does not. Sartre can quickly categorize to create a universal, but that universal is merely the set of all the individual instances thereby summarized: "With [*Chez*] Genet as with all homosexuals . . . " (*SG* 370). Sartre does not generalize the behavior across various categories and varieties. For him, homosexuality exists in each imagined or described individual performance of anal penetration, for he cannot see the real event occurring. Nevertheless, one can be sure that when a situation can potentially be read as having homosexual contents, Sartre will avoid that reading insofar as is possible. Thus, though there is a scene of metaphoric homoerotic masturbation in "Erostrate," it will pass without commentary, even despite the amusing transparency of the image: "From time to time, I entered a men's room [*urinoir*]—even there I paid close attention since there are often neighbors—I took out my revolver and weighed it in my hand" ("E" 264). Since Sartre is constantly creating his own position as witness with Flaubert and since he is always there to ensure that even the invisibility of Gustave's sexuality will be seen, masturbation is both characterized *and* denied as homoerotic: "If I have lingered over these complicated games, which undoubtedly end up with masturbation, it is to indicate that it is not necessary to have recourse to homosexuality to characterize the sexual conduct of Gustave; I prefer to call them *perverse*" (*IF* 694). Of course Sartre is consistent in pointing out that it is not really a question of homosexuality with Flaubert, as once again he saves his subject from that ignominy:

Gustave does not accept himself as homosexual, rightly so, since his passivity demands to be reconstituted by the hugs of a goddess-mother; thus, when he states that he moans under a man, he is trying to convince himself *in front of his mirror* that he is of the other sex; and when his sex *really* palpitates under the caresses of men, as in the Turkish baths, it is necessary that the goal be explicitly nonsexual. (*IF* 703–4)

When a situation so obviously shows the possibility of homoeroticism, Sartre steadfastly maintains his blindness. Commenting in *La*

Nausée on a painting called "The Bachelor's Death," Roquentin notes innocently: "Naked to the waist, the torso somewhat green as befits the dead, the bachelor lay on an unmade bed. The sheets and covers in disorder are signs of a long agony" (*N* 99). The scene is repeated in the study of Flaubert:

Raising themselves up, Gustave and Caroline could surprise Achille-Cléophas in his dissection work: the cadaver is an eminently *manipulable* thing; you undress it, you lay it on a table, you open up its belly. This primitive vision surely played its role in the crisis: the intention of death did not aim so much at the abolition of conscience as at the cadaverous survival *in exteriority* during which Gustave, given over to his parents, would be the innocent object of all their undertakings. (*IF* 1867)

Of course, there is another reading of a naked, though dead, unmarried young man lying on bedsheets in disarray, or lying on the table subject to necrophiliac manipulations by his elders. It is not that the story in *La Nausée* is as obviously about homosexuality as Roquentin seems to believe it is about something else, but rather, this absent reading forms part of a pattern of visibility and blindness that, retrospectively, we can say is already nascent here. At the same time, like the Autodidact and like Sartre himself, Roquentin seems blind to the pederasty that he unwittingly witnesses.

IV. Bad Faith

Homosexuality is obviously a problem for Sartre and will continue to be so throughout his writing career. It is not merely a problem that troubles him on the psychological level. There is certainly something to be said for that, which is one of the reasons that a psychoanalytical reading of Sartre is at the same time so plausible and so disquieting: there is an intimation that the text might somehow spill over into the author's own consciousness (Doubrovsky, in Stambolian and Marks 330–40; Bellemin-Noël). Homosexuality stands out as a problem because it engages both the phenomenology of Sartrean philosophy and the structuring of narrative writing in unsettling ways. His philosophical magnum opus, *L'Etre et le néant*, is not about homosexuality, though the subject does appear at irregular intervals. Rather, *L'Etre et le néant* will try, though without addressing the problem directly, to normalize homosexuality, not from a moral point of view, ultimately without interest to Sartre, but rather from a phenomenological one.

It is always interesting to see which textual details people remember and which they do not. When I mentioned to a friend who has published on Sartre that I was going to discuss the example of bad faith in *L'Etre et le néant* that was based on the "homosexual," he allowed that he did not remember that at all. Elsewhere, in an excellent study of Sartre, Peter Caws discusses the first two examples of bad faith given by Sartre, but not the third (76–77). The third example fits in uncomfortably, or sticks out, or just somehow does not mesh with the two easily assimilable others. Just as a reminder, here are the three examples of bad faith, which Sartre warns us from the beginning have something in common. It is a warning we should keep in mind: "What unity does one find in these different aspects of bad faith? It is a certain art of forming contradictory concepts, that is to say, that unite in themselves an idea and the negation of that idea" (*EN* 92).

First is the well-known example of the man and woman seated in a cafe. Making his move, the man takes the woman's hand and caresses it in a scenario that immediately conjures up the Sartrean intertext of the Autodidact caressing the hand of the young boy in the library. Unwilling to decide for herself what her action and freedom will be, unwilling to return the caress, and unwilling to withdraw her hand, she cuts it off as if it were not a part of her body: this hand does not belong to her, but it is a thing "there," completely separate from her. The second example is equally familiar: again, the scene takes place in a cafe. The waiter in the cafe plays at "being" a waiter; in his bad faith, he sees himself as "being" a waiter in the same way that an inkwell is an inkwell (*EN* 96).

The third example is that of the homosexual and his friend who insists that the homosexual admit his homosexuality. Sartre mentions the guilt that the homosexual often has, and the fact that his existence is frequently determined by his relation to this guilt (*EN* 100). For this homosexual, though he recognizes his "homosexual bent," and though he admits his "faults" one by one, refuses to consider himself "*a pederast.*" So it would seem that he is in bad faith. But he is not alone in that bad faith, for he has a rather censorious friend, existentially speaking, who addresses the supposed bad faith of the homosexual and not the moral content of the action. The friend addresses the narrative of homosexual behavior and not the behavior itself. For the censor, the person "guilty" of being a homosexual has to recognize himself as such and declare straightforwardly—today, we would say "come out"—by saying, "*I am a pederast.*" But is this friend, Sartre asks, not in bad faith as well? For the homosexual, even admitting "his faults" at least, struggles against an oppressive fate, since he knows that "the homosexual is not homosexual as this table is [a] table." The "champion of sincerity," as Sartre puts it, wants his homosexual friend to admit his homosexuality so the champion of sincerity can forgive him. Since for Sartre this implicit attempt to forgive is essential in the friend's behavior, for that alone the champion of sincerity is also in bad faith.

Now what is most profoundly interesting here is that, while the three situations are alike, Sartre feels the need to explain the two-edged sword of bad faith only for the third example. In the example of the woman who abandons her hand while seated at the cafe table, one might well think that the man too is in bad faith because he thinks of her as an object, if he thinks of "her" at all. He has not concerned himself with her freedom and he takes her hand without recognizing her subjectivity. It is not only *pédés sans le savoir* who are in bad faith, but dirty old men in general. For the situation with the waiter, it is much the same: the waiter plays at being a waiter, but the customers demand that he *be* a waiter, in the sense that the table *is* a table. That this is a sign of the alienation of the worker, so be it; it fits equally well under the rubric of Sartrean bad faith. Thus, when we get to the third example, that of the homosexual, and we read that the bad faith is as much on the side of the guilty committer of faults as it is on that of the sincere friend, we can retrospectively project that double bad faith back onto the first two examples. By extension, the absent *giton*, the object of the attentions of the guilty pederast, is presumably innocent, even in his own invisibility. Bad faith is never solitary, we learn from the pederast, but Sartre glosses over that in the first two examples.

Yet if this third example implicitly helps illuminate the missing discussion of bad faith in the first two examples, there is still a double difference that cannot be avowed. First of all, Sartre has taken the initial situation and turned it in a direction that reinforces a religious ethic. If the words "fault" and "guilt" were not enough, the actions of the friend who demands sincerity take effect, so that in fact he can pardon or forgive the pederast for these faults. The supposedly heterosexual friend sets himself up as censor, arbiter, forgiver, and priest. How insightful of Sartre to have foreseen that a part of gay liberation would in fact be the negotiation of the forgiveness involved in statements like "It's OK with me," "Some of my best friends are gay," or "Whatever makes you happy." It remains to be seen whether there might be a statement involved in the expression of *Mitsein* that does not force the friend into a compromised situation. Certainly Sartre himself never finds it. In the third volume of *L'Idiot de la famille*, he introduces an *unheimlich* little aside that continues to show to what extent he believes in the myth of homosexuality as fault or peccadillo, though obviously a fairly harmless one in the greater scheme of things. Homosexuality continues to be defined as a variant that is never freed of its antisocial stigma. It is somehow secondary to heterosexuality; in its nonprimacy, it is somehow mutable. Somehow the fault can be expunged: "I remember this advice given by a psychotherapist to one of my friends who liked very young boys: 'My good sir, you must choose: become a passive homosexual or try heterosexuality' " (*IF* 3:13). And what of the third possibility: become an active homosexual with other adults? Sartre never even mentions it, never even considers the bad faith of the psychotherapist. Sartre cannot accept homosexuality because it is invisible; he cannot condemn it because in so doing he would be moralizing; he cannot pardon it because he too would be in bad faith. Lacking a solution to the problematic of homosexuality in light of the phenomenology he has himself created, he continues to define homosexuality as secondary, as other, as derivative, and ultimately, as not there at all.

The second difference between the third example of bad faith and the first two is clear in every example of homosexuality described in Sartre's work. Homosexuality is a spectator sport, or would be if we could only see it—for we necessarily come back to the problem of perception and the valorization of the visible. In the scene with the waiter or the scene with the woman at the table, there are three loci for the agents. In each case, there are two people in bad faith who are the agents in the situation: the woman and the man at the cafe in the first scene and the waiter and the customer in the second. The third position is that of the observer, with a clear field of vision and a blameless, faultless, guiltless position in which the bad faith of the other stands out. With the example of the "pederast," however, things have changed. Here the second agent is not doing anything but observing his friend. But he is not observing his friend, because the object of the homosexual's conquest is some unnamed, interchangeable *en soi*, the absent *giton* with a phallus or anus, the absent *giton* who will eventually become an ersatz woman anyway. Bereft of the ability truly to observe the scene—for there is nothing to see—the observer is caught between two uncomfortable positions. The observer must accept the argument of the friend, associate with that argument, and still *not excuse* the homosexual's guilt; or else the observer must be assimilated to the absent position, absent homosexual object of desire. In either case, the positions are unacceptable, and some imaginary, ec-static position must be sought from which to observe the whole queer game of guilt and admission. Needless to say, no such position exists; the observer is always infected by one of the other positions already described: that of the homosexual, that of the friend, that of the absent lover. The observer cannot stand away, be ec-static alone; he must share one of the aforementioned positions as the neutral position of the observer becomes infected with a homosexual ecstasy.

We can understand Sartre's philosophical position on homosexuality by reflecting on this *infection* of the observer. The observer cannot stay neutral, for he himself (Sartre's observer, it seems to me, is always presumed masculine) is somehow always tinged with homosexuality. Guilty and shameful over that, he denies that tinge and refuses the implications of his own thought process. This comes from a "nescience," a "not-knowing," that Sartre cannot admit relative to homosexuals: he cannot understand how they can be in a position other than that of bad faith. So even when Sartre finds one who lives his homosexuality, that is, Jean Genet, Sartre will refuse Genet's baroque theatricality to make him the icon of bad faith. There is no surprise here: Sartre's position on women is ostensibly the same. As Simone de Beauvoir shows, even if "one" is immediate as a man, "an other" becomes a woman: that becoming is a social construct and is not inherent in the ontology of the Dasein. Sartre continues to see the accident of thrownness relative to the white male heterosexual, and in so doing, he implicitly grants him(self) a degree of primacy. Sartre just cannot see that the mediation he is forced to invoke for women or homosexuals is a social construct. In this universe into which we have all been thrown, the life of a white male heterosexual is charmed in that he can more readily identify with an immediate image than can a woman or a homosexual. For a woman or a homosexual, there is always a shadowy third between self and image, that shadowy third being precisely the white male heterosexual telling the woman and the homosexual where and at what to look.

The homosexual is other, Sartre keeps telling us; the homosexual, in fact, is the epitome of otherness: "Call to an other. How *to think the other* [Comment *penser autrui*]: 'So-and-so is a pederast.' (Same problem for sincerity with oneself.)" (*CM* 487). And yet the separation is not quite there; the otherness is never as complete in the playing out of the argument as it is in the statement of the opposition. Not that Sartre is homosexual; it would not make one bit of difference here even if he were. Rather, the otherness of the position of the homosexual is never as other as even the naming would suggest. Hence, the predilection for the word "pederast," whose difference from the "normal, white, heterosexual male" is doubly marked: the activity is far removed from the morality of the latter and has the singular virtue of being set, at least in its denotative meaning, in a world far away from the contemporary one; the word is conveniently anachronistic. Moreover, unlike "homosexual," "pederast" does not have a double: the word "heterosexual" is too much like "homosexual" for us to believe in the complete otherness.

Even the act of nomination—"*notre parti pris de nominalisme*" (*IF* 1:686)—thus either staves off or welcomes the infection. Insofar as nomination is concerned, and despite Daniel's continued use of the word "pederast," there will be a recognition through the pages of *Les Chemins de la liberté* that the homosexual is first of all a man, that is to say, a man "like you and me." As Bauer notes, discussing the naming of homosexuals in Sartre's work (in Stambolian and Marks 319–20), the phrase that comes up significantly as a slang word for a homosexual in *Les Chemins de la liberté* is "*un homme pour*": "a man for." Thus the homosexual is still a man, still like the heterosexual, despite the difference of sexual preference or choice. And that similarity gradually takes root in the later works, despite the continued use of the word "pederast" and the continued, though spotty belief in the "otherness" of the homosexual.

Though attached to arguments about original sin and thrownness, the whole discussion of shame is also partly a result of the depiction and conception Sartre has of the homosexual in this world. Shame is involved in my very observation of another as homosexual even though I cannot see him *be* a homosexual. That shame and that guilt show up as figures of the complexity of a world than can neither accept nor refuse homosexuals. The problem of the homosexual is that there is always a measure of identity in the otherness and always a measure of otherness in the sense of identity. And the shame is always there.

When seduction occurs, there is a mixture of reflections of various consciousnesses and there is implicit bad faith. In any seduction, then, one finds a specular element that necessarily involves a homosexual dimension: I am seduced by my own act of seduction, and moreover, I am simultaneously shamed and overjoyed by it. It is no wonder then that the homosexual dimension creeps into the description of the act of seduction: "The beloved, in effect, seizes the lover as an other-object among the others. . . . The lover must thus seduce the beloved; and his love is not distinguished from this enterprise of seduction" (*EN* 421). A passage that can be passed over in the English translation sends up a red flag in French: "L'aimé, en effet, saisit l'amant comme un autre-objet parmi les autres. . . . L'amant doit donc séduire l'aimé; et son amour ne se distingue pas de cette entreprise de séduction." Sartre is using the words "aimé" and "amant," the decidedly masculine terms for lover and beloved. Does Sartre recall Socrates, the discourses of *The Symposium*, Alcibiades at the door? Perhaps, but more likely not. The historical philosophical argument by which all lovers and beloveds were male seems less than exemplary, in the Sartrean sense of the word, because the sexual attraction for the same-sexed other is not at all frequent in the real world (*EN* 458). And, as we all know, discussions of love in classical philosophy often depend on the homoerotic nature of the relation; this is not a model to which one would want to pin existential love.

Perhaps, then, there is a more general philosophical argument to be made in which Sartre is just using generic lovers: the masculine gender includes, we would be told, both the masculine and the feminine. So the contemporary philosophical argument would be that Sartre is just talking about generic lovers, and whatever is generic in French is masculine in grammatical gender. The odd blurring of gender and genre comes back to haunt the work, and, after all, the silent "e" of a hypothetical "aimée" would not have cost anything. That silent "e" would have made the Sartrean phenomenology of love and seduction less ambiguous. After all, Sartre is talking about seduction, and the act of seduction does not seem in Sartrean terms to lend itself to a generic categorization.

Finally, then, even in the most intimate situation, Sartre has forced his writing into a situation where every individual is part of the pervasive system of bad faith. Each subject becomes party to an inertness and to an objectification of self that reflects both the problem of homosexuality or the crisis of identity and what René Girard would term the dangers of mimetic rivalry. At every moment, even the most heterosexual of relations can show itself to be tinged with the guilt, shame, or merely the name of homosexuality. That is a problem that must be eschewed, denied, or turned away; the modus operandi for so doing is the mechanisms associated with bad faith. It is no wonder that the tingling of a caress disappears in favor of some lifeless inert *en soi* of blind identification with one's body even in a moment of *ek-stasis*. Anything, even the cold, clammy hands of dead flesh, is better than admitting that there is a problem in categorization: "In the caress, when I slowly slide my inert hand against the Other's side, I make him [*lui*] feel my flesh and it is that he [*il*] cannot himself [*lui-même*] do except by becoming inert" (*EN* 446). If the indirect object "*lui*" is masculine or feminine, grammar still betrays the author, even here, as the "I" caresses a masculine object. And that inertia, Sartre will tell us, is obscenity itself: "The obscene appears when the body adopts postures that undress it entirely of its acts and reveal the inertia of its flesh" (*EN* 452).

I shall end this chapter on the evocation of that obscenity, for it is as good a break as any. Sartre will take a different approach in the trilogy of war novels. By inventing a homosexual character instead of a situation in which homosexuality occurs, he can perhaps begin to rethink the oppositions and assumptions on which he found it necessary to rely in the early works. Daniel Serano, far from serene, far from being free of guilt, is at least able to look at himself in the mirror without the revulsion that Roquentin feels. At least, for the first time in Sartre's work, someone, Daniel, will be able to *see* homosexuality, and that, at least, is a new beginning.

On Vacation
with Gide and Barthes

I. *Gide's Heart of Darkness*

This chapter started out as an approach to a short piece by Roland
Barthes, *Incidents*, which was published posthumously in 1987. As I
began writing about *Incidents*, I realized that I could not start there
or merely be satisfied with relating this piece to other works by
Barthes, even those that I considered in *The Shock of Men*. Despite
Barthes's avowed admiration for Proust and despite the opposition
that so often sets up Proust and Gide against each other, it was impossible to read *Incidents* without rereading and rethinking André
Gide. In and of itself, the *rapprochement* between the two writers is
nothing new: the classical references and style, the authors' homosexuality, and the authors' Protestantism all are obvious connections.
There have been studies that engage their stylistic *parenté* as well.
Emily Apter makes an analogy between the "grammatical construc-
tions and rhetorical codes" of Gide's writing and the "poststructuralist stylistics of Roland Barthes" (5–6). She notes the references
to Gide in Barthes's own work, Barthes's acknowledgement of Gide's
classicism and style, and notes Gide as the source of references for
both *Roland Barthes* and *Fragments d'un discours amoureux*.

As much as Barthes is a Proustian seeking to write the theoretical equivalent of various passages from the *Recherche*, he is also a Gidean who, like many others in France engaging the problematics of homosexuality and literature, inherited Gide's model of liberation. Although that model might seem out-of-date in an age of sexual liberation, it still insists, and it remains current as the received knowledge about liberation: What could be simpler than the act of self-expression announcing one's freedom? The discourses surrounding that act of self-expression are quite complicated, however, which makes reading *Incidents* far less transparent than it initially seems. In order to read *Incidents*, then, I would hypothesize that one needs to look at a set of Gidean intertexts, specifically the autobiographical and fictional writing about North Africa. My interest in the relation between Barthes and Gide lies not so much in their experiences of homosexuality in North Africa, but in the language and rhetoric used to describe those experiences. Specifically, I want to examine the ramifications of Gide's use of a socially engineered model of dominance that guides Gide's discourse and enables it. That model, in which liberation depends on a colonial or imperialist hierarchy, comes almost silently to Barthes as an obligatory intertext. Barthes will adopt it and use parts of it to his advantage, but he will ultimately try to subvert or disrupt that insistent set of figures in order to free himself from the attendant ironies of Gidean liberation.

In France, the figure of André Gide stands out as arguing for the normalization of the perception of the homosexual while simultaneously insisting on a general liberation of the self. Less obliquely than Proust, whom he rejects, criticizes, and ultimately admires, Gide constructs some straightforward arguments for the acceptance of the normalcy of homosexuality as he writes direct, unapologetic confessions of some of his own experiences. In two works from the same period of his life, Gide makes his strongest arguments for the liberation, recognition, and normalization of the homosexual and homosexuality. The first was his *Corydon*, which I have discussed in the introduction to *The Shock of Men*. *Corydon* was written over a period of years, published privately in 1911, expanded in 1920 and reprinted privately, and finally published by Gallimard in 1924. During the same time, Gide wrote *Si le grain ne meurt*, published in 1921, which is an autobiographical account of his childhood and youth; the more or less simultaneous production of these two works has already been noted by Dollimore (12) as something more than a coincidence.

Before examining passages in Gide's work that determine the figures of homosexuality for him, it is necessary to look at the changing understanding of homosexuality in that work. One of the classics of American Gide criticism is Wallace Fowlie's *André Gide*, which appeared in 1965. The study has several oblique references to Gide's love for Marc Allégret, but it is not until page 170, in a 200-page book, that Fowlie spends any time talking about *Corydon*, Gide's apology for homosexuality, and this discussion occurs in a chapter devoted to Gide and Catholicism. A decade later, on the other side of the Atlantic, Philippe Lejeune approached the question of Gide's homosexuality more directly in *Le Pacte autobiographique*. For Lejeune, much of Gide's writing tends to be oriented toward the production of an *image* of the writer (165). That construct is a fiction that might be weakened by any truthful autobiography whose facts contradict aspects of the image projected by the author. Yet Gide does reveal himself in autobiography several times and, according to Lejeune (173), Gide's intention in so doing is to put an end to the hypocrisy and lies about one thing: his sexuality. In other words, Gide will sacrifice part of his image-building mode in order to liberate himself and textuality from shadows and silence, as well as from rumors and innuendoes. Still, if Gide reveals aspects of his sexual inclination, the autobiography is neither completely liberating nor fully revealing, and Gide keeps certain things in the dark, specifically "the practice and problems of homosexuality" (176–77).

One would think, then, that Gide's forthright presentation of the questions of homosexuality would be natural subject matter for the developing critical patterns of gender studies, a seemingly convenient spot where American theory meets French text, where American rhetoric meets French acceptance. But Gide seems to resist interpretation by gender theory, whereas Proust, Wilde, and Elizabethan drama, among other subjects, seem to welcome gender theory with open arms or at least an open book. Instead of being a means to studying the ramifications of a gendered reading of Gide's work, the often-expressed liberation of the subject seems to stop us from inquiring about the effects of homosexuality on textuality or the relation of homosexuality to other textual elements in Gide's work. And it is to that liberation, that supposedly transparent situation, that I would like to turn, because I think it is the crux of the matter.

I believe the resistance inherent in Gide's work is in part due to a secret architecture in Gide's writing, subsequently carried over to Barthes's work, that subtends the discourse of freedom. This model of discourse is far from the classical modes often ascribed to Gide and the politics of neutrality that supposedly frame the works of Barthes. Despite the rhetoric of the liberation of the subject through the announcement and practice of homosexuality, some of André Gide's works, especially the whole of *L'Immoraliste* and key passages in *Si le grain ne meurt*, construct a discourse of liberation predicated on the inequality of subjects. The liberation of the subject comes at the expense of the subjugation of another; the freedom to be homosexual comes at the expense of someone else's lack of freedom to be homo- or heterosexual. This discourse of inequality cannot, for all that, be avowed, for to do so would vitiate the act of self-liberation. So the discourse of inequality seems to be veiled, hidden, denied, or forgotten in the personal writings; it is significantly transposed in works such as *Les Caves du Vatican* and *Les Faux-Monnayeurs*; and it is by and large displaced by a scientific argument in *Corydon*. But in all three cases, the inequality is still there as the sine qua non for Gide's enactment of a scene of liberation.

This discourse of inequality is a colonialist or imperialist model that can be summed up in one word: Africa. As Edward Said says, "Gide's relationship to Africa belongs to a larger formation of European attitudes and practices toward the continent" (193). In other words, it is part of "a systematic language for dealing with and studying Africa *for* the West." The homosexual liberation of André Gide and the subsequent intertextual freedom of Roland Barthes depend on the continued absence of liberation of the "other." Neither avows the model: Gide will do his best to bury it; Barthes will quietly and discreetly attempt to overthrow it, and failing that, he will turn it into a metadiscourse, a sign at one remove, or its own symbolic representation.

Given Gide's rhetoric of liberation, my insistence on the necessity of this model of inequality may itself seem a perverse reading of Gide, for on the surface, a discourse of dominance and submission would seem to have no place in such a world. Gide's arguments, especially in their pastoral versions, are predicated on a game of freedom and equality. Seizing this will-to-liberation endlessly announced, critics reading Gide have believed him all too easily. An astute, insightful critic such as Jonathan Dollimore sees the relation between the question of homosexual liberation and the mise-en-scène in Africa: "Gide's experience in Africa is one of the most significant modern narratives of homosexual liberation" (12). That narrative of homosexual liberation depends on the continued enslavement of the "other" to the image the white male has made of him; Dollimore does not probe too far to see on what this liberation might be based. In a discussion of *Amyntas*, he falls back on the explanation of Gide's lyricism:

Those [experiences] of Gide's travel journals published as *Amyntas* are even more revealing of this process whereby loss of self becomes a discovery of self; both selves, the centred and the dispersed, being kept alive, both being necessary for the lyrical, unorthodox Western narrative which Gide maps on to the African landscape and his own illicit sexuality within it. (340)

Hence for Dollimore, the strictures imposed on the homosexual by the European model, the laws or mores that make his love "illicit," are freed in a mapping, an act of discovery of that virgin land and that renewed self. But Gide's predication of his freedom on that Africa, his imposition of lyric and prose on the "African landscape," never bring the critic to question what happens to that landscape itself. Yet by every right, one would normally perceive those activities as acts of Western violence. If we consider the African male as the metonymy of that "African landscape," the African male as natural and as wild as all the depictions of that landscape itself, we realize that there is a flip side. Succinctly put, the imposition forces both an enslavement and an illusory freedom: the North African male is condemned to be "natural," forced to be the "noble savage," damned to be the other of the white man seeking freedom and seeing the African male as the figure of that freedom. At every moment, having been found guilty of being natural, the African male must be ready to spring out of the strictures of his imposed European clothing or his own indigenous attire, immediately erect and ready for a quick roll in the sand.

In her study of Gide, Emily Apter also seems to believe in the idealism of the model: "Sexual nomadism is predicated on an economy
of pleasure that undermines the capitalist conventions of exchange:
partners are no longer to be bought and sold, their fidelity guaran-
teed with either sentimental or material bonds; rather, pleasure will
circulate freely" (101). She goes on to say that this "emancipatory
principle of gifts" is "one of the absolute laws" in the *Nourritures* and
that "the same discourse can be found" in *Si le grain ne meurt*. What
of this discourse of liberation, emancipation, free gift-giving, selfless
equality coupled with the subversion of capitalism? Whereas the
"sexual nomadism," with its illusory freedom—illusory because it
too, as Foucault might point out and as Said so brilliantly underlines,
is a product of the capitalist system—might free (or "free") the bourgeois white male, it continues to enslave the Maghrebin male in an
exchange system that is endlessly imposed on him and in which he
has no choice. Moreover, if this emancipation takes place, how can
there be a work like *La Porte étroite*, which Apter (129) calls "one of
the most protracted and frustrating accounts of sexual denial to be
found in the history of literature"? Why bother to deny, if the truth
is already present?

The answer is clear, though the ramifications are not yet so: the
model of colonialism, or more broadly, the model of inequality, is in-
escapably always present, even when hidden or denied. And no cloud
of idealism can fully obfuscate matters, no discourse about an un-
dermined system can change the simple fact of its eternal reinscription mapped onto "the African landscape." Even when Gide is telling
the truth about a sexual encounter in the blazing sands of North
Africa, this truth is the truth of capitalism and imperialism, the truth
of "the white man's burden." Rather than undermining some simplistic version of the capitalist exchange process, such consumption
is fully part of that system, which builds in rules and locations for
such sexual shoplifting, just as allowances for waste and fraud are
built in to any capitalist model. Gide's self-liberation through sex
with Arab boys—at least in the way he describes it and uses it as textual material—is the equivalent, not of some act of freedom, but of a
900 phone line or a *téléphone rose*. As this truth is somehow always an
adequation between the experience and language, mediated through
an ideological filter, Gide is relying on a gap in the truth, which is

the unequal relation necessary to his concept of homosexuality. And no *apologia* depending on Greek pederasty nor any odes in the pastoral vein can completely hide that.

Concerned at not finding in contemporary criticism of Gide what I thought to be the most obvious discursive analyses, I began to think that our understanding of Gide had always been tinged with our will to believe his statements about liberation and to take them at face value. At the same time, we did not see that the liberation was based on a disequilibrium. I am not saying that Gide was a liar nor am I saying that he did not believe in the liberation he so often espoused. What I am saying is that at the heart of that liberation is a Eurocentric argument that is a simulacrum of the dominance of white male heterosexuality. Gide structures his liberation of homosexuality according to heterosexual oppression. Gide's freedom then comes not only at the expense of the Maghrebin male, but also at the expense of the gay European male himself, forced to mime the very power dynamics that made him secondary in the first place. In Gide's universe, the gay European male can be free only if, toward the Maghrebin male, he mimes the system of dominance and submission imposed on the gay European male and on the European woman by the straight European male. This disequilibrium is fundamental to Gide; from it, we can begin to understand Gide's explanations and the lack thereof, both his discourses of freedom and his need for *disponibilité*. And, as for Barthes, what will become clear is that he does realize that the model is in place and he certainly does his utmost to try to displace it. Ever tenacious, it constantly returns: by the end of *Incidents* we learn that once semiotized, he—or we—can never be sign-free again.

Perhaps the most memorable passage on homosexuality in Gide's autobiographical writing comes in *Si le grain ne meurt*. It deals with the protagonist's or author's ostensible loss of virginity with a young North African man. Freedom comes with the awakening of pleasure, the natural love of which the North African male is the shining symbol. Nature takes over, the person is reborn into freedom, and he realizes his own true being. Most interesting, I think, is that this is at least the second time that Gide tells the story; the first time, all the elements are present except for the intimations of a sexual act. As it is described in *Si le grain ne meurt*, the episode is a partial explanation of the mystery and the elisions of the earlier, shrouded version in

L'Immoraliste. A retrospective reading of *L'Immoraliste* through the
lenses offered by much of Gide's later work shows us not that homosexuality is absent but that it is displaced. Gide skirts the issue of homosexuality as sexuality and approaches the question obliquely by
three displacements. First of all, the only conceivable homosexual
situation is one that is pederastic; for Gide, arguing here as elsewhere
about the classical nature of this love, this move is an oft-repeated
strategy. Second, that pederasty is itself translated into a safer, more
obliquely defined homoerotics. And finally, instead of engaging the
question of homosexuality in Europe, the angst-ridden writing of
L'Immoraliste develops a displaced, and therefore "exotic," erotics.
The exotic character of the North African site has none of the faults
of Western civilization; exotic means natural means homoerotic. And
thus, North Africa is the epitome of nature itself, a homoerotic, pederastic nature unveiled in its own self-admitted and self-declared
honesty. These three shifts from Europe to Africa, from homosexuality to pederasty, and from sexuality to erotics combine to displace
the entirety of the situation described in *L'Immoraliste*; only through
Si le grain ne meurt do we realize that Gide installed safety valves in
the earlier work. Thus, in *L'Immoraliste*, these displacements together
produce a somewhat veiled erotic tale whose pith is never fully revealed, but only intimated:

Bachir came back the next day. He sat as he had two days before, took out
his knife, wanted to whittle a piece of wood that was too hard and thrust so
well that he shoved the blade in his thumb. I shuddered in horror; he
laughed, showed the brilliant cut, and was amused at watching his blood
flow. When he laughed, I could see his very white teeth; he licked his wound
with pleasure; his tongue was pink like a cat's tongue. (*Immoraliste* 382)

For Gide, describing the Maghreb and its synecdoche or metonymy
in the North African male, everything is light and liquid; a quick
penetration is done while smiling, in an easy and innocent translation of deflowering into a homoerotic and autoerotic discourse,
which will be repeated in Lafcadio. The white man is aghast; the Maghrebin man laughs. For the shudder and horror exist only in the
one desperately seeking to get rid of his own cultural constraints and
his Protestant guilt.

In *L'Immoraliste*, the possible liberation wallows in the morality of a repressive society and eventually sinks under the weight of the hypocrisy that permits no true act of liberation, either at home or in Africa. Without an articulation of a sexual position, *L'Immoraliste* necessarily falls back on old models of rebellion, in which poaching on one's own land, for example, the lay equivalent of urinating in the holy water, really changes nothing. The Gide of *L'Immoraliste* has not yet found the strategies of what we consider to be the tenets of high Gideanism illustrated in *Les Faux-Monnayeurs* and in *Les Caves du Vatican*: the famous availability (*disponibilité*) and the free act (*l'acte gratuit*). Both of these are a far cry from the repression of *L'Immoraliste*, but they are also a step away from the sexual shoplifting that passes for furtive liberation in *Si le grain ne meurt*. To understand the acts of Gidean freedom, one must follow Gide through his writing to see how homosexuality is first excluded in *L'Immoraliste*, except in the most oblique way, how it is then liberated through the processes already mentioned, and then how finally that liberation replaces homosexuality as the vehicle for the representations of the self.

In *Si le grain ne meurt*, Africa is sex, exoticism, and exotic sex; Africa is seductively clad in a language of freedom and the sublimity of the unknown. Unclad, however, Africa is the incarnation of the tumescent phallus growing to become erect: "Africa! I repeated this mysterious word; I let it swell [*je le gonflais*] with terrors, tempting horrors, waiting, and in the warm night, my gazes plunged wildly toward an oppressive promise wrapped in lightning" (290). Gide can safely circumscribe his action by clothing the continent in the delights of sought-for pleasure, in the garb of a beckoning homosexuality whose truth is now being told. He does this while maintaining the power and transcendence of the ego: the "I" makes the whole continent swell. By his very presence, the figure of the European brings out the tumescence of the continent, its incontinence, and the act of self-liberation. In liberating the self, the ego reins in the incontinent behavior, the naturalness of this unbridled land. Africa beckons him to his freedom, but it is an ironic gesture for a land whose own freedom is endlessly denied. For the white man to be free, and in this case, for him to be a free homosexual white man, it is at the expense of the freedom of the other, the Maghrebin male whose only function is to be a phallus, or for that matter, an anus, for the liberation of the European.

Clad in the language of freedom and the sublimity of the unknown, the Gidean vision of homosexuality depends on the presence
of an unequal dynamic between the two partners. Not for Gide, the
author of *Corydon* reminds us, is the Proustian example in which
there is an equality between partners. Proust's model bends gender
too much; it stretches definitions; there is too much free play. The
danger of Proust's version of homosexuality is that it eliminates the
differences between the two partners. So when it comes to the noble,
honorable version of homosexuality, what Gide calls "well-balanced
[*bien portant*] uranism, or, as you were just saying, *normal pederasty*"
(*Corydon* 30), Proust has nothing to say. For Gide, "well-balanced"
means unequal, means a difference to be negotiated by and for the
ego, while ignoring any reflection on the lack of freedom of the
other. For Gide, homosexuality is normal if and only if there is a difference between the two partners, if and only if the relation is grafted
onto a paradigm of dominance.

The best-known example from the *Recherche* illustrates the matter
quite neatly: the scandal of Charlus and Jupien, for example, is that
their social difference is purely a narrative accident relative to their
sexual encounter. That difference does not count in the action, the
veritable scandal of like calling to like. In the beginning of *Sodome et
Gomorrhe*, Proust's version of the birds and the bees skips dizzyingly
from trope to trope, as I have noted in *The Shock of Men*. No clear
picture of order comes from it because the wealth of examples and
the concatenation of metaphors make all decisions about order, dominance, and structure vague at best, and more likely than not, invalid.

On the other hand, Gide's language of flowers concentrates on the
aspects of dominance, nature, and need that make the model a useful one in the paradigm of pederastic normalcy. Moreover, beyond
the natural argument, *Corydon* ostensibly predicates its cultural argument on the Greek model, and therefore on the relationship of inequality subtending the Greek concept of pederasty. Still, Gide does
not need the dynamics of inequality of Greek love and he does not
stray far from his own implicit model of liberation as he twice refers
in *Corydon* to the model of colonialism. Were it not both an anachro-
nism and an overused term, one could say that Gide literally suffers
in these writings from "internalized homophobia," a fear of "the
same": Gide's acceptance of homosexuality must be based on a dif-

ference that resounds at every level. And even a seemingly liberal
gesture that wards off European xenophobia can hide a discourse
that is not as innocent. The ever-vigilant narrator suggests that the
customs of pederasty came from elsewhere:

> Dear friend, I beg you, don't bring in a question of nationalism here. In
> Africa, where I have traveled, Europeans have persuaded themselves that this
> vice is allowed [*admis*]; the occasion, the beauty of the race helping, they give
> freer reign than in their own countries; that makes the Moslems convinced
> that these tastes come to them from Europe. (*Corydon* 38)

Clearly, Gide is trying to undermine the arguments of his own supposed interlocutors; by rehearsing their theses against his plea for
normalization, he is ostensibly making his own argument stronger.
So we should not quibble with his having brought out this bit of received knowledge about the corruption by Europe of the so-called
inferior races. We should, however, pay attention to the answer given
to skeptical and friendly interlocutor alike.

Pederasty is allowed in Africa: one would assume that it is part of
the natural order of things, especially since Gide depends so much
on the natural argument throughout this book. But no; it is a "vice."
We are given pause to think of this, for after all, this is the argument
against the skeptic, not the skeptic's argument. And moreover, there
is a lure already present: "the beauty of the race." This beauty is
somehow essential, opposed to European transcendence: it is an
eternal quality that contrasts with the development and changes of
European history. The African's timeless beauty is an aestheticization
of the descriptions of his "natural" slavery found in earlier narratives
of colonization, translated by imperialism into late-nineteenth-
century eugenics: the African needs to be dominated for his own
good. Even if this beauty is natural, it calls to the European, forces
him, and imprisons him in a dialectic of desire in which, reduced to
an essence of soulless, mindless "beauty," the African makes the European a prisoner of love. No wonder then that the perversion becomes a "vice": the African male, metonymy of nature, "himself"
robs the European of free will.

The European is imprisoned in the structures into which he has
forced the African. The appeal and attraction of native beauty and
essence are so strong that the model can be generalized: though it is

usually quite helpful, being African is not a requirement. So the imprisonment is not confined to freedom-seeking European homosexuals; even heterosexual Western science is imprisoned in this diabolical game: "Calm down, Darwin is not, as far as I know, more of a
uranist than many another explorer who, circulating among the
naked tribes, were astonished at the beauty of the young men" (*Corydon* 90). No wonder then that in this insistent dialectic of desire, the
European must redetermine the system for himself. Africa calls to
him because it needs the European to right the system. So while
Dollimore (337) sees Gide at one point as "finally capitulating to the
class, racial, and cultural prejudices of his own culture," I see him as
being complicitous, though perhaps unconsciously so, until quite
late, and certainly after he wrote *Les Faux-Monnayeurs*. As Dollimore
notes, "Many years later, in his Journal for January 1933, Gide writes
that he was not unaware of the political realities of colonialism at that
time; it was a feeling of incompetence that prevented him from
speaking" (340n).

Even if it is still based on a model in which desire has to be figured
unequally compared with the earlier *L'Immoraliste*, *Si le grain ne
meurt* manifests a comparative freedom of speech and writing and a
freeing of memory. If it does nothing else, *Corydon* helps Gide free
his writing and *Si le grain ne meurt* is testimony to that liberation.
The barrier has been crossed and the text has left behind the moralizing of the world for a world of choice and availability. When the
veils of morality are lifted, the penetration of this new world occurs
without any symbolic deflowering. The violence and the implied
erotic violence akin to deflowering of the scene in *L'Immoraliste* are
translated in *Si le grain ne meurt* into a mere thread of culture that is
easily cut:

But, seizing the hand he offered me, I made him roll on the ground. His
laughter immediately returned. He bothered little with the complicated
knots of the laces that stood him instead of a belt; taking a little dagger out
of his pocket, he cut the bother in one blow. The clothing fell; he put his
jacket aside and stood there, like a naked god. For a moment, he extended
his slender arms toward the sky, then, laughing, let them fall on me. Perhaps
his body was burning, but it appeared as refreshing as shade to my hands.
How beautiful the sand was! In the adorable splendor of the evening, with
what rays was my joy clothed! (*Grain* 299)

In *Si le grain ne meurt*, Gide discovers a Maghreb where the possibility exists of liberating the self from the weight of a binary system that imprisons a man in the dualities that confuse male, masculine, and heterosexual. Certainly the liberation occurs both for the writer and in the writing, and certainly the writer is sincere in his belief in this liberation. The liberation is based on a model of otherness in which the other is presumed secondary, radically other, and able to be dominated at the same time. The system is wrapped in an ideal of freedom in which the smiling welcome of the "natural" African is considered, if it is considered at all, as his natural state, and not as a part of a dialectic of proxemics, seductions, and exchange with the white men from Europe. What makes this spot capital for Gide's seduction is the possibility of approaching an alterity in which the love of a man for an adolescent is considered as beautiful and as masculine as the love allowed by Western society of a man for a woman. Moreover, the love of a man for another male would be even more masculine, for it is not complicated by women or femininity. Hence, we can understand the Gidean refusal in *Si le grain ne meurt* of a homosexuality tinged with the feminine:

Ali was certainly quite handsome; a white skin, a pure forehead, a well-formed chin, a small mouth, full cheeks, a houri's cheeks; but his beauty had no sway over me; a kind of hardness in the sides of his nose, a kind of indifference in the too perfect curve of his eyebrows, a kind of cruelty in the disdainful sneer of his lips stopped all desire in me; and nothing distanced me more than the effeminate appearance of his whole being, something by which others would undoubtedly have been seduced. (348)

Akin to the inversion that Gide finds repellent in Proust, this femininity is dangerous because it challenges the assumptions on which the argument of the natural is based. The feminine denaturalizes the process of liberation and the discourse of sincerity and forces reflection on the self. The presence of the feminine within the realm of the masculine and natural posits the possible feminization of the ego. For the ego in a "manly" male can stay that way in this paradigm only if he can take the purported *naturalezza* of the Maghrebin male and perceive it as essential and normal. In so doing, the European man finds that same nature at the root of his own, but in his case, it has been perverted by the effeminacies or decadence of Western civilization. It is thus necessary in this context to keep women out and to keep any suggestion of effeminacy at a distance. With that natural ground, the European male can justify his own homosexuality as self-identical normalcy. If, on the other hand, the feminine exists within the realm of this natural maleness, perhaps the role that the ego has played is not as free as he wants the reader to believe. The criticism of effeminate homosexuality will surface again in Barthes. In both cases, aside from appealing to the arguments of nature in the case of Gide and unfettered semioticity in the case of Barthes, the fear of the feminine relates to an unspoken though palpable misogyny that is bound to, albeit not essential to, the homosexuality brought to the fore by Gide and Barthes.

It is the same refusal, explained by the Greek tradition of peder-asty that involves education, training, sponsorship, and erotic or sex-ual love as described by Gide in *Corydon*, that gives rise to a criticism of Proust, whom Gide finds too effeminate. Thus the love of the other is not as easily definable as was thought, for at every moment it engages an idealism that hides a fault. The love of the other em-phasizes pure alterity, conceived as the absence of constraints, the ab-sence of the weight of a civilization that is perverted in its very desire to constrain. Stereotypically, it is "the exotic" that is the sign of this alterity in Gide, Barthes, or Loti, of whom Barthes writes in "Pierre Loti: 'Aziyadé'": "Turk or Maghrebin, the Orient is only the box of a game, the marked term of an alternative: the West or *something else*" (*Degré Zéro* 182). Not coincidentally, Loti himself translates his per-sonal erotics into heterosexual exotics for the sake of safe publication. Moreover, the polarization determines the same identity of the self, freed of all definitions that relate to the woman. There is thus the idealization of a masculine male for whom no sign indicates or hides a feminine side. This is a universe of an idealism without birth, where the same is "always already" there in absolute identity, and where every discourse is filial, including the other in its exotic purity, without being touched or undone by it.

Thus, behind a male-centered idealism joined to a veiled misog-yny, we can see a will to exclude the feminine and the female, evi-dence of a somewhat naive choice: determining the other based on the self. There is also a will to ahistoricism. While refusing the sys-tem of taboos imposed on sexuality by the West, the Gidean relation is blind to the historicity of a situation in which the Maghrebin is forced to play himself as exotic. Opposed to the sincerity of the white man seeking freedom, the Maghrebin male is forced to be an actor in a role designed for him. Even when the Maghrebin is, by his own nature, what we might define as homosexual in the Western world, the "natural," that is, Western-imposed, order forced on the Maghrebin denatures his own inclinations. The Maghrebin is not a white knight, but a dusky knight whose quest it must "naturally" be to liberate the white man's identity, while knowing all the while that he, the Maghrebin, is anything but exotic for himself. What then is at stake in this exoticism?

The deployment of this complex of models that involve liberation of the white man through the imposition of an imperialist discourse, and the hiding of that imposition in a rhetoric of nature relates, quite obviously, to a discourse of power. From the very beginning, the long-dreamed-of trip to the Maghreb is first structured as a flight from Western heterocracy, necessarily defined as an oppressive power. Thus, for the traveler, this trip is presented as a quest for the truth in an uncompromised spot, a Utopian one, completely eroticized. Yet like Robinson Crusoe on his island, as soon as the white man is freed from his cultural yoke, he wastes no time in reestablishing a colonial world around him in which he once again has all the power.

According to this model, the traveler believes that his action of escaping from one power structure, its pressures, and the *perceived* oppression of heterocratic Western society would lead him to total personal liberation. Yet these actions are no more a flight toward that liberation than they are a nostalgic repetition of Socratic Athens. Looking for his liberation, the white man participates in an ideology of domination that reactivates the dialectic of the master and the slave, and even refigures this domination in the terms of a victimization: as Hegel says, the white man becomes the slave of the slave. Whether it be the theft of the scissors in *L'Immoraliste* or a whole series of pathetic incidents in Barthes's work, it is always a question of a vision of the Maghreb determined by the structuring of a system of power that alone gives meaning to the erotic.

In the light of the homosexual liberation that is conflated with liberation *tout court*, it is not surprising to see a reworking of the colonial model in writings in which sexual liberation is itself reasonably marginalized. Directly present in *L'Immoraliste*, it feeds the beginning notions of *disponibilité* proffered by Ménalque in that work. And if the formulae of *disponibilité* and *l'acte gratuit* far exceed the local instance of self-liberation posited in the acts of sexual freedom, they nevertheless depend on the same model. At the same time, the origin of that true liberation is a model that depends on inequality, the model of homosexuality outlined in *Si le grain ne meurt*. Significantly, the colonial model appears in quotation in *Les Caves du Vatican* and *Les Faux-Monnayeurs*; framed, under control, and even alienated from the subject when the direct sexual question is absent, the model can serve as a reference at a distance. Far from the painful concept of freedom as an act of self-liberation, these two books attenuate human relations. Distant from the immediacy of sex, the subjects become secondary to the societal bond between them, and the sexual act itself is perhaps now seen as an impossible, utopian positing of immediacy. There is no escape, however, from the bonds of sociality: in *Les Faux-Monnayeurs*, Bernard Profitendieu tries to escape the imposed bonds of the social, only to return at the end of the novel.

These two books marginalize the problematic of homosexuality; the author prefers to give hints about autoerotic and homoerotic behavior, rather than engaging the matter head on. Hints of the sexual model still resurface but in quotation: in the one direct auto- and homoerotic scene in *Les Caves du Vatican*, in which Lafcadio inflicts wounds on his own thigh, Gide is sure to interrupt the flow of the writing with a reference to Algeria (716). Much later, when Lafcadio is about to commit the *acte gratuit* of killing Amédée Fleurissoire by throwing him from the train, Gide puts a quotation from Conrad's *Lord Jim* as the epigraph: "One thing alone can cure us from being ourselves" (821; in English in the text). Thus, at the two critical moments in the work that relate to a liberation of the self, Gide recalls the repressed African land written over by Western cartography. At the same time, because of the act of quotation, one could presume that the act of self-liberation through this colonial model was both a failure and a dead end. Incapable of success, unable to find another path, Gide turns from sex to social bonds, from the yoking of two to the general intertwining of the many, from the false act of liberation that subjugates another to the *acte gratuit* that frees through anarchy and entropy.

Significantly, Gide's presentation of the model occurs at one remove: whereas in *L'Immoraliste* and *Si le grain ne meurt* there is a literal trip to North Africa, here there is merely a written reference. The first reference to Algeria is found in a note in Lafcadio's private notebook, and, as if to underline what he is telling us, Gide notes that the remark comes "after a blank page." The latter reference, the quote from *Lord Jim*, is also at one remove, and shows by its source the extent to which the colonial model is intertwined with Gide's sense of personal liberation. And as for the representation of the *acte gratuit* here, we remember that Amédée Fleurissoire is using the ticket of Julius de Baraglioul, an erstwhile novelist; Amédée is a reference to Julius, found at one remove. The same scene of homoerotic behavior is remarked in *Les Faux-Monnayeurs* with a reference to North Africa, as Edouard, another version of the novelist, watches his nephew steal and subsequently return a book—a guide to Algeria (999).

In these books, Gide translates that remembered liberation into antisocial behavior. Even the anarchy of the *acte gratuit*, in escaping the colonial model, needs a victim. In every case, whether it is the *acte gratuit* or the liberation of the self through homosexual sex in North Africa, there is something far less savory in common: every scenario depends on the victimization of the other. The gratuitous murder in *Les Caves du Vatican* takes the odious bourgeois as the propitiatory victim, sacrificed for freedom and availability. As a bourgeois, the victim is undoubtedly far from innocent in Gide's eyes, in that the victim is considered to be the stereotypical exploiter of society. Yet ironically, who is more of a victim in this world of egocentric ideology than the bourgeois himself, who has sacrificed all availability and all real identity to social position, status, and the transcendental signifier of money? Killing a bourgeois to proclaim one's freedom or refusing bourgeois paternity may be an effective tactic in a workers' novel, but in a middle-class novel in which the supreme value is the value of the self, one is killing the supreme victim.

Gide, to my mind, never solves the problem imposed by his concept of freedom. Exploring the ramifications of the sexual/colonial

model in the later works is far beyond the scope of this introduction—which was, after all, originally just the pre-text for reading
Barthes. So we shall return to North Africa, quotation marks removed, footnotes erased, North Africa in all its semiotic glory, and
we shall see what Barthes undertakes in his descriptions of that homoerotic, homosexual semiotic world unto itself.

II. *How Can One Be Maghrebin?*

Here I will examine how Barthes explores the power structures and
semiotics of desire as they are interpreted and inscribed in the North
African locale. Specifically, I would like to show that, coming out of
a structuralism that builds its projects *ex nihilo*, Barthes uncomfortably inherits the residue of a colonial discourse that organizes his
very vision of North Africa and thus his transcription of desire in
North Africa. That residue, the *part maudite* of structure, will become the locus on which that eternal "other" remainder lies: the
marks of the self and its desires that cannot be absorbed into the
structures of structuralism. Second, while Barthes's writing is not as
dramatic as Gide's various scenes of liberation in the North African
sun, it shows the liberation of the author *en voie de développement*. In
Barthes, the conflict is not between compulsory heterosexuality and
a hidden homosexuality but between a desire to participate in a cultural doxology that tends to marginalize homosexuality and a refusal
of that doxology for sexual and theoretical reasons. Barthes always
seems to sense his participation in and simultaneous distance from
the cultural canon and its doxas. The liberation then for Barthes is
from the structures of Occidental thought, from the structures of
structuralism, from the ascesis of the writing ego, and toward an expression of desire, the latter especially finding a most sympathetic
reading in D. A. Miller's *Bringing Out Roland Barthes*. Along with key
works like *S/Z* and *Le Plaisir du texte*, which I looked at in *The Shock
of Men*, *Incidents* is part of the sea-change in Barthes's thought. And
third, the various traces, residues, and marks of the subject, the mix-
tures of memory and desire, and the blanks and gaps all prod Barthes
to produce a nonstructuralist reading of his object, an object for
which his own admitted fascination and trans-fiction find a language

and a place. Finally, to understand the system, Barthes becomes absorbed by it in unexpected ways.

To understand Barthes's unique work *Incidents*, we may ask questions that Roland Barthes might have asked had he, the literary critic, read this work after publication. How can the object of a discourse be delimited when it has a double minority status? How can some other discourse, as neutral as it may be, state the doubly other, even if that neutrality can be said—and by whom?—to exist? How can this doubly other come to speak? The *locus standi* of such a double alterity has been refused twice, the locus of discourse has been reduced twice to silence. Writing about the doubled minority voice in the work of Lorraine Hansberry, an African-American woman, Adrienne Rich calls this a "double erasure" (14). And who would do the giving of the right to speak or write, who would bestow the honor of speaking? And in that giving, would the very exchange not reinforce the minority and therefore somehow excluded nature of the other discourse? In short, would the very gift not nullify whatever followed? Putting the doubly minority voice in an emphatic position can be accomplished, if at all, only sequentially, in two movements, two deconstructions, as it were, of two separate oppositions. Each would regulate and regularize the voice of one of these silences, but the two could never be done in concert. In specific, it is a question of showing the interrelations of two networks of power and discourse: nationality and sexuality. We must see the discourse of Maghrebin homosexuality.

The problem cannot be resolved in a simple way because, if for no other reason, we are seeing it through Western eyes. In other words, the object here is not to see what Maghrebin homosexuality might be for itself, but rather what it might be defined as in another language and another sexual discourse, and how it might be related to them. To let the Maghrebin speak, he must be forced to speak against his will through a linguistic violence, as subtle as it may be. For the Maghrebin does not define himself in the language of the other except as "other": other when compared to the "right," that is, European, speaker, and other to the language itself. The definition of the self that the Maghrebin has in French is by definition always postcolonial. He is forced to use the language in which he is defined

as "Maghrebin," defined according to a law in which he is always
other from what he is; he is linguistically alienated from himself.
French is not his language, even if he is a "Beur," a person of North
African origin born in France for whom French is a native tongue; a
hundred times a day he is forced to recognize that the language is not
his, for he cannot say "*nos ancêtres les Gaulois.*" What goes for the
"Beur" is even truer for the "real" Maghrebin from North Africa, a
native Algerian, Moroccan, or Tunisian, who speaks some French.
Whether at home or in France, he is subject to a linguistic system
that promises, but never delivers, freedom from alterity by perfect
mastery of the language he can never master, by definition. Writing
of the French-speaking Negro of the Antilles, Frantz Fanon says
something that could as easily be applied to the Maghrebin: "[He]
will be proportionally whiter—that is, he will come closer to being a
real human being—in direct ratio to his mastery of the French language" (18). But his reality is never complete.

As far as homosexuality is concerned, the superficial evidence certainly shows the categorization to be less restrictive. Certainly, the
homosexual can often be invisible in a society where the dominant
law of sexuality, even as it allows certain freedoms to others, remains
that of heterosexuality. It thus remains to discover what might happen when these two categories meet. It is not solely a question of determining what the subcategory of "homosexual Maghrebin" or
"Maghrebin homosexual" might be, for in so doing, we would still
remain on the level of a dominant discourse that seeks not to understand but to categorize. The categories themselves are part of an imposed Western system: the category of "Maghrebin" more obviously
comes from a nationalistic and oppositional system, that of "homosexual" is equally Eurocentric in nature. There is no need to cite extensive anthropological and sociological tracts to understand to what
extent the behavior called "homosexual" in the West depends on a
social discourse of heterosexual propagation. In other cultures, the
opposition is not between heterosexual and homosexual as defined by
our categorizations of sexual behavior, but between the acceptable
and the taboo. To give only the most obvious example, in some cultures this would be the opposition between active and passive roles
in anal intercourse, the former being considered acceptable, even if
nominally forbidden, and the latter, paradoxically, demeaned.

Thus the definition of "Maghrebin homosexual" is always subjected to our dominant doubly Eurocentric law, and thus is doubly false. Or it is triply false: we impose a Western model on the Maghrebin male forced to parade as other, that is, not European, and as natural, openly homosexual and free of the repressive constraints on sexuality afforded by Europe. Even if we get beyond simple oppositions from the West—say, that between homosexual and heterosexual—and arrive at a more indigenous concept of the taboo and the acceptable, we tend to reduce the other to that essentialist opposition. As Malek Chebel warns Western readers in his excellent book on sexuality in the Maghreb, the "omnipresence of the active/passive couple" should neither blind us to the variety of aspects of Maghrebin homosexuality, nor be perceived as giving the complete meaning of Maghrebin homosexuality (18). In short, the image of homosexuality, paraded about and even donned as a disguise by the North African male involved in a postcolonial system of exchange, hides a complex system of sexuality that may, in any individual case, include a homosexual component. This homosexual component, however, is not necessarily the signified to which the signifiers imposed by European culture refer. And thus, on a very real level, the Maghrebin homosexual (as opposed to the "Maghrebin homosexual" defined by the West), is necessarily alienated from who he is.

This is not to say that one only has to let this person speak in his own language, for we would never know to what extent other constraints were imposed. In fact, it is necessary to try to understand the subject that flees our discourse and our objectification of the other. In this case I want to examine how this problem has been dealt with by someone who, as much as any of his contemporaries, had extensive insight into the ramifications of the constraints imposed by any discourse. Reading Roland Barthes's *Incidents*, a diary of jottings about a stay in Morocco, one is immediately struck by the difference of the work, so untypically Barthesian, lacking the polish and the verve of his other works. How do we read this roughness? We should not be fooled by the superficial differences: the mechanisms of *Incidents* are those of the public Barthes; the lack of polish only makes the "hidden architecture" a bit more visible. The work is crisscrossed by reading problems, not the least of which is the unpublished and private nature of a work consisting of short jottings in a diary not fully intended for publication, at least when it was written. As we know, Barthes took pride in writing only *sur commande*; one wonders then about the status of a written work with no "order," a work that never had any definite reader projected as the possible audience. Though the editor says that "it was ready to be printed and Roland Barthes thought of publishing it in *Tel Quel*" (8), it never appeared. What kind of text would this be for Barthes, where the pedagogical possibilities are reduced to zero? Without the other, any game of seduction vanishes, and though the work deals with sexuality, it does not exchange this sexuality for signs. Without that exchange of sexuality and sign, not the body of the author, nor that of the other, nor that of the text—a locus in which signs and sexuality are mixed—can be emphasized.

Barthes comes to the Maghreb knowing that it is linguistically structured by power and not by some purported *naturalezza*. The Maghreb is a literary locus in which equality is always replaced by a power play of difference. In linguistic terms, this means that the one who gives language—the French dominator—is "always already" in the locus of the "I": he uses the familiar "*tu*" with the other, for the neutrality of the "*vous*" would imply some imaginary equality between the two individuals. Language itself repeats the colonial model of power whose contents Barthes already seems to be rejecting but whose forms continue to insist. On the other hand, the "*tu*" used by the Maghrebin is something amusing or childlike. Though he might be useful for sex, the Maghrebin can never be the linguistic or cultural peer of a French citizen, who must, at least in the context of this essay, be white and male. The Maghrebin has no right to what Sartre called a *pour soi*.

It is perhaps the insistence of a linguistic model with a memory that makes counterexamples so rare. One of the few exceptions is found in a work by Guy Hocquenghem, *La Beauté du métis*, who attempts to seek linguistic liberation: "Love speaks to me only in other languages" (10). Still, Hocquenghem uses French as a means of communication and recognizes that linguistic difference means difference and distance. Even in this case, the line between the signifier and the signified, or between sign and referent, is always brought to the fore: "Like in Japanese theater, where the gesture and voice are split, your [*ta*] voice is here, but its echo is there, in your home, in your language" (12). French dominates semiotically with its images, its organization of space, and its truths. The rest is dangerous. If the Maghrebin is allowed to structure space, death always awaits as the ultimate meaning because Occidental dominance has been voided, as can be seen in the death of Alexandre in Tournier's *Les Météores* or even in the most well-known heterosexual version of the same story, Camus's *L'Etranger*. Without the Western sign, be it the linguistic structure or the individual who metonymically represents the power structure of colonial dominance, there can be no meaning for the Western individual. He must therefore find death, the absence of his—and I mean "his"—meaning.

The Maghrebin is always displaced because he cannot express his desire for, of, or against the other outside of the structures imposed *by* the other. The Maghrebin can never be where he will: he is constantly banished from there. Thus, starting with a utopia, we have seen that there is a system that reproduces the closed structures of the colony, the seraglio, and the prison, despite all of the possible variations. A good part of the subjugation of the Maghrebin relates to the systematic domination by Western heterosexuality as it is inscribed within a sadistic colonial discourse. In other words, these two discourses are the same: the Maghrebin woman becomes invisible, or, as Genet says in *Les Paravents*, "ugly," and the Maghrebin male replaces her in the locus of rape: "It's Saïd who would be jumped, not his wife" (48).

III. Barthes in Morocco

What could Barthes's project be? Can we speak of this readerless writing that can be read despite the author, despite the structures of power and discourse from which it can never wholly escape? Barthes has firsthand knowledge of the mythology of the colonized. In *Mythologies*, for example, there is a short piece entitled "African Grammar" that deals with the official vocabulary—the double-talk—of African affairs, that is, the state version of Africanism or Africanist discourse discussed by Said (193). That official discourse is "a language charged with making norms and facts coincide and with giving a cynical reality the air of a noble morality" (155). We would be selling Barthes short if we thought he did not see everything we have just described. So how can we begin to read his *Incidents*?

Incidental at first glance, these *Incidents* are part of the same theoretical and textual revolution as *S/Z* and *Le Plaisir du texte*. Faced with an unsignable orientation of desire and confronted with sexual orientation in an Oriental key, semiotics and structuralism retreat. These Moroccan incidents are testimony to the flight of the structuralist sign that cannot represent or even signify his desire; no set code is found adequate, no system of signs meets his needs. Ultimately, Barthes writes against his own received knowledge of structuralism and its signs. This work, I hypothesize, is an attempt—an essay—in defining what might be a homosexual semiotics that functions without necessarily depending on the structures to which homosexuality had been assigned: the infamous closet, the secret space, the confessional act of self-liberation, the translation from male to female, the glory of crime, the shame of the event. Barthes is writing a work that has been voided of all those little boxes that structured and oriented desire in other works. Like other writings of the era, it is a rereading of previous textualities that had been accepted as viable; in this case, Barthes is reading Gide and rewriting the results of that reading.

In *Incidents*, the closure and the bivalent opposition necessary to structuralism are put into question, eventually to be rejected. While *S/Z* makes the object-text implode by showing that the gaps between the real, the signifier, and the signified are willfully forgotten in realist writing and reading, *Incidents* questions the validity of the sign itself. No real interferes, for there is no real to lodge there. Signifiers and signifieds are engulfed in a desire that cannot be circumscribed in neutral language. Moreover, there is no explicit questioning of generic, literary, or world history here, even though every word seems at the very least to question the unsaid colonial background on which Gidean liberation is predicated. Given the more or less nonexistent status of the work as act of communication, the absence of overt revision of the models needs no explanation; Barthes has to profess nothing here, though he has much to profess.

For all these reasons and because of the appearance of desire as a motive force, it would be difficult to find the law and to discern the order of these *Incidents* that have no incidence, these fragments that are part of no totality. No logic is followed and there are even fewer causal or hermeneutic relations. Still, we can attempt to answer two questions. First, what is the status here of the relations between the author (or a "Frenchman") and Maghrebin men? And then, what is the status of sexuality at this point in the writer's career, a point at which we know that his work is undergoing a complete textual revolution? There seems to be a relation between the entry of the desiring subject into the game and the gradual appearance of a more personal kind of writing, a writing expressing desire, and known, for lack of a better term, though perhaps not entirely correctly, as poststructuralist writing.

Incidents starts with a structuralist model, soon to be abandoned in favor of a nonoppositional mixture, a combination of sign and object, of desire and its inscription, of self and other. At the beginning of *Incidents*, it is a question of describing a world marked by the categories of structuralism. Thus, on the first page, there is a classical (that is, structuralist) opposition between order and disorder: "The barman, at a station, alighted to gather a red geranium. He put it in a glass of water between the coffeemaker and the rather dirty collection of soiled cups and napkins" (23). Immediately thereafter, Barthes capitalizes "Désordre" and promotes it to being the transcendental sign of this world marked by anger, madness, and gesticulation: "In the little Socco square, blue shirt in the wind, figure of Disorder, an angry boy/waiter (that is here having all the signs of madness) gestures and curses a European (*Go home!*)" (23; italicized English Barthes's own). Thus Barthes starts by opposing two cultures, one hot, mad, gesticulating (that is, nonwritten), and disordered, the other, cold, ordered, and logical.

One culture, though perhaps chaotic, has the value of being indigenous. It tries to refuse the imperialism associated with Europeans, a lingering ideology that continues to kill the native even after independence. Yet the logic of the dominant culture to which Barthes himself belongs is limited in its knowledge. As its power shrinks, though it never fully disappears, so too does it become more and more apparent that the epistemological absolutism on which it prides itself is a sham, as is its own self-justification as the mimetic representation of the natural law. Even if the shrinking of Western ideology leaves nothing in its wake but a vision of the alienated other, the alienation shows the law itself to have been a specious imposition, not on "nature," as Gide would have had it, but on another, equally complex system of representations: "Two old American women grab an old blind man and force him to cross the street. But this Oedipus would have preferred money: money, money, not help" (24). This Maghrebin heat cannot keep its uniqueness and pure alterity for long. There is always the possibility of mutation and corruption. This blind man, for example, is caught up in the mercenary system, but we will never know if it is willingly or not.

So what should prove to be a set of stable values within the system of the other never quite maintains itself as stable. Even royalty seeks to convert the unknown—the incomprehensible, the unheard, the unexpected—into the extreme determined by the dominant system: "Heard the King's Cousin, with a beautiful black skin, was passing for an American black, by pretending not to understand Arabic" (24). To pass for a black American is the supreme irony in this bivalent value system. As a member of the royal family, this cousin should dominate as would any other African prince, but he is subjected to the postcolonial law according to which his nobility is always vulnerable to domination by white purity. While passing for an American black, a real victim of a continuing system of domination and difference, the king's cousin becomes a tourist so he can wear the imaginary white skin of which Fanon writes. As a tourist, the king's cousin is automatically classified as a member of the dominant society, the dominant class, and therefore, has the color of dominance as his assigned skin color.

It has nothing to do with his color or his background, but rather depends on the fact that he is perceived by others as a tourist and therefore, whatever the color of his skin, as white. This image of an imaginary white skin in a character who could have come from Fanon's study allows us to return to our preliminary question: What happens in a discourse with double minority status? Barthes perceives irony where Fanon calls to revolution. Perhaps the difference is that Fanon is writing in the early fifties, when France's colonies were still intact, and he was writing about the Antilles, whose status as *départements d'outre-mer* differs politically from that of the former North African colonies or of Algeria. Or perhaps it is Barthes himself who is wearing an imaginary white skin. As a homosexual male, he passes invisibly for his own other, the white heterosexual male, defined by the system that creates his subjectivity as the norm and zero-degree of the subject. In the North African sun, any European man alone may be viewed by the indigenous population as "homosexual," that is, as someone who has come to this spot to be penetrated. Wearing that invisible white skin for other whites, Barthes suddenly becomes the negation of the negation. In the eyes of the other, Barthes may in fact be "homosexual," unavowed other of the dominant European male. After the game of the king's cousin, image of the author of this work, discourse clearly falls under the ironic sway of a double bind: one cannot escape the system, but one can get the juicy role whichever side one chooses. For Barthes, the problem is the imposition of the master trope; while he recognizes its necessity, he cannot accept irony as the figure of the erotic. Most of all, the insistence of irony would mean that the violence associated with Gide's system of domination could never be fully overcome, no matter how often it was translated symbolically into other models and other figures.

Whereas a nonironic position is impossible, an ironic position de-eroticizes the situation for the master semiotician. To counter the devastation of the erotic imposed by irony, Barthes posits a new kind of master trope, produced by conceiving of alterity instead of identity as the base on which to build. If the same always implies the other, and if that implication leads to an endless round of negating negations, perhaps by positing the other as having primacy, Barthes could envision a semiotic system that would involve less subterfuge, less role-playing, and far less irony. A new system needs a new sign and Barthes conceives of the mixed as the basis of the system: by refusing a semiotics of identity that says "a equals a" and an oppositional semiotics that says "a is not b," Barthes hopes to show the intertwining figures of the system from the very beginning. Intertwined self and other, *corps-à-corps amoureux*, the mixed or the maculate is the figure of desire.

For Barthes there are no more oppositions and no more structures of domination: it is the inseparable stain, the sign of the other in the same, or for that matter, that of the same in the other, that makes the same other to itself, fixes the interest of the perceiver, and becomes the *punctum*, the point at which the subject sees himself or herself caught in alterity. Barthes will later define this punctum against a *studium* in his book on photography, *La Chambre claire*. In that book,

he writes that the studium is "the application of the taste for someone to a thing, a sort of general investment that is strong but without any particular acuity" (*CC* 48). The punctum, which comes to
"bother [*déranger*] the studium," is "the chance event that in and of
itself stings me [*me point*], but also wounds me and grabs me" (*CC*
49). Thus the punctum is defined against something (the studium),
but is inseparable from it; in fact it penetrates the studium: "a shot, a
little hole, a little spot, a little cut" (*CC* 49). The punctum will be the
name eventually given to the maculate that insists, the spot that penetrates, the desire that is marked from without and from within. And
even the chance event marked by the punctum (for it also means a
roll of the dice) is akin to the cruising in which chance plays such an
important part (Bell; Chambers).

The macula designates the sign joined to the object.[1] The mixture
and the heteroclite count for Barthes, the more imperceptible the
difference the better. As it is indelible, the sign is also the stain in its
lowest form; the punctum is a sign of the mixed that will not unmix
for love or money. For example, a man dressed entirely in white and
drinking milk has "a spot, a light coat of shit, as of a pigeon, on his
immaculate hood" (25). The insistence of the heteroclite ensures that
Barthes falls neither into an essentialism nor into a dialectic of
power, though this latter creeps back at numerous points in a ludic
mode. Yet we should not go so far as to believe that all traces of older
models disappear; for Barthes, textuality is always a palimpsest re-
plete with catachreses. Completely separated from their original
models, essentialism, dominance, and irony are refigured in inverted
commas. At numerous points they return in a playful logomachy that
is the Barthesian equivalent of sexual foreplay.

The heteroclite here seems to be the confrontation not of nature
and culture, but of two systems of representation or two complex
semioticities. To use a well-known Lacanian example from "The Insistence of the Letter" (499–500), the absence in a culture of two
doors with "Men" and "Women" written on them does not mean
that a) natives do not urinate or b) natives are more natural. In fact,

---

1. Cf.: "A fine, almost sweet boy, whose hands are already a bit thick, suddenly, in
a flash, evinces the gesture of the 'little guy': flicking his cigarette ash with his nail"
(24). Compare to that the sign about to disappear: "The five-year-old kid, in shorts
and a hat: knocks on a door, spits, touches his crotch" (26).

according to Lacan, the sign shows that Western man has made an imperative of "the laws of urinary segregation" that he (*sic*) shares with the great majority of primitive societies. This mixture must always be determined by language even if it cannot be anatomized according to the laws of form or the division between self and other that still weighs so heavily upon Western consciousness. The mixed and the maculate then show us through word-pictures, as in Jean-François Lyotard's "space of the figural," what no Aristotelian discourse could: every discourse is itself an encounter of semioticities; we posit unity through exclusion. Playing with the language, dancing with the maculate of the language, one can seduce and be seduced without falling prey to the most deadly of insistent, denotative, essentialist meanings.

This is neither a linguistic nor an erotic utopia. The mixture must always be determined by language, and whatever Barthes does, language still has its rules. These rules do not necessarily apply inherently to the maculae, for which no independent semiotics exists. Even a law of violence may interfere, one that by its very nature as neutral and self-identical tends to reproduce the power structures that Barthes finds to be anathema to his personal Maghrebin erotics: "Hunting long hairs: Rafaelito maintains that his father cut his hair while he was sleeping. Others saw that the cops forcibly cut hair in the street: revolt and repression even of the boys' black hair" (24). The law of violence, the negation given by the Lacanian father, is too reminiscent of the Occidental division and decision to be valid in his erotic re-signing of this world.

The mixture of objects, the mélange of signs, is thus also a linguistic and behavioral fetish. In fact, it is the very mixture of the two kinds of fetish: the behavior that recalls a series of mnemic traces or psychological inscriptions and the semiotic fetish that recalls a series of individual actions or imagined behaviors. Thus, even fetishistically, the mixture functions for Barthes as a mise-en-abîme of its own status of mélange. The mixture insists at both the macroscopic and the microscopic level. At times, the locus at which the maculate occurs within the inseparable dyad is perceived as an image that is "always already" given: "The child discovered in the hall was sleeping in a box, his head emerged as if cut" (26). The images of the space thus resist the law that separates subject from object, the

Western law of laws. The image is what cannot be assigned; it is a locus from which the punctum itself may seem to have fled. More precisely, punctum and studium have so thoroughly intertwined that they cover the same space. We might call the image "surrealistic," but a better term would be "cinematic," the kind of photograph where punctum and studium inseparably overlap. In this expansion of the singular punctum into the generalized maculate, the erotic point of the simplest images, which is the impossibility of complete detachment, is replaced by the diffusion of the erotic throughout a space:

On the road from Marrakesh to Beni-Mellal: a poor teenager, Abdelkhaïm, who does not speak French, carries a round country basket. I give him a ride for a few hundred meters. He has hardly gotten in the car when he pulls a teapot out of his basket and hands me a cup of hot tea (how is it hot?); then he gets out and disappears along the side of the road. (54)

Like other images in the book, this one is cinematic and its essence cannot be touched, as it always seems beyond the reach of the semiotician's analyses. In every case, the image either does not reveal the point of the mixture or it shows many points at once, though without irony. In such cases of multiple points of contact, the erotic fills the space as no single point dominates:

But also: at Settat, I picked up a twelve-year-old boy who was hitching; he carries a big plastic bag full of oranges, tangerines, and a package wrapped in awful grocer's paper. Wise, serious, reserved, he holds it tight on his knees in the hollow of his djellaba. His name is Abdellatif. Out in the country, without a village in sight, he asks me to stop and shows me the plain: he is going out there. He kisses my hand and hands me two dirhams (undoubtedly the price of the bus, which he had readied and held tight in his hand). (52)

Thus the locus of the erotic is the mixed. The mixture then is also the call to the other in jouissance itself, what might be called the moment of purity of the spot: "Abder—wants a clean towel, which, out of the religious fear of impurity, has to be put down separately, to cleanse him later of love" (25). The erotic appears with the contact between two object-subjects, two object-signs. They are bodies and words in a space and a structure in which neither can be given a priori. This means that neither the body nor language can be posited as the same from which the other and the doubly other come, to be defined as other by Western metaphysics and erotics. The macula is the sign of this mixture, though it cannot be separated from it: it exists only as a spot, only as a sign of the mixture it signifies as it spots. There, on the object of discourse, everything is suddenly made less "other" by this welcome of the somewhat deictic nature of the sign in its failure to mean: "Aliwa (a pretty name to be repeated tirelessly) likes white, spotless pants (late in the season), but, given the local lack of comfort, there is always a spot on this milky white" (31). In this world, the sign marks the man-object as being both the one who has no right to subjectivity and the one who is a fetish, a sign joined to the object, all viewed by the master semiotician:

A young, serious man, well-dressed in a gray suit and wearing a gold bracelet, with fine clean hands, smoking red Olympic cigarettes, drinking tea, speaking with enough intensity (a government worker? one of those who slow down files?), lets a thread of saliva fall on his knee; his companion brings it to his attention. (34)

Thus the sign resists the semiotics that determines the object seen as an object of discourse. The sign detours the system from signifying something other than itself: "A certain Ahmed, near the station, wears a sky blue sweater with a nice spot of orange dirt on the front" (35). For Barthes, the possibility of signification sometimes suffices; the process does not have to be completed, subject to the Occidental gaze of closure. Sometimes the *béance* of signification, like the famous gap between two articles of clothing noted in *Le Plaisir du texte* (19), is all that is needed for there to be "semierotics."

If the sign is no longer integrated into a logical classifying system, how can there be meaning? Perhaps it is the will to say, and not meaning, that is rubbed away, a will to say that comes from a subject defined by the criteria of Western semiotics. For the system of a subject that goes beyond the limits of structuralism to be elaborated, the subject must be presented. For this to be done, he, she, or it must be placed in the middle of a discourse that is still semiocentric. Yet what is targeted by the subject of the discourse immediately challenges the constitution of discursive subjectivity through the systems of enunciation and the laws of semioticity. This challenge is the emergence of desire in a subversion of signs, subjects, and meanings. The subject is not the one speaking, the one who "announces the present instance of discourse containing *I*," as Benveniste (252) defines the subject. No: the subject is the one who desires. And the one who desires needs another subject: the one announcing (pointing, pricking, chancing) the present instance of desire. This other subject is the one to whom the rights to enunciation and the proper have been refused, the one for whom signs do not separate from their referents.

The sign of desire is seen at a zero degree. It depends on the visible as much as does the cinematic image. Here, for example, the sign is a gesture:

> Relation between his very fine, cared-for, clean hands (he had just washed them), and the way in which he showed them, turned them, used them, while speaking, in the little movements of *pied-noir* gestures. Relation between the extreme fineness of his black socks, as of the highest quality, and the way he stuck out his leg. (47)

The text remains ambiguous: Is it a *pied noir* doubled in a sign of black socks who is assimilated by this spotlike semioticity to a Maghrebin or a Maghrebin who is like a *pied noir*? In other words, has the Maghrebin learned to be "French" by copying what the metropolis would consider the B-movie version of the *pied-noir*, or has the *pied-noir* become a caricatural version of himself? In either case, the sign-gesture clearly remains attached to its object that has become or will become a fetish.

Moreover, the signs and the other objects of desire, the Maghrebins themselves, seem to be separated from any systematic approach. To contemplate a Maghrebin, the object of desire of a subject awakening as such, is essentially to see the contingent and the juxtaposed: "A teapot for mint tea, in solid metal, without a plastic knob, bought with the help and company of the Moroccan middleweight boxing champion" (28). The juxtaposition of the purchase with the muscular body of the young man can mean nothing, for every sign is "always already" linked to its object. From that it is only a short step to the chance occurrence, to the erotic defined as a chance occurrence, as an unexpected meeting, indeed, as nothing more than the story of a teapot. Without designating himself specifically as such, Barthes, as well as his objects of desire, becomes a Baudelairian *flâneur*. The heterosexual of the nineteenth century is transformed into a homosexual and transported from the streets of Paris to those of North

Africa: "Abdessalam, an intern in Tetouan, seems to have come this morning to Tangier (I meet him by chance) to buy an antiarthritic cream and a whistling cap for a kettle" (29).[2]

Thus, Barthes's Maghrebin erotics occurs in semiotics to go beyond it. Barthes's semierotics is defined by starting with structures that disappear once they have been enunciated. His erotics finally occurs according to the effect of a subject that the author is always in the process of outstripping or upheaving. The effect of the subject occurs through Western discourses, but the desystematization of subjects and desire in the Maghreb results in the derailing of the system. Still the mixture remains: the Maghrebin is submitted to a linguistic, discursive, and differential system of the white man by simultaneously surrendering to and escaping from it. Though it appears to be an artificial separation, we need to consider this mixture in two versions: one in which the body is in the fore, and the other in which discourse itself is in the forefront.

The first division is between the masculine and the feminine, though we know from the beginning that this division occurs within the masculine, for the veiled, cloistered woman is paradoxically not found within this opposition. The feminine occurs within the masculine, and takes place in flight, in passivity, and in absence: "Selam, a veteran from Tangiers, snickers because he has met three Italians who wasted his time: 'They thought I was feminine!' " (32). As has already been noted, there is a blending between this position of differentiation and a misogyny never wholly denied nor ever fully avowed. In that, Barthes is miming the position of the other whom he wants to make the locutor, not the interlocutor. From time to time, there may be a confusion because of clothing, but afterwards, there is always a correction: "A Negro, hooded in his white djellaba, becomes so black that I take his face for the *litham* of a woman" (54).

In a way, then, Barthes buys into the position of the other, for whom there is only one visible gender. It is a convenient co-option, for it allows him to continue his erotic game instead of bemoaning,

2. Baudelaire appears in a passage that could be understood as the mise-en-abîme of the desire of the *flâneur*: "The Moroccan student, with large teeth and slightly receding gums, a short beard, is a student at the Lille Catholic school, because in his village in the High Atlas, he had a white father. He reads (or does not read) *The Flowers of Evil*" (56).

as any good liberal might, the fate of the North African woman. In this world, such confusion can be dangerous, just as the woman herself is dangerous, captivating, and deadly: a witch. Her very presence can confuse signs, for the woman is perceived to distort meanings, to force oppositions, and to demand by her very presence, as contingent as it may be, that the fetishistic division of the sexes be replaced by an oppositional separation of the sexes. And it matters little that it is undoubtedly the man who first demanded this separation and who, "to protect women," created the structures of the seraglio. He formed it for his freedom, but the woman's veil veils him as well and limits his liberty at the very heart of his definition of the masculine: "The Gardens of Chella: a gangly adolescent, with smooth hair, dressed all in white, with little boots below his white jeans, accompanied by his two veiled sisters, looks at me a long time and spits: refusal or contingency?" (37).

Thus there are two versions of the feminine. One is weak, found within the masculine, perhaps to be disdained, but harmless in any case. The other, the female feminine, which can be counterfeited by a game of veils, is perceived as being potentially dangerous. The first version of the feminine, the one found within the masculine, is separated by a fuzzy, variable, changing border between the two zones. The line is relative, determined in part by the perceiver, the reader, or the master of language and/or of action. The line between the masculine and the gendered feminine is an absolute and to cross it means to go into a forbidden zone and to have violated a taboo. Thus to be a male and to have some feminine behavior, understood stereotypically as some version of passivity, is at worst to be disdained. To be a woman, however, or to become a woman, is the implication of the possibility of danger and death: "A very poor hitchhiker who goes from city to city looking for work (very nice eyes) tells me a dark story about a jitney (we are in a vague forest) whose driver was assassinated by four passengers disguised as women" (54).

On the other hand, what cannot be dangerous in this system is the masculine announced as such in some variation or another. No matter how much conniving there is and no matter how much the realm of the masculine turns into a game of one-upmanship, there is never any real danger: " 'Monsieur, remember [*rappelle-toi*], you should never pick up a Moroccan you don't know as a hitchhiker,' this Moroccan tells me whom I pick up hitching and whom I do not know" (55). Here the irony has reached the level of the body, a rhetorical fetish ever more precious for Barthes, by his translation of the fetishbody into fetish-sign. Thus on the erotico-linguistic level, Barthes appreciates whatever touches on this position, seen as something artificial or as an other in which bivalent oppositions dissolve. Within these Maghrebin incidents appears a natural Derridean:

Farid, met in Jour et Nuit, rails against a beggar who asks me first for a cigarette, then, having gotten it, for money "to eat." This schema of progressive exploitation (rather banal) seems to make him indignant: "See how he pays you back for having given in!" Yet, a minute later, as I leave him and give him my whole cigarette pack, which he takes without thanking me, I hear him ask me for 5,000 francs "to eat." I burst out laughing; he alleges *difference* (everyone here says he is different, since he considers himself not as a person, but as a need). (36)

As the reader will have guessed, *Incidents* is about sex. Or more accurately, it is about sex organs. What would, one wonders, the sex organs of a "need" be, as distinct from those of a person? Always the good professor, Barthes gives a French lesson that winds up in philology: "Three young Chleuhs, on the cliff, insist on a French lesson. 'How do you say . . . ?' Answering them, I realize that sexual apparatus fits in an occlusive paradigm: *cul/con/queue* [ass/cunt/prick]. Instant philologists, they themselves are amazed" (108). What is not said is even more interesting: What are the words in their language? Do these young Maghrebin men touch themselves to indicate what they want to know? How do they indicate "cunt"? This Arab freedom of expression confronts the driest French paradigm imaginable, in a language that shows, by a chance coincidence of sounds, the will to closure and occlusion that opposes sex and bodies, sex and sex, body and body.

If this is about sex, then, as we have already figured out, it must be Arab-style sex. For Barthes, this means that the signs and the gestures are not distinguished from their origin, do not leave their locus, and never become writing. It must mean, in the most profound way, that "cunt" has no name in this world, for its name is always separated from the organ, the singular exception in this world of proxemics and maculae. In this world, the female genitalia are always metaphorically and metonymically veiled to protect them. But it is not only protection enforced by the men who have proprietary rights to these organs: the fathers protecting them when the women are virgins, the husbands protecting them when the women are wives. It is also that they must be shielded from the naming process, for in this world, the name, like any other sign, is attached to its referent. To name the female genitalia is to come in contact with them, thus violating social taboos, sullying oneself and them as they are named, and perhaps even becoming feminine oneself in the process. No, it is better to veil those organs, to divorce them from the processes of nomination and meaning that depend on the presence of the referent. Thus these Maghrebin versions of semiotics are homosexual: unnamed and unseen, women remain out of the public discourse of exchange about sexuality in order to be kept entirely in the economic law of family exchanges and orders.

Writing is a game between men. When there is writing, it serves to destroy distance by restating it: " 'I feel I am going to love you. What a bore. What to do?'—Give me your address" (42). As insignificant as a sign may be, it must disappear when it is separated from the body. This piece is a singularity, the only text by Barthes written against writing. For example, for a boy who has nothing and who asks for a souvenir of Paris, Barthes brings back a bronze Eiffel Tower (37). The sign of France or of the French phallus must be empty of usefulness and meaning. It will be valuable in the act of giving itself, the giving of oneself that accompanies the sign, an act that returns the object-sign to its use as a sign of desire (and not of the Eiffel Tower itself) for the boy. Thus every separate(d) sign must be annihilated or returned to its origin and gestural nature.

As I have said, *Incidents* is about sex. Still, it is sex caught up in the gestural and in differential nonopposition: "Demonstration of phonological pertinence: a young salesman in the bazaar (rather fetching): *tu/ti* [you/'yi'] (not pertinent) *veux tapis / taper* [want a carpet / to screw] (pertinent)?" (31). Despite the best efforts, be they Barthes's emulation of the system of the other, or a sympathetic critical reading, this sex story still seems to be caught in the stereotypical opposition between active and passive penetration. Barthes seems to try to flee it: "Little teacher from Marrakesh: 'I will do anything you want,' ['*Je ferai tout ce que vous voudrez*,'] he says, full of effusion, good will, and with complicity in his eyes. And that means: *I'll screw you* [*je vous niquerai*] and only that" (53–54). Nothing is more deeroticized for Barthes than a use of language where there is no ambiguity, no play, no erotic gape or slippage. In the case of the rather fetching salesman in the bazaar, the ambiguity is not resolved and it is therefore still seductive. In fact, we will never know for sure if the salesman was talking about carpets or sex. On the other hand, with the teacher, who uses the polite form (*vous*), everything is all too clear. In the first case, the Moroccan, inept master of the finer points of the French language, is nevertheless a master of erotic games without ever knowing it. On the other hand, the teacher, Gallicized because he has been educated in the French system, cannot but wind up in the poverty of opposition. Having mastered the dominant language, the teacher wins the game of mastery but loses his poetry and erotics in the process. For him, there are only detached gestures, maybe ironic, maybe not. For teachers, be they French or Gallicized Moroccans, it is only a question of a vulgar farce, even when faced with the poetics of a talking phallus named Proust:

A certain Jean, a young professor—of what?—, leans over my book: "I could never swallow that guy (Proust) [*J'ai jamais pu me le farcir, celui-là (Proust)*]; but I feel it coming." His friend Pierre, bewildered, disdainful, and dry (indifferent to the answer): "Do you take notes?" (57)

Everyone knows that the bodies of two men can be connected genito-anally in only two topological ways. In these *Incidents* as much as in *Fragments d'un discours amoureux*, the writing subject engaged in a playful logomachy is reduced to the finite physicality of his body only as a last resort. Even if language becomes a game of tag or hide and seek, even if language has no truth, the body may be deferred: "Visit by an unknown boy, sent by his friend: 'What do you want? Why have you come?—It's nature!' (Other, another time: 'It's tenderness!')" (37). For the body, present, silent (that is, without a tongue), cannot be erotic. A homosexual should think himself in paradise on earth in a place where each and every one is ready to penetrate him; for Barthes at least, such mechanical predictability is far from interesting, for it is no better than a doxa of foreseeable sexual behavior.

On the other hand, when it is a question of making the male organ, the linguistic phallus, speak, or of speaking of it to integrate it into a system of linguistic dominance, affection appears. In one case, it has to do with entering a linguistic system entirely framed by colonialism: " 'Papa,' an old, charming batty Englishman, does without his lunch *by sympathy* during Ramadan (*by sympathy* for the little circumcised boys)" (32; emphasized English in original). By now the colonialism is completely vestigial and merely the sign for Barthes of a linguistic and erotic seduction. In another case, the linguistico-phallic fetish is irresistibly conjugated and yoked to the body: "Gérard, born of a French father and local mother, wants to show me the path of the Golden Gazelle; he spreads his legs in the car to show me his bait; then, like a rare sweetmeat, a last irresistible argument: 'You know, my thing, it's not cut!' " (56).

Thus the opposition between penetrater and penetrated is understood as such only in a telelinguistic world in which the sign is separated from the gesture and the body. Where signs are far from the objects they represent, the referents ironically become too solid, finite, and fixed to be of erotic interest to Barthes. Yet replaced in a proxemic world, the signs return to the mélange of the maculate; this game of bodies is veiled by a poetry that is hallucinatory in its displacements:

His pals say of H. that he is "very sensual" (enunciation made even more troubling by the dryness of the *pied noir* accent): for me, H. becomes the "Very Sensual." Still, the meaning of this nickname is finally guessed: H. takes it up the ass [*se fait niquer*]. (42)

So not even the scorn felt by the Maghrebin population for the passive role in anal intercourse can dissuade Barthes from his pleasure at the game of love. This same poetry can exist far from the sexual arena, but in any case, it is what makes Barthes cherish the other:

In front of a dancing bearded man, the King's Cousin tells me: he's a philosopher. To be a philosopher, he says, you need four things: 1) to have a diploma in Arabic; 2) to travel a lot; 3) to have contacts with other philosophers; 4) to be far from reality, by the seaside, for example. (29)

The Arab does not divide the world as we do, longtime, jaded, blasé structuralists that we are. The Arab resists the division into metaphors and metonymies, all directed according to a plan that we still seem to assume without the slightest hesitation. For the Arab, metaphoric distance is always brought back to be annihilated by metonymico-sensual proximity.[3] Even the absence of poetry, the prosaic world of the newspaper story, the political, is brought back to proximity and thus even the banal or the awful become eroticized:

> Abdellatif—so voluptuous—peremptorily justifies the hangings in Baghdad. The guilt of the accused is obvious because the trial was so quick: thus the case was clear. Contradiction between the brutality of this stupidity and the fresh warmth of his body, the availability of his hands, which I continue, rather absentmindedly, to hold and caress while he does his catechism of vengeance. (36)

The meeting, a mixture of bodies and signs, would thus be "charming," even if at first no charm appears to come from it: "Azemmour: bought a tureen in white metal, whose seller, young and toothless, proposes a meeting 'in his bachelor flat [*dans sa garçon-nière*]' " (58). For the meeting is always the occasion for Barthes to quote, though inaccurately in this case: it is doubtful that the young, toothless man said "in *his* bachelor flat." It may be a case of free indirect discourse, but it is also the chance for Barthes to show himself a winner in a little logomachy, regardless of the end result on the physical level. This boy, a body with a phallus, has a hole as well, a toothless mouth, and speaks French badly, as do the members of the little Verdurin clan, so many of whom seem to be afflicted with one form of dysphasia or another. The locus of language remains attached to the locus of the subject and determines its activity. At the same time, although the various games of language and bodies finish more or less simultaneously, they are not coterminous in all respects. While the game of bodies depends on a bivalent, though not necessarily oppositional, logic, the linguistic game depends on rhetoric and dialectics. Barthes conquers through language:

3. See, for example, the following quotation: "Mohammed L., met one morning toward ten o'clock, is clean with sweetness and sleep. He has just arisen, he says, because late last night, he wrote lines for a play he is writing 'without characters, without a plot, etc.' Another, little Mohammed, said he wrote poems, 'in order not to get bored.' Here, poetry allows you *to go to bed late*" (43).

Driss A. does not know that cum [*foutre*] is called cum; he calls it shit [*merde*]: "Watch out, the shit is going to come out": there is nothing more traumatic.

Another Slaoui (Gymnastic Mohammed) says dryly and precisely: *to ejaculate*: "Watch out, I am going to ejaculate." (38)

The right word, or, for that matter, the wrong word, can be reinterpreted according to the logic of the dominant linguistic partner, Barthes, regardless of his sexual role. He is still the master of the game. Could this be nothing more than renting bodies and the purchase of words, taken, seized, ravished, and thus separated as fetishes themselves, all performed by the recidivist semiotician? Is Roland Barthes condemned to a Gideanism coupled with an unhappy awareness of that condemnation?

Certainly Barthes is cognizant of the intermittent logomachy, the verbal translation of the Gidean discourses that hide a structure of power and dominance. And to that extent, Barthes remains a scion of Gide. In a sense, the erotics and politics can never be fully disengaged from each other. Whatever he does, Barthes will always be the European male in the Maghreb. If for no other reason than the phenomenological one, he will always be taken at first glance as one of "them." Yet at the same time, there is another subtle shading that moves Barthes away from the model.

Consider the literature professor again, the writer of *Sur Racine*, who knows of what he speaks. He does not fail to remark his knowledge, our knowledge as well, as we read, with Barthes, the Maghrebin male who unbeknownst to himself may have a career as a declaimer of classical theater: "A Racinian beginning: with sweet complacency: 'You see me? You wish to touch me? [*Vous me voulez toucher?*]' " (34). Once again, Barthes dominates linguistically as the literature professor in full command of his subject. But what does that literary dominance mean? That Barthes is a poet, that he uses language to create, reflect, and dream, but not necessarily to dominate physically according to the bivalent power model. For if caught in a seemingly inescapable Gideanism, Barthes has another literary master, not Racine, but Gide's alternative, Proust. Barthes's Proustianism, his recognition of the inevitability of these situations, and his desire to write a novel are all the same thing, which amounts to a difference from the Gidean model of liberation through dominance.

Ever the good Proustian, Barthes knows that one is always a captive, if not to the other, then at least to writing.

At the heart of this rather disparate work in which the laws are neither generic nor extradiegetic, there is a fragment of a minimalist novel. It is not a novel in the sense of a developed plot, but there is enough continuity among four fragments for a minimalist tale. They deal with a certain Amidou described as a character in a novel, subjected both to French literature (which Barthes has mastered) and to Barthes's own personal poetics. Significantly, the literature this time is not the fatality of Racinian love, but the resolution of Molière's comedy:

Amidou, high school junior, future gymnastics teacher, met one morning in the mud of the Flea Market, poor and nice, his raincoat too short, his big shoes faded and worn out, his beautiful Moroccan eyes, his hair frizzy, has "to reflect" on "Molière's comedy" for tomorrow.

(Amidou: I prefer to suppress the H, for: sweet like starch [*l'amidon*], inflammable like tinder [*l'amadou*].) (44)

Of all the boys in this work, Amidou is the only one who is equal to Barthes himself as a poet. And, at the same time, Barthes is equal to Amidou, who is a poet in a language that is neither his own (Arabic) nor completely other (pure French). For Barthes has become a lover in a semiotics that is neither his own (French) nor completely other (pure Maghrebin). The literary dominance of Barthes meets the hybrid poetry of the other, and Barthes suggests in this little novel, in fact, *by* this little novel, that the Gideanism can at least be temporarily overturned. Amidou's language and his name are part of the hybrid of Maghrebin French that has French signifiers (most of the time) and Arab signifieds (all of the time). Yet he can produce poetry, and, just as his name causes Barthes to dream poetically, his vocabulary does the same: "I like Amidou's vocabulary: *to dream* and *to burst* for *to get hard* [*bander*] and *to come* [*jouir*]. *To burst* is of plant life, splashing, dispersing, disseminating; *to come* is moral, narcissistic, full, closed" (44–45). Spotted as perceived, spotted as maculate, Barthes too is caught (up) in the hybrid system. In the end, Barthes also dreams: the critic has an erection.

What can we say after that, once we have seen and uncovered that which, like Tartuffe, "I should not see," once we have uncovered our critical father's nakedness? Obviously, the image of this Maghreb and of these Maghrebins "always already" eroticized according to the rules of an erotics of the dominant culture does not simply disappear. And this country whose image Barthes sketches remains subjected to certain of the models inherited from colonialism. These Moroccan boys, who are materially poor, depend on their own submission to the law of the other, his money, and his language; they dominate, if at all, with their bodies, in the sexual act, and then only in a non-dialectical logic. At the same time, we learn the lesson of *Incidents* along with the author. Just as the work deforms structures and semi-otics, it teaches the beginning of a new lesson to the master: here and now, if only for a moment, Roland Barthes writes a novel, abandons the system, frees himself for an instant. Here and now, blissfully erect, Roland Barthes permits himself to dream.

Cippus: Guibert

Now this Story is destined to raise a modest cippus in
which witness is given the life of the one who left me
all his goods and his thought.

Honoré de Balzac, *Louis Lambert*

To write in the dark?
To write until the end?
To end it all to avoid the fear of death?

Hervé Guibert, *Cytomégalovirus*

I. The Unnameable

Even within the literature of illness, the discourses and narratives associated with AIDS occupy a special niche, unheard of certainly since
the times of plague narratives. Tales of syphilis, of tuberculosis, and
of madness or its more modern version, neurosis, have had currency
throughout the centuries, and the nineteenth and early twentieth
centuries used this literary subgenre to great effect: *La Dame aux
Camélias*, *Le Horla*, *The Magic Mountain*, the *Recherche* (or its myth),
Zeno's Conscience; the list goes on and on. By and large, through the
circumscription effected by the discourses of the nineteenth century,
not the least of which was the discursive inscriptions of the advances
of medical knowledge, this tradition of the literature of illness became normalized. Discourse kept madness and sickness behind a
protective barrier and while the reader risked no infection, literature
risked no corruption.

Of late, there has been a significant change with the appearance
of the discourses of AIDS. Distinct from the neatly circumscribed
discourses of tuberculosis that match the enclosure of the sanatoria,
distinct from the more dangerous narratives of venereal disease circumscribed by a moat of scientific commentary and admonishing,

moralizing discourses, AIDS narratives have been subject from their inception to an external fear. Outside the individual discourse reigns an apocalyptic tone that may force the discourses of AIDS in certain directions: AIDS, perhaps, cannot speak as it would. The narratives may not reflect the truth of the person living with AIDS (PLA) because the narrative is always subjected to a pressure from without that forces the narrative implicitly or explicitly to respond to the lack of circumscription, to the apocalyptic tone, and to the voices of "reason." Even the contained AIDS narrative may be dangerous: in the United States, in the framework of a media campaign entitled "America Responds to AIDS," you cannot get the information directly and succinctly; the only way to get real information is to make a toll-free telephone call. We are constantly told that AIDS knows no boundaries, but that seems to hide a belief that AIDS can infect even through the very channels of communication. The image of AIDS is thus like the classic image of homosexuality itself: ostensibly restricted to a small group, it is somehow able to infiltrate everywhere. It is the image of surreptitious homosexuality, the image of a vampire lying quietly in wait; it is the image of Satan's minions.

Moreover, given the uncertain peripeteia of the manifestations of the illness, the so-called opportunistic infections, as opposed to, for example, the codified stages of syphilis or the progressive consumption of tuberculosis, AIDS has a wide range of paths to take to reach its final moments. Ironically, then, at least from the point of view of the literary critic, the AIDS narrative has an infinity of possibilities brought on by the imprisonment of the illness: the AIDS victim is certainly condemned, but like the Sartrean Dasein, he or she is condemned to live a kind of freedom, a freedom to struggle, a freedom he or she may never have imagined before. For any writer, the disease is a chance to write as never before. For the writer who is also a PLA, he or she has the possibility of leading a struggle against death and the inexorable beating of the clock in a way that renegotiates the pact of fiction and autobiography implicitly or explicitly made with the reader, who, by the way, must accept the narrative as a risk-free experience. The AIDS narrative of a PLA hovers between genres, between an (auto)biographical narrative and fiction, between a documentary and an invention.

And there is something additional for a select few, the authors engaging questions of reflexivity in literature and the student of literature: the truest, though most insidious, aspect of AIDS is that the retrovirus mimes the subject. The openness to opportunistic infection is also the lack of recognition or representation of the other, even at the level of the cells of the body. AIDS kills because it destroys otherness, confuses self and other, mixes substance and representation, and rewrites the codes of the self. No wonder, then, that Hervé Guibert talks about counterfeit paintings in *L'Homme au chapeau rouge* or confesses, "And the results are faxed back, here's another kind of jargon I like to use: words for new tools that didn't exist in books written ten years earlier" (*PC* 105). AIDS questions identity and difference, for it occurs when the world of simulacra collapses into the world of origins and singularities. Long after the end of a culture of propitiatory sacrifice, long after the act of representation included that violence at the level of representation to banish it from the realm of the real, AIDS is death by mimesis.

The first phases of AIDS will have been a rare moment in the history of literature. It appears on the horizon as the incomprehensible, mysterious catch-all term for a polymorphous medical condition known early on by the ill-fitting, fatally misleading names of "gay cancer" and "gay plague." Despite these early terms in popular parlance, science, in an official discourse, named it "Acquired Immune Deficiency Syndrome." As Susan Sontag notes, AIDS is the "first major illness known by an acronym" (28). AIDS does not have, as she puts it, "natural borders." The very identity of the disease, illness, or condition "is designed for purposes of investigation and with tabulation and surveillance by medical and other bureaucracies in view." This supposedly neutral scientific term quickly became part of official language. Absorbed directly into the language of power, that medical terminology named everything and nothing at once. Bureaucracy seized the word: here was a convenient acronym by which to name the unknown, label the victims, and isolate them from the healthy. The codification even helped make the mortality rate more accurate, though in recent years we have learned that even the definition of the disease excludes some PLA's, especially women, people of color, and third-world victims, because of the way in which knowledge of the disease developed, with the white gay male community as the reference group. The naming of the disease, as well as its well-announced, well-known "origin" within the "gay" and therefore "other" community, made the naming itself part of a scourge. From the early eighties on, the dissemination of information about the disease separated groups, tried to use it to protect the "innocent" from the "guilty," tragically doing what AIDS itself does not do: distinguish between one and another. Whether out of ignorance or calculation, the result of distinguishing among communities has had the same results. Randy Shilts has documented the tragic dimensions of laissez-faire public health in response to the AIDS crisis in the United States. More recently, in France, the tainting of the blood supply after the knowledge was available to provide blood free of HIV has seemed to make hemophiliacs a "dispensable" population.

Perhaps because of the enormity of the death toll, perhaps because of the incomprehensibility of a disease that attacks on many fronts at once, perhaps because of the galloping rate at which it has infiltrated every stratum of the human community, AIDS had no poetic dimension, no literariness with which it entered the world of writing. The only name it had was the scientific one; it entered writing as a fact of life and a fact of death.

II. Textual Seropositivity

I do not ever remember being as struck both by the presence of the author and the *difference* of writing as I was with Hervé Guibert. As was the case for many other readers and critics, I discovered his writing with a book called *A l'ami qui ne m'a pas sauvé la vie*, the detailed exposition in novel form of the early stages of his AIDS. From that point, I followed his work both backwards and forwards. Backwards, through the books he wrote before *A l'ami*; forwards through the final volumes that give what I think is the most complete literary account to date of a human being and a writer, two minds, two modes occupying the same body and grappling with this terminal disease. The extreme nature of Guibert's situation brings into focus and into question the disposition, organization, and structures of the literary work and, once again, blurs the line between fact and fiction.

In this chapter, I will examine the literary dimension of the extreme nature of this illness as it is figured principally in *A l'ami*, which is Guibert's first "full-length study" of his encounter with

AIDS. I will also look at two other works, though in less detail, since many of the textual problems of these works are already laid out in *A l'ami*: *Le Protocole compassionnel* and *Cytomégalovirus*. The former is the continuation of *A l'ami*; the latter is the chronicle of a hospital stay toward the end of the author's life. Even a cursory reading of these works shows that the lines between genres, as I have suggested above, are blurred. As Guibert himself notes in *Le Protocole compassionnel*: "It is when what I write takes the form of a diary that I have the greatest impression of fiction" (87). Is the "I" of a PLA writing fiction, writing fiction about AIDS, or, for that matter, writing a diary about AIDS, still in the position to distinguish between genres? Or, to ask a more radical question, does the "I" of a PLA bring into question everyone's distinctions between genres? Can we be so sure now that our previous distinctions were correct?

If the reader will forgive me a brief personal excursion, I would like to relate, anecdotally, my own confusion (in the French and English senses of the word). I had originally discovered Guibert at the FNAC. Though immediately taken with his writing, that is to say, immediately captivated by the work of a very talented author, I did not begin to question the generic implications of these works until much later; I let them sit unproblematically, *tantôt* fiction, *tantôt* autobiography. But on December 30, 1991, I was sitting in San Francisco International Airport, and as I was waiting for the plane, I was reading that morning's *New York Times*. The newspaper contained an obituary for Hervé Guibert, who had died on the twenty-seventh. For me, the irony was chronological: anyone reading this book knows that the holy days of professors of literature in North America are the twenty-seventh through the thirtieth of December every year, the days in which the annual meeting of the Modern Language Association takes place. There thousands of us had been, existing in a worldless, maybe almost lifeless, stretch of sacred time punctuated by conferences, meetings, interviews, rumors, and assignations. All of this had run its course in the exact time it took from Guibert's real death in France to my reading of the death in the *New York Times* that final afternoon. Two chronologies, two kinds of discourses: an official discourse of newspaper obituaries; a critical discourse that took place in a dystopian elsewhere that had no contact with the reality around it. In short, I realized that even when introduced into a critical discourse, AIDS does not exist except in an "out there" detached from the subject and separate from the reader. In the realm of the photograph, Douglas Crimp has brought this point home in his excellent article on the photographic representation of people with AIDS and on "giving AIDS a human face." Can a personal narrative give AIDS a human face? Can it meet its reader? And if so, where does that meeting take place?

This difference relative to the critical and aesthetic discourses of AIDS was driven home by the arrival a few weeks later of two of Guibert's last books: *L'Homme au chapeau rouge* and *Cytomégalovirus*. As is often the case with books published in France, there was a little red wrapper around the cover, a paper band serving to draw the shopper's attention to the book on the display counters (Derrida, *Signéponge* 148–51). Among the various items on such bands, there is often a picture of the author, plus his or her name, the title of the book, and the name of the publisher. On the novel *L'Homme au chapeau rouge*, we find one variation: in addition to the title of this new book are the titles of two previous books, *A l'ami qui ne m'a pas sauvé la vie* and *Le Protocole compassionnel*, plus the name "Gallimard." Along with the written words, there is a picture of Guibert, a thin face in which the organs and features seem almost too big for the shrunken, gaunt head. It is, perhaps, an earlier photo than the photographs on other covers; still, it has been chosen as an icon for the dying/dead author. Guibert is staring through the glass of a window that reflects the world of the viewer; Guibert, however, is separated from the reader, distant from the outside world. In his world, on the other hand, are some bookshelves on which various books and other objects can be seen. His name, though, does not appear on the front of the promotional strip; it is printed on the back in small type, as unremarkable as possible, more an index of what strip it is or to what book the assembly-line worker should attach it than a part of the advertising ploy.

In its own way, the band on the other book is also incomplete: it is nothing more than the author's name, that of the publisher, and a picture of Guibert's eyes, the eyes constantly threatened by blindness throughout the hundred short pages of *Cytomégalovirus*, a book that deals with the reflections of Guibert on a hospital stay for the opportunistic AIDS infection that gives the book its title. They are the eyes of someone who may go blind, but that is not the point. They are the eyes of a dead man. This book, published posthumously in January 1992, has the picture of a dead man on its cover, someone for whom it does not matter now whether he is about to go blind or not. As Barthes says in *La Chambre claire* of a figure in a historical photo: "He is dead and he is going to die" (149). Guibert, condemned by the ravages of various opportunistic infections, is the new version of that man.

This illustration is actually turned into a quotation of sorts with *Mon valet et moi*, published in September 1991, right before the author's death. Again, there is a band on the cover. This one is wide, coming more than halfway up the book. On the band is the author's name looming large and a smaller, more discreet "Seuil," the name of the publishing house, a word that is ironically the threshold between life and death that Guibert is about to cross. The rest of the band is a photo of the author, who seems to be sitting on the ground in front of what looks like a lichen-stained wall. He appears to be looking straight into the camera, as he stares directly into the eyes of the viewer who, in turn, is in the process of viewing what is now a corpse. Guibert's long legs are brought up in front of his body and his arms lean on his knees, with his hands hanging out in front of him. The picture is uncanny, *unheimlich*, for one remembers that the photo on the cover of *Mon valet et moi* is a quote of another photo, which, like a literary intertext, seems to repeat and point to, yet simultaneously change, a previously produced image. In this case, the interimage could not be missed, for it is also found in a last book: the reader will undoubtedly remember the photo I have already mentioned of a condemned prisoner in *La Chambre claire*, about whom Barthes says, "He is dead and he is going to die." Missing in Guibert's photo are the physical shackles that bind the wrists of the man who has attempted to commit an assassination, but the rest is the same. In this case, it is Guibert's own body, the AIDS-ravaged body of the subject of the photo, that binds his hands, that shows that he too is dead and is about to die. In that his photo replaces the photo within *La Chambre claire* and the missing photo of the moribund Barthes, tragically wounded, that cannot be shown. Death must, we think, have its dignity, except where AIDS patients are concerned.

Three incomplete strips indicate the separation, the incompleteness, and ultimately the death sentence of the author, whom we know is already dead. The eyes stare at the reader from beyond the grave, but the reader will not be affected by the stare, because on one strip, the reader is safely separated from Guibert by a piece of glass that quarantines the author as if he were another Hannibal Lecter ready to eat, or at least infect, the reader. And this is not an exaggeration: the reader must be kept safe from the infection. The reader can, of course, be prompted by a simulacrum of the disease, its translation into text: "In fact I wrote a letter [*Ami*] that was directly telefaxed into the heart of 100,000 people, it is extraordinary. I'm now writing them a new letter" (*PC* 121). But the reader must be separated from it, for if he or she were to come into contact with the disease of which the work is a record, she or he might in fact have to deal with the impossible situation of this writing. It is not that the reader risks a real infection, but realizes the dreadful fact that, through his writing, a dead man is calling to the public to read AIDS, a tetragrammaton for the end of the twentieth century, writing on the wall that so far has resisted complete interpretation.

Protected from the text or at least forewarned to gird himself or herself in a metaphoric body condom, the reader should be able to discern what is going on in a work about AIDS, in these works about AIDS, without fearing the damage that an AIDS-text might wreak. What is this damage? Certainly it is not infection by AIDS. It would not be in France, but only in a mythical country like the United States that people fear being infected by something they read or hear about. No, the fear is that the effect of AIDS will be the destruction of the work as a text. If the reader has too close a contact with the AIDS-infected writer, the reader may miss the signifiers. The risk of the AIDS-infected text is the loss of the textual space, the loss of the text itself in favor of a sympathy that blinds the reader to what he or she is reading. "AIDS" risks being the only readable signifier in such a way that it becomes not a transcendental signifier but a transcendental signified, a four-letter word that means what it says. Everything is AIDS.

If we are to understand the implications of this textuality and if we are to understand what AIDS might mean in a literary work, we need to maintain some separation from the virus, from the soulfulness of the writer looking at us through space, across the bars of a prison cell, through the viewing panel of a morgue. Like Auschwitz, which itself names the unnameable and which is a term that repeatedly comes up in Guibert's work, AIDS is an all-consuming signifier. That very word must be kept at a distance in order to prevent it from overwhelming the work and our interaction with it. To understand what textual AIDS is, to understand its mutations, we must let it occur in its contradictory varieties; we must try to understand the mutations, contradictions, and inconsistencies that the catch-all nature of such a signifier produces.

The basic problem concerns the interplay between language, textuality, and the literary, on the one hand, and the all-consuming nature of AIDS, on the other. If we can write about AIDS and its function in and as the subject, we should be prepared for three things, the first of which is the juggernautlike nature of AIDS as signifier. Moreover, in his or her fight against AIDS, a fight against something that is, as I write, still inexorable, the subject is constantly trying to remain true to himself or herself before AIDS, as well as trying to maintain the identity of the subject faced with the insistent mutation by which AIDS takes over body and mind. So the second effect is communicational: AIDS takes over the order of subject pronouns, changes the relation of pronoun to pronoun: AIDS forces us to rethink the reciprocity of the I-thou relation. The "I" is less and less complete as each day goes on; the subject decreases in potency, viability, and stamina. He or she becomes the locus of more and more opportunistic infections: AIDS-related dementia or cytomegalovirus (CMV), pneumocystic pneumonia (PCP), or Kaposi's sarcoma (KS) makes the subject's every thought, word, and breath less and less his or hers. The subject is not only reduced, like Balzac's wild ass's skin, but also changed. As AIDS becomes the deadly simulacrum of the subject, the original subject becomes more and more other to itself and to its pre-AIDS past.

So too the relation changes between any interlocutor and that subject. For Guibert, the position of the interlocutor includes both a friend or relation within his world and an addressee or *destinataire* at the other end of the communicational model. The presence of AIDS in an affective relation begins to structure the entirety of the relation;

the dynamics of the relation, the order of pronouns, and the very acts of communication are all reoriented by AIDS, the ever-present third party to any dyad. Both for the protagonist and his real interlocutor and for the author/narrator and his presumably sympathetic reader, new relations arise that involve the "I" of narration and the "I" of action in a different complex. The addressee is called from some complex combination of "I" and other, some nexus of self and disease. And the reader or interlocutor recognizes this alteration as well as the inability to distinguish alterity from identity. AIDS kills by mimesis, even unto the structuring of a protocol of discourse and its pronouns.

Finally, AIDS interrupts the natural flow of discourses by insisting over and over again on its own presence as the subject and object of all discourse. As is the case for the life in concentration camps described in Primo Levi's *The Periodic Table*, in Guibert's writing there is an effort to use multiple discourses to try to explain what no one single discourse can express. The discourse of the subject has no word for AIDS, no language to define its introduction into the subject; the language of medicine has no discourse to engage the subject that preexists the infection. Or more exactly, the subject of the medical discourse is a three-stage object of discourse defined by the absence, presence, and ultimate activity of the virus. In no case is the subject there as such; there are, rather, three separate subjects unintegrated with one another.

To read Guibert now means to read with him, even if our knowledge is always more complete than his own. For the first time in a long time we have the resurgence of a narrator who knows less than the reader, less than the literary structures imply, less than the real world. The technique, longstanding in its literary history, focus of many experiments in early twentieth-century fiction, comes back, but with a vengeance. If Guibert the man knows that he is dying, at the beginning of *A l'ami* at least, he is also the narrator who does not know to what extent he is dead. The disease is a reminder of that mortality and the eyes that we finally see on the cover of *Cytomégalovirus* are wide open but about to be shut forever. It is information that we now have, that we know from the very first words of *A l'ami*, even if the eyes of the narrator are temporarily closed to the fact of his own death:

I had AIDS for three months. More exactly, for three months I thought that I was condemned by that deadly disease called AIDS. Now I was not imagining things, I was really infected, the test that had turned out positive showed this, as well as analyses that had showed that my blood had begun to fail. But, at the end of three months, an extraordinary chance made me believe, and made me almost certain, that I could escape from this disease that everyone still thought to be incurable. Just as I had told no one except a handful of friends that I was condemned, I admitted to no one except these few friends that I was going to get out of it, that I would be, through this extraordinary chance, one of the first survivors in the world of this inexorable disease. (*Ami* 9)

A l'ami is the dawning realization that a timer is running down. Writing with AIDS, Guibert is already in the position of having the end of the story present from the beginning. Hope against hope, the denial of each and every victim, and the possibility of a miraculous survival are of course the natural, standard reactions expected when there is a death sentence. It is a hope that lingers even in *Le Protocole compassionnel*: "Shall I arise from my coffin as I arise from my bed, holding on to the edges or falling, now that, thanks to the DDI of the dead dancer, I believe in the myth of rebirth?" (*PC* 123). The possibility of a reprieve takes the form of the denial of the very language used to describe this syndrome.

AIDS is the disease whose descriptions and protocols have not taken into account the discourse of the ego that stands up against the inexorable progress of a disease by producing a language that will outlast the subject, and thus be relatively immortal. And yet there is a delay, the time of writing, that is the distinction between the literariness of the work that speaks of death in every word and the real time that has, for the moment, delayed the outcome. Tense and time differ in the literary work dealing with AIDS; they diverge, as the time and tense it takes to narrate the disease both stay the deathknell and recall it. If the tocsin rings with every stroke of the pen, between those strokes a continuing textuality can be both read and celebrated.

From the first, there is an opposition between the mortality and finitude implied in the scientific language and the self-affirming nature of the discourse of the ego that does not fit into the patterns of the objective discourse of death. This individual's body will be the

one that fights AIDS. His or her discourse will be the one that finds
the loophole in the language of science. His or her *locus standi* will be
the one that wins back the territory for the ego against the parasitic
chatter of the disease that takes every opportunity to speak and
drown out all others by extending a welcome mat to every opportunistic infection. With the weapon of authorial language against the
disease, Guibert will do what no medicine can do, what no doctor
can solve, and what no alternative can engage. He will write against
the disease by reforming it for his own textuality and reshaping it for
his life. He alone will render it harmless by translating AIDS into a
textuality of life: "I undertake a new book to have a companion, an
interlocutor, someone with whom to eat and sleep, next to whom to
dream and have nightmares, the only friend now tenable" (*Ami* 12).

AIDS reshapes the possibilities of discourse and intercourse, and
reframes the very words on the page as a discourse of death addressed to no one in particular and to everyone in general. For Guibert, AIDS defines the parameters of a discourse that is now his by
default, for in it he is subject to a double alienation in word and deed.
In deed, for he cannot do what he has done, cannot be the same as he
was, and cannot exchange in the same ways he had. A person with
AIDS is blocked from the exchange system as a subject: no part of
himself or herself can be safely given. The ego is safely quarantined
behind the glass of a window, behind the latex of a condom, or behind a wall of discourse that prevents his or her words from being
read in any other way than as those of a person with AIDS. AIDS
threatens to become his or her essence, and what was there before
AIDS, the congealed experiences and memories of existence, has to
wage an endless fight against the insurgent infection merely to maintain some semblance of identity. And even as the life of the PLA is
often extended by medical intervention, especially if one is a white
occidental male, the PLA's words are blocked by the discourse of
medical science, which each day takes over more and more of the
space allotted to the subject for his or her own words. Fifteen years
ago, could anyone have imagined the presence of acronyms like PCP,
CMV, or KS in a literary work?

As a writer, Guibert is intent on combating this double block. It is
not that he is rampantly violating the social contract imposed on a
PLA, which amounts to not letting his or her bodily fluids contami-

nate another. Nor do I mean that with his writing he is refusing to let AIDS be the objective correlative to which every word is related: the objective meaning of every sentence and the redefinition of every writerly act. Even if almost all is taken away and even if there is but a scrap of identity that survives the onslaught of this disease, Guibert will not let the other determine his act of writing. If he chooses to write about AIDS, it is as a writer who explores the extreme nature of the condition—and the reader familiar with Guibert knows how much he revels in writing about extremes long before *A l'ami*—and not as a literary victim whose language has been reduced to a bare, shadowy fragment of itself. The refusal is double. One refusal is the act of rebellion itself that, at every turn, tries to wrest the author's life, and thus his writing, back from the forced submissions it undergoes. To say "no" to some medical discourse is perhaps to shorten one's existence, but it is also to reclaim some of that existence from the new I-thou couple that seems to be the condition and its treatments, or their metonymy in the form of the doctors for whom the individual is a "patient." The condition "says" something by producing a new symptom or allowing in a new opportunistic infection. The "thou" of medicine responds with a new treatment to silence the latest manifestation of the disease:

> In two years my relations with Dr. Chandi have become so intense and so intimate, despite the minimal level of informality we have, I believe he so identifies with me and with the suffering I can handle that he no longer asks me to do certain things that he knows are painful to me, or that I no longer allow him to do even if he asks. I refuse to allow to appear in the dark square of the scale the dotted red numbers that always indicate a lower weight. I refuse endoscopies: fibroscopies, sigmoidoscopies, alveolar washes, tubes down my throat, up my ass, in my lungs; I gave at the office [*j'ai déjà donné*]. (*PC* 28)

The second refusal is the act of generalization of the contents to the act of writing itself. If the first refusal says "no" to a dehumanization process or at least to a mutation of the relations of the human subject and a fortiori the writing subject, the second refusal is of the disease as something wholly different, at least as far as the act of writing is concerned. No matter how extreme the situation, and no matter what changes are forced by AIDS in the writing subject, it is still something to be written about. As such, even in its complete revolution in human relations, it is something that lets writing be writing. Once again, the goal established for writing is to make present something that is absent. And what cannot be accomplished on the level of one's existence is accomplished through writing itself:

> I attacked his nipples anew, and rapidly, mechanically, he kneeled before me, his hands imaginarily tied behind his back, to rub his lips against my fly, begging me in his tremblings and groans, to give him my body again, to free him from the pain I was imposing on him. To write that today, so far from him, gives me an erection in an organ that has been inactive and inert for weeks. (*Ami* 156)

Yet does such making present risk infecting the reader with some mimetic version of AIDS? Certainly the dangers of writing have never seemed more immediate; infection by writing might make the reader textually seropositive. Who else can read such a work? Certainly not someone who thinks that AIDS happens only to "them."

There is an act of cognizance of the disease, of the announcement of the disease, and of the stakes of the disease that reforms the communicational model, even from the very beginning. The disease does divide the world into HIV+ and HIV− individuals. That immediate division is tempered by a swift understanding that AIDS mimes even the communicational model of the world by reproducing the same model, though with a twist: "I feel that I now have interesting relations only with those who know" (*Ami* 16). This is echoed later, when the visible nature of the disease is unmistakable: "We [Guibert and a waiter] were already in different worlds: separated by an invisible mirror that is the passage from life to death and which knows death from life" (*HCR* 40–41). Arguably, then, the messages within a system could be the same as they always were, but one needs to be a clued-in receiver in order to perceive knowledgeably and thus respond with messages of interest. It is not that the knowledge changes the message, reforms the model, or even has an influence on the system. It is rather that there is a recognition for those who know that the system is already infected from the beginning. For them, there is always another message, always the same message of death lurking within the system; the communicational model is marked by a fatalism that seems to resurge out of the romantic narratives of sickness with which the nineteenth century filled its libraries and bookstores. In every other respect, the system is the same. There can be messages in this system whose contents are specific to the codes of the system, but basically they are not different from those in the real world: "The last analyses, dated November 18, gave me a T-cell count of 368, a healthy man has between 500 and 2000" (*Ami* 13).

The initial sense, then, of the communicational system in which AIDS participates is that it is a virtual model, even a simulacrum of the non-AIDS system, but parasited from within by the very reason for its existence. Thus the initial model of the system is a metalepsis of AIDS itself. The virus mimes the host body and mimes the structures offered by that body, but its every move is geared toward self-replication and self-perpetuation. If AIDS structures the system, there are no messages other than the tautological one: this is a system that contains AIDS. In the short run, there is no better model than that of the virtual universe that looks like the system, but which is in fact a deadly game of Pacman that we know will sooner or later come to an end:

Before AIDS appeared, an inventor of electronic games had drawn the progression of AIDS in blood. On the video-game screen for teenagers, blood was a labyrinth in which Pacman ran around, a yellow chomper moved by a control, who ate everything in his path, emptying out the various hallways of their plankton, simultaneously threatened by the proliferating appearance of even more gluttonous red chompers. (*Ami* 13)

Once we remember, however, that in order not to "go gentle into that good night," an author must remain an author, that *this* author must remain an author insofar as he is able to do so, the game changes. And when he can no longer use his own power of words, he still can recognize that the act of usurpation was fought at every step of the way: "A funny dictionary could be written about AIDS terminology: the candidate is a fungus that announces its candidacy to take power in your throat, your esophagus, your stomach, and eats them" (*CMV* 21).

To be meaningful, the communicational system that engages AIDS in this struggle must not simply be a safe simulacrum of the old system, but rather must take the parasite and normalize it. Now it may seem an aberration to consider a disease, especially this disease, something normal. Yet in order to make the disease strange, in order to give it a literary tenor, and especially, in order to explore the philosophical, literary, and even metaphysical implications of AIDS, the author must turn it into a part of the system. AIDS must be a given, much like the world given to realism, instead of a parasite that destroys normalcy. Guibert is quite correct medically, but even more correct literarily, when he says that:

AIDS is not really a disease, it simplifies things to say that it is, it is a state of weakness and abandon that opens the cage of the animal within, to which I am obliged to give complete powers for it to eat me alive, to which I allow to do to my living body what it was getting ready to do on my corpse to make it disintegrate. The spores of pneumocystic pneumonia that are boa constrictors for the lungs and breath and those of toxoplasmosis that ruin one's mind are present within every man; quite simply the equilibrium of his immune system prevents them from being accepted, and AIDS gives them a green light, as it opens the floodgates of destruction. (*Ami* 17)

Once Guibert has taken control of the initial discourse of the disease he can make his last excursions literary ventures. The last thing an author wants to do is to simplify, to lose the subtlety, or to die for lack of words. If excess verbiage is to be eschewed, it is also true that in order for the text to make the most of his AIDS, Guibert must explore what it means, what the poetry and philosophy of AIDS might be. And if they do not yet exist, he will invent them. Thus he must refuse the death sentence in every word that the parasitic model offers, because the message is always the same. Just as he gives over his body as the sacrificial subject to the AIDS virus and as he might eventually have to abandon his very mind because of toxoplasmosis or AIDS-related dementia, he must put into question the very categories of heterogeneity and homogeneity: Is this virus me, does it define me, is it other, is it alien, can I describe it? The uncomfortable answer is already known: it is both me and not me; it is different and the same. Or, in other words, I am both it and not it, just as it is I and not-I all at once.

Certainly the borderline nature of AIDS, in its existence between same and other, presents a constant problem for its literary inscription. What discourse can take it on? What discourse is adequate to the inscription of AIDS that, while pinpointing it, does not do the same violence to the body as the virus itself? For the literary version of the undecidability between same and other of this virus means that the sign of the virus is not distinct from the referent: the otherness does not occur, precisely because there is an inability to distinguish between what preexists the sign as thing (self or other) and what is apposite to it. No wonder then that one of the first attempts to understand the literary implications of AIDS involves making a map, one that changes over time, as it represents the time for the sentence to be carried out:

I have never suffered as little as when I learned that I had AIDS; I am very attentive to the manifestations of the virus's progress; I seem to know the cartography of its colonizations, its assaults, and its retreats, I think I know where it waits and where it attacks, I feel the zones as yet untouched, but this struggle within me, quite real organically, as the scientific analyses show, is for now nothing, wait a while, good fellow, given the certainly fictive ailments that assail me. (*Ami* 45)

By making his body the corpus/corpse as well as the object of the literary, medical, or philosophical gaze, Guibert hopes to inscribe it correctly. Reminiscent of the anatomization of the woman in nineteenth-century fiction, scion of emblem poetry, this means of mapping out the problem changes what we know to be the question of the reflexivity of the subject into the objective task of reading signs as a prelude to writing. If he is the subject undergoing the manifestations of the virus, he is also the object being examined almost dispassionately by the cartographer or map reader who remains unchanged by the observation. So one of the first strategies deployed, and one that will continue to be a safety valve throughout, is the description and recognition of the state of being alienated from one's body. This is not me, Guibert seems to be saying, but the fictional possibilities afforded in a battle sketched out in these pages, of which you, the reader, and I, the cartographer, have the game plan. Or, in other words, we have all seen the same movies: "the surgeon and his team now looked like cannibal Martians bent over their feast; the image had itself become Hitchcockian" (*HCR* 42). Out of necessity, the authorial mind is distanced from the patient's body, yet both the intertwining of body and mind, and more generally that of healthy and ill parts of the individual, will have to be transcribed or at least subject to transcription.

The semidetached map reader will soon fade into a complex of the partial subject who recognizes that his words come and go, as they play on the undecidability of the system. For Guibert, AIDS becomes the test of writing, and writing becomes the test of a disease that only for some is summarized into the specious bivalency of HIV+ and HIV−. If everyone is always already potentially HIV+, then the name of the game has changed and, no longer content merely to record otherness or to make the familiar strange, literature itself must begin to grapple with the familiarity of the strange. With that paradox, the fundamental irony of the disease, AIDS will have entered literature and found a voice beyond the thunders of officialdom.

III. The Legend on the Map

Guibert's image of "the cartography of its colonizations" (45), used as he speaks about the gradual progress of the disease in his body, brings to the fore a "whole host" of images. Implied here is a complete discourse and ideology of dominance and domination, and generally a textuality of the exclusion of the native, the indigenous, and the natural. To map a territory is to bring it into one's fold and to create a legend about one's knowledge of the place, the legend at the bottom of a map that tells us what the symbols mean. Who is to say that this is the appropriate legend, that a map of a colonized territory in any way corresponds to the vision of the territory held by those who live there, people who do not consider it a territory at all? The legend is just that, a code for the translations of symbols, for the reassertion of dominance, but it is the alphabet of an ideology, the code of an untruth, if not a bald-faced lie. What legends does AIDS tell? Of this I am not yet sure. Endlessly exploring the possibilities, Guibert brings into focus several versions of the legend before returning to his original, imperfect literary discourse. In the pages ahead I would like to follow at least one of the legends, the legend of medical discourse that believes it names what it talks about.

At the same time, Guibert remains an author, a literary figure in his own writings, and a user of language attempting to integrate into that writing the medical discourse foisted upon him out of necessity and accepted out of desperation. And even with or in those last breaths, perhaps as a writer, he can give a new turn to literary lan-

guage: "I'm waiting for someone to give me an IV (I love using professional language; with the cytomegalovirus, I won't have an 'LP,' a
spinal tap [lumbar puncture]); I'll take it lying down, it's eight P.M.
and I'm tired" (*CMV* 15). The exchange may be simple, but the original exchange of bodily fluids was simple as well. In a translation of
the postmodern Eucharist, he will exchange his own blood for ink,
and even use his own blood as ink in the writing of this sacrifice of
one too young to die. There is a quiet heroism in these pages, postmodern in tone, Greek in inspiration:

> Perhaps a vein that has burst is quite beautiful: a spurt that shoots every-
> where, an explosion of red blood [*un sang d'artifice bien rouge*], a bouquet of
> blood. As soon as I think about it, my blood starts to percolate in the little
> plastic tubes. No, it is not a vein bursting, just a reflux of blood. (*CMV* 38)

Yet there is only so much blood to be given, and there is less and less
ink to be had, a paucity already figured in *Le Protocole compassionnel*.
It is as if Guibert knows that the well will eventually run dry: "I
would like to take a photo of ink bottles, I collected some these two
years in Rome, and all of them drawn, I really like these ink bottles"
(*PC* 119). At some point, writing will no longer be able to attenuate
the disease through the imposition of a literary model; at some point
the disease will catch up to the text, and after that there will be darkness and silence.

   Integrating the medical discourse means giving oneself over to it,
allowing oneself to be vampirized, as it were, even at the most intimate level. For one suddenly becomes a patient, one is no longer
oneself, and even those who "mean well" participate in the dissolu-
tion of the subject: "my two great-aunts who become pitiless vam-
pires who drink in my strength to the last drop of blood as soon as
they find a wound in which to be engulfed" (*Ami* 189). It is a short
step from that well-meaning, yet ill-fated bloodletting to another. To
allow oneself to become wholly a patient and not be oneself is to allow the angel of death to write the literary work. Soon there will be
neither blood nor ink, only water:

> When a nurse gives me the IV, I can't help thinking that maybe it's just wa-
> ter, "since he's going to croak anyway," and thinking about the three lesbian
> nurses in Tübingen who liquidated old men by shoving a small spoon under
> their tongues and drowning their lungs. (*CMV* 17)

Obviously, the authorial solution is a resistance to this discourse, the only resistance he has left: Guibert realizes that even in naming a disease, a symptom, and a medical fact, the discourses of medicine do not name him. If he no longer knows exactly what he is, he is still sure of *who* he is as a sentient being and as an author. From the very first, Guibert recognizes that medicine itself, whether in linguistic or physical form, is invasive:

[I]t was useless to try to use a tongue depressor on me, for my tongue had refused all contact since I was young. I preferred to open my mouth very wide as the luminous bundle approached, using pressure on the throat muscles to contract, to push my uvula toward the deepest part of my palate. (*Ami* 19)

No one needs a map here to realize that the homosexual author is painting a very clear picture: there was never any need to invade my body or to rape me with the tools of the other; I willingly opened my throat to be penetrated to the deepest point possible. If the gag reflex is natural, the form it takes, says Guibert, is different in me: whereas a "straight" man might gag during an act of fellatio, that is no problem for Guibert; a straight man accepts the tongue depressor because, for him, it is not an act of fellatio, and that is precisely why Guibert does gag. It is a rape by another discourse; it is another world that invades his own.

In the pre-AIDS phase of his life, there is thus resistance to the invasive procedures by which medicine defines itself. So it is not at all surprising to find that the initial depictions of medical discourses present a noninvasive form of medicine, the only one he can initially stand. What we have come to think of as standard medical practice for AIDS would, after the initial diagnosis, involve an invasive procedure of one sort or another. Each of these procedures is surgical or pharmacological, specific for each set of symptoms or each disease permitted entry by AIDS into the body. Yet at least in the beginning of his writing about AIDS, Guibert is deferring the eventual invasion: he will not be subject to the abbreviations of hard, cold medicine, but will choose a path that is as discursively rich as the one afforded to the pre-AIDS author. So one doctor, with the amusing name of Dr. Lérisson, that is, the hedgehog, says to him: "You are one of the most spasmophilic beings I have ever met" (*Ami* 44). Another, named Dr. Aron, a name that echoes one of the most famous

French AIDS cases, that of Jean-Paul Aron, who made AIDS "his" in "Mon SIDA," says, "I have found the disease . . . its most understandable name is dysmorphophobia, that is to say, you find every form of deformity odious" (*Ami* 46).

The first diagnosis comes from a homeopathic doctor, the second, from a neighborhood general practitioner whose office appears as if nothing has changed in a century. True to the image of times past, the general practitioner's solution is to give Guibert a prescription for antidepressive drugs. In neither case does the doctor invade the body; in neither case does the doctor realize what AIDS means; in neither case can the doctor do much of anything. Decidedly, the modern disease needs modern medicine. When the homeopathic, holistic, or sympathetic approach is eventually eschewed, it is at the price of colonization, rape, internment, and the recognition of the constant presence of death. Once the invasion by medicine starts, it is clear that the clock is ticking; as soon as Guibert gets to the hospital, which has previously been evacuated, he is reminded of a concentration camp. The hospital is "like a phantom hospital at the end of the world. I was remembering my visit to Dachau. The last inhabited island was that of AIDS, with its white silhouettes behind the frosted glass" (*Ami* 50). To enter this world means to give up control over one's life and to allow one's body constantly to be invaded in an act of reinscription of the disease. Each set of tests, such as blood-taking for analysis, each set of pharmacological cures, whether by pills or intravenous mechanism, and each eventual surgical operation echoes the entry of the retrovirus into the body. The Dachau referred to in *A l'ami* turns into a reference to the death camp of Auschwitz in *Le Protocole compassionnel*, as the frighteningly *unheimlich* nature of the metaphor reminds us of the seeming inexorability of the death sentence. A mere reference is enough; since the metaphor is transparent, it can be introduced as speech in inverted commas: it becomes part of a gallows humor that no longer seeks to explain, but to defy the situation at hand, as Guibert's friend Jules now calls him "Baby Auschwitz" (*PC* 110).

Just as Auschwitz redefines time and space for the prisoners within the camp, AIDS also infects those parameters of existence; it changes the perception of time and space. From Guibert, we learn that the closure of space and the distention of time, along with a certain hallucinatory, imagined reversibility to the latter, are what redefine those parameters for AIDS: "The hospital room is an insidious cocoon that slowly but surely makes the real space outside, even the hallway, frightening" (*CMV* 47). Yet it is not merely in the last moments that there is a recognition of the changes in space; it changes with the very onset of AIDS. The body becomes a new world, distinct from the body that one always had; it is a world filled with unknowns, new discoveries, and parts one never knew one had. All of these are discovered at the price of their integral nature: AIDS uncovers the fault lying dormant, the PCP already present, and the diathesis for KS; AIDS re-marks them as it allows them to be activated. So, too, the body is, as a whole, always about to go through another mutation and another incarnation as a leaky monad, where another hole will appear if one hole is plugged through a stopgap measure.

For this writer, then, there is a loss of control over how and where literature will be produced. If he is writing of AIDS, of "his" AIDS, there is the recognition that this AIDS is precisely not "his," that he is, at least in part, "its." It is no longer "his AIDS," but he is "its Guibert." The function of the writer is to try to recapture what once was his, his body, his tongue or writing hand trapped into a discourse that is not his own, and especially his mind as it is constantly drawn to thinking about the loss of ego and the loss of control over his body: "This unleashed body brutally kneaded by the masseur to give it life again, and which he left panting, warm, tingling, as if exulted by his work, I saw it again every morning in the Auschwitzian panorama offered by the full-size mirror in the bathroom" (*PC* 14–15). The struggle to recapture this identity is not part of some deluded nostalgia that seeks to recapture the territories lost to colonization. Rather, as Guibert sees it, the writer's task is to internalize the discourse of AIDS in order to make it literary, to defuse it and diffuse it, and, insofar as possible, to neutralize it. One of the possibilities is to make himself look as if he in fact does have AIDS. His friend Jules cuts off the author's blond curls: "to sculpt all of a sudden a long, angular face, somewhat emaciated, with a high forehead, a bitter look on the lips, a head unknown to me and to others" (*Ami* 89). To write, he welcomes the parasitic invasion of his body, of his whole existence. It is a welcome to a parasitic discourse in a way that mimics

the open-mouthed gape of fellatio or, oddly enough, the anal intercourse that was the probable means of entry of the virus into the
body. It is a welcome that distinguishes the discourse of AIDS from
the virus itself: with AIDS in the body, there is no neutralization possible, no countermeasure except a delay of one sort or another that
slows down, but never arrests, the inexorable beating of time. To the
extent that the discourse of AIDS can be integrated into the literary
discourse, however, it will not be harming him as a writer: he can,
with the discourses of AIDS, as invasive as they are, make text.

   I have just alluded to the fact that the reorganization of space is
accompanied by a reordering of time in the writing of this AIDS.
Obviously, there is the recognition, second to none, that there is an
unstoppable clock:

If life was only the foreshadowing of death, endlessly torturing us with the
uncertainty of our expiration date, AIDS, by fixing a certified limit to life, six
years of being HIV+ plus two years in the best of cases with AZT or several
months without it, made us men fully conscious of our lives, and freed us
from our ignorance. (*Ami* 182)

What we understand as the irreversibility of time takes a completely
different form. Time is counted in a double movement, forward toward death and backward toward the specific moment of infection,
the origin of the infection for the individual, which at least in this
case (Guibert's literature), remains unknown. Time beats backwards
in a revisionist way; there is a constant review of the past and an endless repetition of events and nonevents. The review tries to negotiate the critical nature of the present moment by orchestrating what
happened, what did not happen, what *might* have happened, in the
sense of not having happened, but still being a hypothetical possibility, and what *may* have happened, a hypothetical reconstruction of
the past:

In this chronology that encircles and marks the auguries of the disease over
eight years, even though it is now known that the incubation period is
between four-and-a-half and eight years, according to Stéphane, physiological accidents are no less decisive than sexual encounters, nor the premoni-
tions than the wishes to try to erase them. It is that chronology that is becoming my plan, except when I discover that progression is born of disorder.
(*Ami* 59)

Henceforth the progress of time, figured normally as the gradual building of a life, means rather the progress of an infection whose manifestations and consequences will eventually destroy that life.

The chronological effect of the disease accelerates time for the body, while keeping the perception of duration the same in a general sense and slowing it down during any medical intervention. Thus the body rapidly ages, and the recognition of this aging increases the split between the mind and the body that is more and more alienated from the ego. The beginning of the second volume of these works paints the picture of a decrepit old man in whose body the aging process (which amounts to saying "the movement toward death") has galloped:

> [A]n old man's body had taken possession of my own 35-year-old man's body, it was probably that in the diminution of my forces, I had gone way beyond my father who had just turned 70, I'm 95, like my great-aunt Suzanne who is powerless; I no longer take baths because I can no longer get out of the bathtub and I no longer crouch under the shower as I liked to do to warm me up in the morning, for the power of my legs, even slightly crossed, and of my arms on the edges of the tub is no longer enough to get me out. (*PC* 10)

The mind moves away from the body, yet recognizes in this other inhabiting the same frame that there is a familiar sameness, a future actualized in the present, yet far different from the future that might otherwise have been. The mind separates from the body: recognizing the other, it sees the body as being subject to a time line that is not that of the mind, the internal measure of duration, or that of the literary work. The mind must recognize the domination of the time line of the body, yet the only means Guibert has of making himself aware of the difference is in the recognition of the unified self as an image of another. The only means of notating it is in the perspective on time afforded by literature. In the first case, the eventual reunification comes at the expense of the liberty of the ego, for realizing that it is his body's time that is right means realizing the full extent of condemnation, even if, from time to time, there is a forlorn hope:

> This confrontation every morning with my nudity in the mirror was a fundamental experience, renewed each day, I cannot say that the perspective it offered helped me get out of bed. Nor can I say that I had pity for this guy,

it depended on the day; sometimes I have the impression that he'll make it out alive since people returned from Auschwitz; other times, it is clear that he is condemned, ineluctably heading toward his grave. (*PC* 15)

What do we make of the time of literature which normally follows a rhythm that responds to its own internal needs that abridge or distend according to the exigencies of textuality? And, we might add, if there is a domination of the literary work by the time of the body, normally the furthest thing from literary time imaginable, can literary functions be saved when bodily functions fail? This is not at all a cavalier attitude, for we are reading literary works: *A l'ami* and *Le Protocole compassionnel* are both classified as novels, perhaps to protect the reader from the truth, perhaps to give the reader a textual condom that protects him or her from becoming textually seropositive. Given that classification, we expect some reference to or even some distinction from the amorphous generic parameters of the novelistic. Those include the passage of time determined by narrative, internal motivation, or description. Here, however, time is determined by a physiological change that is in no way the necessary, substantive meat of literature: rather, the body is sacrificed, and from that sacrifice comes the literary nature of the work. Guibert accepts the time clock of his body, the ticking time bomb set to explode in the not-too-distant future, as a replacement for the motivations of the literary. His body has turned around, and turned literature around, in a reflection that shows the endless spinning of words as the only other measure outside of the medical parameters of reality: "In 1990 I'm 95 years old, though I was born in 1955. There has been a rotation, an accelerated gyration, that spun me around like a ride at the fair, and crushed my limbs in a mixer" (*PC* 111). As long as there are words to be spoken or written, there is life present. Since his body has been taken from him, he makes a steadfast effort to assimilate the discourses of the other and continue, not to hope against hope, but to fulfill a literary function, lead where it may.

Literary time per se no longer exists, for to posit a fictional time line would mean that there might be some ending to these books other than the end the reader already knows. There are no peripetiae too improbable and no literary tricks whatsoever that can change the outcome; there is no *deus ex machina*, no "Reader, I married him," no "boy meets boy, boy loses boy, boy gets boy" to give us an ending in which he lives happily ever after. Guibert knows that his reader knows that there is no survival of this Auschwitz, and that the process of "selection" of which Primo Levi writes so passionately in *Survival at Auschwitz* and *If This Be a Man* does not separate those who survive from those who do not, but merely moves some further back in a line that is one-directional and inflexible. Instead of the literary time that would imply a fiction, a rhythm is created that balances the various times of the acceleration of the body, the distention of medical time, and the slowing down of mental time. Literature will happen as a series of ictuses, syncopations, accelerations, saccades, and slowdowns, rhythms that parallel the changing rhythms of his life, sounds, articulations, and intersections that are the mirror for the medical event of which he has become the subject:

And I write my book in the void, I build it, balance it, think about its general rhythm and about the cracks in its joints, its breaks and continuities, the interweaving of its plots, its liveliness, I write my book without pen or paper under the mosquito netting, heading toward oblivion. (*PC* 153)

IV. Parallel Discourses

The shrinking of time, the gradual diminution of powers, and the ever-widening swath cut by the disease all inform the very possibilities of the literary text for Guibert. At first, AIDS is a challenge to writing itself, as the author's initial reaction is to shrink, hide, run away, or even commit suicide if it seems necessary: "I was to have lunch with my editor and discuss the advance provided by my new contract, which would allow me to go round the world in an iron lung or blow my brains out with a gold bullet" (*Ami* 55–56). Literature is what has gone before and what has been heretofore viable enough to provide the author with a livelihood. His writing is the means by which he could eventually assure a sweet death. In that, by its very existence, literature ironically serves to reinforce its own iterative function that repeats what has gone before, even if that "going before" is off in the future: since AIDS assures death, Guibert's literature will reinscribe that eventual death as a dramatic, suicidal, or pathetic figure of his own textuality. No one can take that literary death away from him; no one can reinscribe his death in an other-than-literary fashion if he chooses to be the new Werther.

Yet to solve the problem that way is not to write the literature of AIDS, this series of books of which *A l'ami* will be the first and of which, from the authorial point of view, there will never be a discrete set; Guibert will never have a clear agenda or plan for the series. AIDS will determine every word, yet if he is to maintain both literary presence and honesty, he must let his own literary considerations as an author determine what he writes. Not surprising, then, is a retreat from AIDS as the counter to the extreme of the Wertherian reinscription of the death of the author. He proposes a new project:

with the announcement of my death I had been seized with the desire to write all possible books, all those that I had not yet written, even if I risked writing them badly, a funny, nasty book, then a philosophical book, and to devour these books almost simultaneously in the shrunken margin of time and to devour time with them, voraciously, and to write not only the books of my anticipated maturity, but also, like arrows, the very slowly ripened books of my old age. (*Ami* 70)

In a sense, this infinity of possibilities is what will and will not be accomplished, or what will have been and will not have been accomplished once the end of the set is marked by the death of the author. The infinity of possibilities is enacted at each turn. AIDS limns the picture so extensively that it becomes the only possible subject, even when the book is philosophical, slowly ripened, nasty, or whatever. AIDS is the subject of the text, but it remains to discover in what language the subject can be written.

No language already given can account for this new extreme in the human condition. As I have mentioned, in the nineteenth century, tuberculosis developed a whole literature and there was an intermetaphoric relation between the disease and literature as a whole. As much as there were texts in all realms dealing with the effects of tuberculosis, phthisis, or consumption on an individual, ranging from *La Dame aux camélias* to *The Magic Mountain*, tuberculosis itself became a metaphor for other things: for sicknesses of the soul, and for the heart's desperations. Earlier and later, other diseases fulfilled similar functions, though perhaps never with so much continuity or intensity, whether it is the plague inscribed in various Renaissance texts, Poe's "The Masque of the Red Death," or Camus's *The Plague*, the heart disease in Ford Madox Ford's *The Good Soldier*, or the cancer that figures on a regular basis in twentieth-century fiction.

No extreme of the human condition ever comes with its own discourse already prepared and already able to explain the extreme. Such a supposition would necessarily show that the extreme is not that at all, that it is already inscribed within the possibilities of pre-existing language, and that literature serves merely to reinscribe something already known and not to explain something new. Like the Holocaust, AIDS must necessarily not yet be in literature. When we first come upon AIDS in literature, in a play like Larry Kramer's *The Normal Heart*, it is inscribed within the realm of the known: this is a new disease, and a deadly disease at that, but its resonances are inscribable within the standards of literary discourse. It is only after a while that the impossibility of tacit inscription becomes evident. As Kramer goes beyond his own writing to be one of the initial promulgators of ACT-UP, Guibert writes texts that are the literary equivalent of ACT-UP: no previous situation can explain the need, the behavior, and the struggle. After Guibert, the AIDS text cannot ever be the same: Guibert has provided the struggle with words, the vocabulary, painfully discovered, and the discourses, experimentally interwoven, with which AIDS finds its literary voice, in which AIDS is "outed" in literature.

Not coincidentally, one of the future writing projects mentioned by Guibert is a book of philosophy; I would go so far as to say that *A l'ami* is in part that projected philosophical text. As there is a dawning realization that no one book can inscribe AIDS, the philosophical threads of this book interweave to help explain AIDS within the literary text, endlessly forming it, endlessly miming the possibilities. And that miming is anathema to philosophy from Plato on: AIDS reigns as a simulacrum of life, as the simulacrum of a disease (for it is not a disease itself), and as the simulacrum of death: the PLA is always in the process of dying, but once he or she is dead, the AIDS is gone as well.

A l'ami contains a thinly disguised portrait of the philosopher Michel Foucault in the character of the ironically named Muzil, a fact not lost in almost every review of the book, and discussed as well in a short article by Raymond Bellour. The character's name conjures up the author of *Young Törless*, with its homosexual overtones, the same author of *The Man Without Qualities*, an oddly apt apposition for a person with AIDS suddenly subject to endless inscription from the outside and subject to modification at every point by AIDS. Muzil is a philosopher dying of AIDS, a carefully scripted portrait of a well-known individual from the provinces, whose father was a doctor (114), who gave seminars in California (29–30), and who cultivated a taste for leather and bondage and discipline: "In a closet in the apartment which, according to a holographic will, was off-limits to the family, Stéphane had found a big bag filled with whips, leather hoods, leashes, bits, and handcuffs" (*Ami* 29).

Fine, the reader will say, here is a character who resembles Michel Foucault, but so what? By what right does this critic, who is admittedly reading this text in the light of poststructuralist discourse, introduce the *bête noire* of twentieth-century literary endeavor, the so-called "truth" behind the character? It is a much-decried process that gave us Agostinelli behind Proust's Albertine, for example, and that made money for editorial houses that published books with copious scholarly notes that explained to the reader that the character of Mr. So-and-so is based on a little-known individual whom the author encountered during a certain weekend while on a jaunt in the South of France. By what right does the critic say that "Muzil" is based on "Foucault" and to what end? What does it matter that Guibert actually knew Michel Foucault, who was a professor at the Collège de France, and who was the author of, among other things, the three volumes of *The History of Sexuality* and a shorter piece entitled "What Is an Author?"

One could develop a whole scenario for a critical take on the texts of Foucault in which the matters Foucault discusses function as interpretemes for Guibert's text. Specifically, Foucault's writing would provide the philosophical resonances permitting the literary structures of Guibert's writing to make sense on a philosophical level. That critical take would undoubtedly include the disappearance of the subject as a critical point in textuality until the resurgence of the function of the subject in the third volume of *The History of Sexuality*: the point of sickness is the undeniable moment at which the subject comes home to himself, or herself, despite all the possible epistemes in which that subject might have functioned, despite all the discursive constraints on subjectivity provided by any given episteme. Yet the same Foucault, as I have noted, wrote "What Is an Author?," in which he makes the telling remark, "Where a work had the duty of creating immortality, it now attains the right to kill, to become the murderer of its author" (*Language* 117). This is the philosopher who ends the same article with a complete damning of the fetishizing of the subject: "What matter who's speaking?" (138).

To introduce Foucault as the voice behind Muzil, over and above the fact that Guibert knew Foucault and was his neighbor and friend, is simultaneously to erase Foucault by Foucault's very words. At the same time, we must remember that Foucault's death from AIDS was one of the first AIDS-related deaths of a famous Frenchman. But as soon as Foucault had died from AIDS, that death was covered up and bruited about almost in the same breath. Foucault did or did not die of AIDS, said the voices of reason, the newspapers, and the various other media and university gossip lines. In *Libération*, left-leaning, hypocrisy-challenging newspaper, there was a famous debate about the shamefulness of the death. The same newspaper published a graveside photo of Foucault's interment in which everyone was identified except the very obvious Jacques Derrida, fellow poststructuralist, fellow questioner of the validity of the subject. As Guibert says in an earlier version of Foucault's death, entitled "Les secrets d'un homme":

> They stole his death from him, and he had wanted to be its master. They stole even the truth of his death from him, who had been the master of the truth. And it was especially necessary not to pronounce the name of the leprosy, they would disguise the name on the death certificate, they would give disinformation [*faux communiqués*] to the press. (*MLV* 108)

Brought into question, the validity of Foucault's presence behind Muzil then might seem a spurious appeal to an older vision of literature's relation to the reality behind it. Even if "Muzil" is "Foucault," what does it matter? It is not the simple mirror image of some real philosopher behind a fictional character that is important but rather the specularity of the position. The Foucault that counts is the Foucault who first became known to a large number of intellectuals through *Les Mots et les choses*, in which he creates a specular reading of Velásquez' painting *Las Meninas*: the reader of the painting—the reader of the book—occupies the impossible specular position of the king himself. It is the Foucault of Derrida's critique of Foucault in *L'écriture et la différence*, in which Derrida shows that Foucault's reading of madness necessarily predicates madness on the precedence and valorization of sanity (51–97).

Understanding Foucault behind Muzil means seeing the simultaneous presence and absence of the author, the simultaneous construction and deconstruction of the image-text, and the presence and absence of AIDS in Foucault who did or did not die of the disease. Understanding Foucault behind Muzil means that the whole discourse of AIDS is put into a specular perspective that is the measure of change effected by the disease "that is not one"; it means that the return of the subject occurs, as it must, at the moment at which the subject is least free and least able to exercise its purported independence or even measure the extent to which it is controlled by some pervasive episteme. Foucault behind Muzil means the disappearance of the author and the struggle to regain authority against AIDS, which speaks endlessly in a foreign, invasive discourse that is always identical to itself if understood teleologically. If, as it is said, "Silence = Death" (for not to speak about AIDS is to guarantee death), it is also true that the discourse of AIDS, when AIDS itself speaks, is the discourse of death.

The reality of Foucault behind Muzil shows that the realization of this singularity that is the combination of the philosopher with the human being is the very figure that Guibert needs for his own writing. To use an old saw: if Foucault had not existed, had not written, and had not died as he did, Guibert would have needed to invent him. No more important philosophical situation exists for Guibert than this one: the discourse of philosophy clearly expresses both the impossibility of this textuality—a writing about, with, and against AIDS—while maintaining the purity of the subject; this is combined with anguish at the realization that such purity is not possible. The position is mirrored in a mise-en-abîme in the story itself, a recognition that the impossible discourse of AIDS is there despite its impossibility:

[D]uring the semester that had preceded the death of Muzil, the three of us had often evoked this vacation, Stéphane believed it sincerely, as did I, and in his double discourse of lucidity and trap [*leurre*], Muzil made us believe that he too believed in this imminent vacation, until the day that, as we needed to prepare, he told Stéphane (who told me after Muzil's death) behind my back that he had never believed this trip possible. (*Ami* 116)

The truth is that one is dying, a truth that cannot be admitted, even if it is, as is the case for Guibert, told outright. For the admission of dying is always coupled with the trap of continuing. There has been a change from Foucault's position that does not admit the impending death, but the double discourse has not changed: for Guibert, the discourse of lucidity and the discourse of the trap remain the same. Writing will continue as long as possible, staving off, in the world of simulacra, what appears to be a juggernaut in the real world: "Night here: struggle against a steamroller pushing ahead, I dare not say blindly, without a driver. If you don't resist, if you don't run, you get crushed. Might as well do it, it's better to remain a human being than a bloody wafer" (*CMV* 24). And that, then, is both the trap and the salvation: that somehow the writing will perpetuate the life that is slowly ebbing away at the level of the real and is quickly becoming solidified into art at the level of the text.

The mise-en-abîme is repeated as the philosopher himself offers a gift of books that will perhaps show or teach how to die. There is no point in seeking some justification in the writings of the real philosopher behind Muzil, for Guibert's story tells us all we need to know. Guibert recounts how he has discovered a painting entitled *Après le duel*, done by a certain nineteenth-century Italian painter named Antonio Mancini when the artist was about twenty years old. The strong homoerotic element is brought to the surface: the subject of the picture is a young man dressed in mourning after a duel. Moreover, Guibert tells us that Mancini had used a young man as a model with whom he himself was smitten, and, if that were not enough, Mancini was eventually put into a psychiatric hospital by his family, apparently, we surmise, for his eccentric desires. In any case, Mancini was buried with a copy of "the *Manual* of Epictetus, that follows the *Thoughts* of Marcus Aurelius, in the yellow Garnier-Flammarion copy covered in opaque cellophane paper Muzil took from his library a few months before his death to give to me as one of his favorite books" (*Ami* 75).

Each story feeds into the impossible situation that joins the discourse of truth (AIDS), which alone is an endless self-fulfilling prophecy, and the discourse of representation: the possibility of continuing along in literature independent of the fact that looms over all. The stories join the fiction of Muzil to the truth of Foucault, but the truth of Foucault is that there was no truth about his disease, no truth in the caption for the photo of his burial that had Jacques Derrida's name patently missing, and no truth in the sequence of letters in *Libération* that appeared following the incident. The truth of Muzil/Foucault is that he teaches someone how to die and how to have been an artist (like Mancini) by giving him Epictetus and Marcus Aurelius, while all the while ignoring the Stoic truth of death. AIDS denies death its dignity, and in doing so it makes the literature of death an impossible discourse that can no longer find anything to praise: "Muzil, who was going to die a few months later, told me at that time that he would soon write [like Marcus Aurelius] an encomium [*éloge*] dedicated to me, to me, who undoubtedly had never been able to teach him anything" (*Ami* 76). Retransformed into an *énoncé* in a novel, this statement echoes in a different way: what he can teach "Muzil" is how to write about AIDS; what he can write is the last volume of *The History of Sexuality*.

The philosophical discourse in Guibert's novel is one means of entering the impossible world of AIDS and its literature and of staking out what a literature of AIDS might eventually be. There is no sustained philosophical treatise nor any preaching to the choir of readers of a philosophy that might explain what is to follow. Rather, the key moments of a certain philosophy and the cryptic presence of a certain philosopher are used to set up an episteme for AIDS in which the eventuality of certain discourses and certain *énoncés* becomes possible and from which, at least theoretically, certain others are rejected. The death of the philosopher makes this literature possible, as it is the articulation of a death that can no longer distinguish between truth and falsity, can no longer give a "history of sexuality," and can no longer serve as a critical tool in any guise. It does provide a point at which a kind of discourse can appear that is seemingly strange to the novel, the discourse of medicine. As "Muzil" stops being a writer, he is dispersed into a new set of doubles: the owner of a set of sexual devices found in a closet off-limits to his family both is and is not the mourned son of that family of physicians. For now,

Guibert will put that sexuality back into the closet and participate vicariously in this act of filiation; Guibert will become Foucault's double, he too, the son of medical discourse, and he will use this discourse to try to further his text.

Two matters need to be brought to the fore: the function of the detail in general and the presence of the medical detail in particular. The verisimilar detail in a realist text such as "Un Coeur simple," as Roland Barthes tells us in "L'Effet de réel," has as its purpose to say "We are the real" (*Bruissement* 174). As these details are "supposed to denote the real directly, they do nothing but signify it, though without saying so." In other words, the realist detail becomes the verisimilar detail used to help create the aura of verisimilitude that we, subject to the selfsame ideology promulgated by the text in question, take as the representation of the real. Similarly, writing of Balzacian realism, Naomi Schor says that it is "an *anxious detailism*, preoccupied with ensuring its own legitimacy" (*Detail* 141). What holds for Balzac and Flaubert in their similar use of and exploitation of the detail is put into question as realism gives way to modernism and postmodernism. In modernism, one might argue, the detail occupies the locus of an undecidability that vacillates between the signaling of a metaphoric link—in that it has replaced the metonymy of realism—and an accident or a superfluity. Since in modernism there is no absolute baseline objectively given that might be reproduced as an ideology of dominance, even in fostering an ideological position, the detail always puts the position into question instead of securing it.

If he was initially a postmodernist, Guibert is anything but that in these realist works, unless we consider that writing about AIDS makes him a postmodernist. Do we read medical details as realist signs of verisimilitude or as ambiguous signs of the modern or postmodern? Perhaps the medical detail is a special case: if it functions in Balzac, Flaubert, and, most obviously, Zola as a sign of the system of the real, it also functions as a sign of the discourses of medicine. As Foucault points out in *The Birth of the Clinic* and as Barthes reiterates in his study "Semiology and Medicine" in *L'Aventure sémiologique*, the signs, glances, and symptoms of medicine occupy a special semiotic plane. While intersecting with the textual planes and discourses of everyday life, medical semiotics brings a specific view and set of meanings to the fore in a way different from the semiotics of veri-similitude. For Foucault and Barthes, "to read a disease is to give it a name" (Barthes, *Aventure* 280). Thus in a sense medical semiology is the opposite of literary semiology, and is certainly the opposite of the literary semiology of the twentieth century, which in many ways consists of unnaming: of making strange, of spinning a story, and of weaving prose.

What then is the case of the medical detail introduced into the literary text? What history does it bring? To what semiology does it pay its allegiance? The presence of a medical detail in the text reflects the literary ideology into which it is inserted, but brings to that ideological position the look, the history, and the naming associated with the medical sign. Thus, on the first level, the descriptions of tuberculosis in Dumas's *La Dame aux camélias*—to take an example I have already used—refer to a romanticized ideology of passion and to an evanescence of the female within the system. Diseases in Balzac, Flaubert, or Zola are signs of the verisimilar. Again, in Mann's *The Magic Mountain*, the tuberculosis refers to a humanistic ideology of creativity, as does medical discourse in Proust's *Recherche*. At the same time, the medical detail in each of these works introduces another world, one in which giving a character a disease means necessarily following a medical protocol. It does a work no good to have a tubercular character gallivant about unless you want to kill her off fairly early: at least in the age of modern medicine and realist narrative, the medical detail forces the text to go in a certain direction that may or may not conflict with what nonmedical literature would choose. In other words, standing at the intersection of the Boulevard Saint Germain and the Boulevard Saint Michel, a character could go four ways, and find a different set of circumstances at each turn, so as to make the possible set of events almost infinite in nature. On the other hand, a character afflicted with tuberculosis has fewer choices if the text is to be meaningful: there is no point giving a character tuberculosis and then pretending that he or she does not have the disease.

With AIDS, however, things are topsy-turvy once again: we never know what the next medical detail might be, what course will be taken, or what effect the medical discourse will have. AIDS forces postmodernism to mime realism, not the realism of certainty and verisimilitude but that of chance, undecidability, and the ruptures and miasmas that are the hidden life of the realist text. AIDS falsifies medicine to its roots because one detail always leads to another, and another, not one of which is predictable literarily in the literary text:

[T]o have it analyzed, five different doctors who had felt it [a ganglion] during the month of observation had demanded the biopsy; only one big shot [*ponte*] consulted on the phone thought that an aspiration-biopsy would do, but once I was on the operating table, the surgeon told me that the aspiration would have no results, because the ganglion was too hard, and that it was necessary to cut off a piece. (*HCR* 11)

To introduce the discourse of medicine into the literary text is once again to create a simulacrum of the subject. Since AIDS has taken over the author's body and since acts of free will seem to be less and less possible, the medical discourse will speak in his place. But first of all, medical discourse divides the world into a "we" and a "they," not opposed to one another, but separate from one another. And if the discourses of medicine cover up as much as they explain and are no more the product of a unified "we" where AIDS is concerned than are the sufferers, medical discourse does not acknowledge its act of repression of variance in opinion. Medical discourse stands as a monolith; yet AIDS becomes a linguistic apartheid into which Guibert, one among many, is newly thrust, as if there had been some big bang, or gang bang, that suddenly split the world in two:

The doctor who announced my results to me was odious, and I welcomed his news quite coldly, to be done as quickly as possible with this man who did his work assembly-line fashion, thirty seconds and a smile for those who were HIV−, from five to fifteen minutes of a "personalized" interview for those who were HIV+. (*Ami* 147)

The PLA does not exist for medicine as much as does a category of individual who is HIV+, a vague grouping that is completely depersonalized and desubjectified. For medicine, the HIV+ individual becomes someone *at whom* one talks in a "personalized" way, which means that this doctor-to-patient talk happens in a completely depersonalized way. Nothing is as far from the subject of the HIV+ person as is this discourse that remarks the fracture, opening, or fault in his or her subject, the metaphoric locus in which AIDS has entered but which is incapable of remarking anything else. And specifically nothing addresses the fact that this "fault" is still merely one part (although the deadliest) of a complex individual who has foci completely unrelated to this positivity or negativity.

The world is divided into those who are HIV+ and those who are not. Again, from Guibert's point of view, the only valid position is that everyone is potentially HIV+ and therefore, no one can truly be HIV− as an absolute essential position. The HIV+ person immediately develops a new vocabulary, one that no longer corresponds to the states of his or her soul, the repressions of his or her subjectivity, or the engagement of his or her being. Rather, the subject internalizes the medical discourse so that at least at certain times and in certain phases of the development of the disease, he or she mimes the position of the medical gaze. Looking at himself, Guibert sees not the subject, nor any *présence à soi*, but the alienation forced by the discourse of symptomology. Ultimately, it is only mythical American millionaires (*CMV* 45) who can buy a new set of eyes. And thus, ultimately, the eyes that see or do not see with a fixed gaze are Guibert's own, even if they are the eyes of a blind man: "I ask her if the blindness provoked by the megalo is white or black. She answers, 'It changes depending on how the virus has advanced' " (*CMV* 82). In the end, then, his sight or blindness, his gaze in any case, is wholly his, returned to him when medicine is no longer of any use. For now, however, the invisible world of medical symptoms, ascertainable only through tests, becomes the visible semiotics that define him as someone condemned or someone who may have been given a temporary stay of execution. Free will fades away in a game of counts, symptoms, and numbers. The doctor says to Guibert: "Shingles, the fungus now, and your T-cell count would allow you to enter the research group" (*Ami* 157). Guibert's fate is in the keeping of the mysteries coursing through his bloodstream, the activity of the virus, and not the movements of his mind or body.

It is particularly painful for an openly gay man or woman to realize this reimprisonment in a new model that is not of his or her own creation, for the rhetoric of gay liberation, if not its whole reality, has been deeply influenced by concepts of existential freedom. If the reality of gay liberation has at times turned into a manifestation of the reign of the practico-inert, the individual still often feels that the actions of his or her subject are of consequence to him or her alone. The advent of AIDS has changed all that, and has forced a reexamination of the activity of the subject caught in a serious, even deadly, game that threatens every imaginable concept of free will. Moreover, for an author like Guibert who has previously delighted in the celebration of his unique subjectivity, AIDS places numerous constraints on his ability to function as such a gay author.

One solution is to accept the very challenge that AIDS offers to an author, to turn, for example, the seriousness of symptomology into a literary constraint that encourages creation. So the variation in a T-cell count becomes analogous to a chess game played with Thomas Bernhard, author to author, across the miles (214–15). Or the very symptoms and their treatments become the poetic litany of a new sort of creation that measures pain and its relief according to the variations of "the oscillometer of my anguish several thousandths of a millimeter" (*Ami* 137):

Since I had learned of the definite presence of the HIV virus in my body, covering at some unknown point either my lymphatic system, my nervous system, or my brain, polishing its weapons, set to go off in six years as a time bomb, without mentioning the fungus under my tongue that had stabilized and which we had given up caring for, I had various secondary diseases that Dr. Chandi had treated, often over the phone, one after another: patches of eczema on my shoulders treated with a 0.1 percent Locoïd cortisone cream, diarrhea treated with Ercéfuryl 200, one pill every four hours for three days, a doubtful sty treated with Dacrin eyewash and an aureomycin cream. (*Ami* 167)

No symptom is too subtle or too invisible to resist being textualized, not as the sign of the disease and its ravages, but as the sign of a new, rewritten relation of the subject to the text he is producing. His work becomes symptom and balm, as we read, internalize, and react to its minutiae. No one can fail to react to the dedication of the sequel, *Le Protocole compassionnel*, to "All those women and men who wrote me for *A l'ami qui ne m'a pas sauvé la vie*. Each one of your letters upset me" (*PC* 7).

V. Safe Sex

Would I like to jerk off until my blood stood still, until my hand flew off my wrist? (*Ami* 218–19)

If AIDS wreaks one greatest havoc on the individual before he or she is in the final stages of agony, it is the absolute revolution brought about in human relations. With one simple blood test, the entire world of the socialized individual changes. Of course, the initial reactions of some are frightfully predictable, those who fade away, shrink from continuing friendships, disappear, and run from all contact. More crucial to our understanding of the changed subject is what happens to the internalized sense of intimacy, the conception not only of an "I" or "me" but of a "we" or "us." And that is changed with one word, one announcement, and one realization that the world is forever different. And we should not think that the recognition of the validity of "safe sex," "safer sex," or *SSR* (*sexe sans risques*) is the same for seronegative individuals and seropositive ones. The seronegative individual practicing safe sex acts out of an egoistic motivation: it is he or she who does not want to become infected by the invisible scourge to which the other may or may not be host. The seropositive individual, reaffirming his or her participation in the social contract as a member of the community of humans, is protecting the other from the known. It is ironic, then, that just as there is an exclusion from the community that he or she once knew as a cohesive social unit, the seropositive individual can reaffirm his or her membership in that community by a veiled, sheathed action that is at once potentially the most dangerous and the most life-affirming: sex with AIDS.

At least potentially, the sexual activity of a PLA, while obviously the most dangerous activity imaginable in this realm for a seronegative partner outside of a shared needle, is also the one, if suitably categorized as "safer sex," that may do the most to lessen the complete alienation of the PLA. At least on the literary level, Guibert can take the impediment and make it "suddenly prosperous like a condom factory" (*Ami* 171). And yet it is not so easy, for the very presence of the safety is a sign of the omnipotence of the disease. On the phenomenological and literary levels, the condom is the same as the disease. If, as I have indicated, everyone is potentially HIV+, except in a country like the United States with its murderous myths of perpetual virginity and abstinence, then the protective condom of safe sex is as much a sign of the disease as is the T-cell count that is a part of medical discourse. Understandably, then, even when there is no risk, the very reaffirmation that states that the PLA is still a part, or again a part, of the human community is the barrier beyond which no subject can go or come: "It had become difficult for Jules and me to screw again, of course there was no longer any risk except for a reciprocal recontamination, but the virus stood there between our bodies like a ghost pushing them off/away" (*Ami* 155).

AIDS comes between. In so doing, it turns the couple of the "we" into a ménage à trois in which the virus is always the dominant member, the one that decides for the two others. The "we" is never again a dual pronoun, and if we consider the number two to be the limit of a pair, or dyad, if we thus refuse the three-way category assigned to the AIDS-infected couple, we are forced to conclude that even phenomenologically, the presence of AIDS diminishes the individual until he or she is somewhat less than a subject, somewhat more than the collection of symptoms to be sure, but at every point, less than what the individual might be. With AIDS present, a corresponding absence within the individual penetrates to the very core of his or her being. At the same time, AIDS takes on more and more of the characteristics of the subject acting both singly and in a dyad. AIDS becomes the subject of discourse, the subject of action, and the only approved position, to which all the others must surrender: "On the other hand, the virus, which had taken on an almost corporeal existence in becoming a certified thing, as opposed to one just feared, had hardened a process of disgust at Jules's body, even against her will" (*Ami* 155).

One might think that the diminution could find its compensation in the sexual activity of two seropositive individuals who would then form the ironic double of a couple of two seronegative individuals. In neither case is there risk of infection (though unsafe sex between seropositive individuals increases the risk of the exchange of the microbes of opportunistic infection and there are indications that different strains of the AIDS virus act synergistically). In the case of two seropositive individuals, each subject can be whole again, at least in the brief moments of the embrace, for no artificial barrier nor any sheath is needed that would otherwise sign AIDS as an indelible signature. In the case of two seropositive individuals, the subject should reappear, but it does not:

> Jules came to spend a week in Rome, and his presence only increased my panic. Two AIDS were too much from one man, since I had the feeling that we formed one being, without a mirror between us, and that it was my own voice I heard when I spoke to him on the telephone, and that it was my own body that I took over when I took his between my arms, these two foyers of latent infection had become intolerable within one body. (*Ami* 169)

How can we understand this position that seems at first to be so unlikely? It goes to the very core of the function of AIDS within, or as, the literary text. AIDS is so insidious in every aspect of its manifestations that it continues to mime the position of the subject even when that miming no longer has any function. AIDS destroys the subject by installing itself in the place of the subject. In the most secret embrace between two seropositive individuals, there is the recognition that the complete flowering of AIDS, like no other known disease, means that even the idealized image of the other and the alienated image of the self are infected as well. AIDS leaves no position free from its parasitic behavior and nothing untouched by its powerful means of creating simulacra. If the literature of AIDS has caught both literature, through the entirety of its manifestations as a locus, and philosophy, in which there is a constant struggle with and against simulacra, then every position has been usurped by simulacra. As long as we maintain the separate positions defined for the narrative text—the narrator, the subject, the narratee, the implied author—each of them will become laden with the AIDS virus. In this case, the subject, his ideal image, and his definition of the other within the dyad have AIDS. And for the subject in such a condition, his implied reader has AIDS too. No matter how far the real reader is from the realities of seropositivity, he or she too is infected, on the phenomenological level, with the all-consuming virus.

Yet there is a hope held out, a slim one, but seemingly viable. One of the realities of the extremes of literature is the reorganization of pronouns and referents. It is no longer so easy to assume, as Benveniste quite rightly does for the realm of "normal" communication, that, for example, "I" refers to the speaker of the discourse containing "I" at that moment. The PLA writing is somewhat less than a subject at the same time he or she is joined to a greater subject, the subject in simulacrum that is both AIDS and the discourses of symptomology. What hope is there for the literary text when at every point there is the tautological recognition of the fact and discourses of AIDS? For Guibert at least, there is the possibility of a complex interweaving of strands, from "I," "you," and "he," from the discourses of a "they" that provide succor and death in the same sentence, from the collective "you" that reads the death of the author in every line. For Guibert, there is the possibility of a new knowledge, a new science, and a new set of paradigms; he has been given the mixed blessing of a reapprenticeship in the world of writing, living, and dying:

At a point when he did not think we were infected, Jules told me that AIDS is a marvelous disease. And it is true that I discovered something smooth and dazzling in its atrociousness, it was certainly an inexorable disease, but it did not make lightning progress, it was a step-by-step disease, a very long staircase that certainly led to death but whose every step represented an unequal apprenticeship, it was a disease that gave the time to die, and which gave death the time to live, the time to discover time and to discover life, it was somewhat of an ingenious modern invention that had been transmitted to us by those green monkeys from Africa. (*Ami* 181)

For now, Guibert will at least attempt to make the invasion something that he can live with, and write by. But it cannot last forever. As the end of his writing and his life approaches, the final stage is there. No recasting of pronouns can help, for in his death he is alone: "I read (only today, accidentally) that DHPJ, the antiviral drug I get intravenously every day, irreversibly blocks the reproduction of sperm, but what the fuck do I have to do with fucking at this point?" (*CMV* 92). If, as he says a few pages earlier, this writing is the only way to forget (64), we must ultimately recognize that for us, this reading is one more way to remember.

Reference Matter

Works Cited

Apter, Emily. *André Gide and the Codes of Homotextuality.* Saratoga, Calif.: Anma Libri [Stanford French and Italian Studies], 1987.

Artaud, Antonin. *Œuvres complètes.* 24 vols. Paris: Gallimard, 1961–88.

Balakian, Anna. *Surrealism: The Road to the Absolute.* New York: E.P. Dutton, 1970 [2nd ed., rev.].

Balzac, Honoré de. *Louis Lambert.* In *La Comédie humaine.* Paris: Seuil [Intégrale], 1966. 7:285–324.

Barbedette, Gilles, and Michel Carassou. *Paris Gay 1925.* Paris: Presses de la Renaissance, 1981.

Barish, Jonas. *The Antitheatrical Prejudice.* Berkeley: University of California Press, 1981.

Barthes, Roland. *L'Aventure sémiologique.* Paris: Seuil, 1985.

———. *Le Bruissement de la langue. Essais critiques IV.* Paris: Seuil, 1984.

———. *La Chambre claire. Note sur la photographie.* Paris: Editions de l'Etoile. Cahiers du Cinéma. Gallimard. Seuil, 1980.

———. *Le Degré zéro de l'écriture suivi de Nouveaux essais critiques.* Paris: Seuil [Points], 1972.

———. *Incidents.* Paris: Seuil, 1987.

———. *Mythologies.* Paris: Seuil, 1957.

———. *Le Plaisir du texte.* Paris: Seuil, 1973.

Bataille, Georges. "René Crevel. *Le clavecin de Diderot,*" in *Œuvres complètes,* vol. 1. Paris: Gallimard, 1970. 326–27.

Bauer, George H. "Pretexts for Texts: Sartre and Barthes Before Genet and Camus." *L'Esprit Créateur* 27.3 (1987): 89–99.

Beauvoir, Simone de. *Le Deuxième Sexe.* 2 vols. Paris: Gallimard [Idées], 1949.

Bell, David F. *Circumstances: Chance in the Literary Text.* Lincoln: University of Nebraska Press, 1993.

Bellemin-Noël, Jean. "Le Diamant noir: échographie d' 'Erostrate.' " *Littérature* 64 (1986): 71–89.

Bellour, Raymond. "H.G./F." *Grand Street* 10.6 (1991): 79–80.

Benveniste, Emile. *Problèmes de linguistique générale,* vol. 1. Paris: Gallimard [TEL], 1966.

Bosquet, Alain. *Conversations with Dali.* Trans. Joachim Neugroschel. New York: E.P. Dutton, 1969.

Breton, André. *Œuvres complètes,* vol. 1. Ed. Marguerite Bonnet et al. Paris: Gallimard [Pléiade], 1988.

Breton, André, et al., "Recherches sur la sexualité." *La Révolution surréaliste* 11 (1928): 32–40.

Buisine, Alain. *Laideurs de Sartre.* Lille: Presses Universitaires de Lille, 1986.

Buot, François. *René Crevel.* Paris: Grasset, 1991.

Cabelguenne, Fabienne. "René Crevel: écrire—mourir. Le drame de l'écriture." *Littératures* 18 (1988): 101–7.

Camus, Renaud. *Chroniques achriennes.* Paris: P.O.L., 1984.

Carassou, Michel. "René Crevel entre la mère et la putain." *Obliques* 14–15 (1977): 23–26.

———. *René Crevel.* Paris: Fayard, 1989.

Caws, Peter. *Sartre.* London: Routledge & Kegan Paul, 1979 [additional notes 1984].

Chambers, Ross. "Poaching and Pastiche: Reproducing the Gay Subculture." *Canadian Review of Comparative Literature* 21.1–2 (1994): 169–92.

Chebel, Malek. *L'Esprit de sérail. Perversions et marginalités sexuelles au Maghreb.* Paris: Lieu Commun, 1988.

Chénieux-Gendron, Jacqueline. *Le Surréalisme.* Paris: Presses Universitaires de France, 1984.

Cohen-Solal, Annie. *Sartre 1905–1980.* Paris: Gallimard, 1985.

Courtot, Claude. *René Crevel.* Paris: Editions Pierre Seghers, 1969.

Crevel, René. *Babylone.* Paris: Pauvert, 1975.

———. *Détours.* Paris: Pauvert, 1985.

———. *L'Esprit contre la raison et autres écrits surréalistes.* Paris: Pauvert, 1986.

———. *Etes-vous fous?* Paris: Gallimard [L'Imaginaire], 1929 [rpt. 1988].

———. *Mon corps et moi.* Paris: Pauvert, 1979.

———. *Les Pieds dans le plat.* Paris: Pauvert, 1979.

———. *Le Roman cassé et derniers écrits.* Paris: Pauvert, 1989.

Crimp, Douglas. "Portraits of People with AIDS." In *Cultural Studies*, ed. Lawrence Grossberg, Cary Nelson, and Paula Treichler. New York: Routledge, 1992. 117–31.

Deleuze, Gilles, and Félix Guattari. *L'Anti-Oedipe. Capitalisme et schizophrénie.* Paris: Minuit, 1972.

Derrida, Jacques. *De la grammatologie.* Paris: Minuit, 1967.

———. *L'écriture et la différence.* Paris: Seuil, 1967.

———. *Signéponge. Signsponge.* Trans. Richard Rand. New York: Columbia University Press, 1984.

Descombes, Vincent. *Proust. Philosophie du roman.* Paris: Minuit, 1987.

Dollimore, Jonathan. *Sexual Dissidence: Augustine to Wilde, Freud to Foucault.* New York: Oxford University Press, 1991.

Duvert, Tony. *L'Enfant au masculin.* Paris: Editions de Minuit, 1980.

Fanon, Frantz. *Black Skin, White Masks.* Trans. Charles Lam Markmann. New York: Grove Weidenfeld, 1967.

Foucault, Michel. *Language, Counter-Memory, Practice. Selected Essays and Interviews by Michel Foucault.* Ed. Donald F. Bouchard. Ithaca, N.Y.: Cornell University Press, 1977.

Fourny, Jean-François, and Charles D. Minahen, eds. *Sartre Revisited* (forthcoming).

Fowlie, Wallace. *André Gide.* New York: Macmillan, 1965.

Gauthier, Xavière. *Surréalisme et sexualité.* Paris: Gallimard, 1971.

Genet, Jean. *Les Paravents.* Paris: L'Arbalète, 1976.

Gide, André. *Corydon.* Paris: Gallimard, 1925.

———. *Romans. Récits et soties. Œuvres lyriques.* Paris: Gallimard [Pléiade], 1958.

———. *Si le grain ne meurt.* Paris: Gallimard [Folio], 1955.

Goldthorpe, Rhiannon. *Sartre: Literature and Theory.* Cambridge: Cambridge University Press, 1984.

Guibert, Hervé. *A l'ami qui ne m'a pas sauvé la vie.* Paris: Gallimard, 1990.

———. *Cytomégalovirus.* Paris: Seuil, 1992.

———. *L'Homme au chapeau rouge.* Paris: Gallimard, 1992.

———. *Mauve le vierge.* Paris: Gallimard, 1988.

———. *Mon valet et moi.* Paris: Seuil, 1991.

———. *Le Protocole compassionnel.* Paris: Gallimard, 1991.

Harvey, Robert. *Search for a Father: Sartre, Paternity, and the Question of Ethics.* Ann Arbor: University of Michigan Press, 1991.

———. "Sidéens/Sidaïques: French Discourses on AIDS." *Contemporary French Civilization* 16.2 (1992): 308–35.

Hocquenghem, Guy. *La Beauté du métis. Réflexions d'un francophobe.* Paris: Editions Ramsay, 1979.

Works Cited

Hollier, Denis. *Politique de la prose. Jean-Paul Sartre et l'an quarante.* Paris: Gallimard, 1982.

Howells, Christina. *Sartre: The Necessity of Freedom.* New York: Cambridge University Press, 1987.

Kopelson, Kevin. *Love's Litany: The Writing of Modern Homoerotics.* Stanford: Stanford University Press, 1994.

Lacan, Jacques. *Ecrits.* Paris: Seuil, 1966.

Laqueur, Thomas. *Making Sex: Body and Gender from the Greeks to Freud.* Cambridge, Mass.: Harvard University Press, 1990.

Lejeune, Philippe. *Le Pacte autobiographique.* Paris: Seuil, 1975.

Linkhorn, Renée. "Les Faces antithétiques de l'érotisme chez René Crevel." *French Literature Series* 10 (1983): 80–87.

Lyotard, Jean-François. *Discours, figure.* Paris: Klincksieck, 1971.

Mehlman, Jeffrey. *A Structural Study of Autobiography: Proust, Leiris, Sartre, Lévi-Strauss.* Ithaca, N.Y.: Cornell University Press, 1974.

Meltzer, Françoise. *Salome and the Dance of Writing.* Chicago: University of Chicago Press, 1987.

Miller, D. A. *Bringing Out Roland Barthes.* Berkeley: University of California Press, 1992.

Morin, Louis. "Le Jour n'a rien repeint. (René Crevel et le surréalisme)." *Nouvelle Revue Française* 15 (1967): 953–61.

Pacaly, Josette. *Sartre au miroir.* Paris: Klincksieck, 1980.

Pierre, José, ed. *Recherches sur la sexualité. Janvier 1928–août 1932. Archives du surréalisme 4.* Paris: Gallimard, 1990.

Plato. *Lysis. Symposium. Gorgias.* Trans. W. R. M. Lamb. Cambridge, Mass.: Harvard University Press [Loeb Classical Library], 1975.

———. *Theaetetus,* in *Theaetetus. Sophist.* Trans. Harold North Fowler. Cambridge, Mass.: Harvard University Press [Loeb Classical Library], 1921 [rpt. 1977].

Proust, Marcel. *A la recherche du temps perdu.* 4 vols. Paris: Gallimard, 1987–89.

Pucciani, Oreste F. "Saint Sartre et l'homosexualité: ébauche d'une lecture homosexuelle du 'Saint Genet.'" *Les Temps modernes* 46 (1990): 638–57.

Rich, Adrienne. *Blood, Bread, and Poetry. Selected Prose, 1979–1985.* New York: Norton, 1986.

Rochester, Myrna Bell. *René Crevel: Le Pays des miroirs absolus.* Saratoga, Calif.: Anma Libri, 1978.

Said, Edward W. *Culture and Imperialism.* New York: Alfred A. Knopf, 1993.

Sartre, Jean-Paul. *Baudelaire.* Paris: Gallimard [Idées], 1963.

———. *Cahiers pour une morale.* Paris: Gallimard, 1983.

———. *Ecrits de jeunesse.* Paris: Gallimard, 1990.

———. *L'Etre et le néant. Essai d'ontologie phénoménologique.* Paris: Gallimard [TEL], 1943.

———. "Gide vivant," in *Situations, IV. Portraits.* Paris: Gallimard, 1964. 85–89.

———. *L'Idiot de la famille. Gustave Flaubert de 1821 à 1957.* 3 vols. Paris: Gallimard, 1971–72.

———. *Œuvres romanesques.* Paris: Gallimard [Pléiade], 1981.

———. *Saint Genet. Comédien et martyr.* Paris: Gallimard, 1952.

———. *Vérité et existence.* Paris: Gallimard, 1989.

Schehr, Lawrence. "Artaud's Revolution: Nowhere to Turn," *Romance Notes* 33.2 (1993): 109–17.

———. *The Shock of Men.* Stanford: Stanford University Press, 1995.

Schor, Naomi. *Reading in Detail: Aesthetics and the Feminine.* New York: Methuen, 1987.

Sedgwick, Eve Kosofsky. *Epistemology of the Closet.* Berkeley: University of California Press, 1990.

Shilts, Randy. *And the Band Played On: Politics, People, and the AIDS Epidemic.* New York: St. Martin's Press, 1987.

Sichère, Bernard. "Sartre et Genet: une scène." *Les Temps modernes* 46 (1990): 614–37.

Sontag, Susan. *AIDS and Its Metaphors.* New York: Farrar, Straus and Giroux, 1989.

Stambolian, George, and Elaine Marks, eds. *Homosexualities and French Literature: Cultural Contexts / Critical Texts.* Ithaca, N.Y.: Cornell University Press, 1979.

Stein, Gertrude. *The Autobiography of Alice B. Toklas.* New York: Vintage, 1961.

Symonds, John Addington. *A Problem in Greek Ethics.* In *Male Love: A Problem in Greek Ethics and Other Writings*, ed. John Lauritsen. New York: Pagan Press, 1983. 1–73.

Thucydides. *History of the Peloponnesian War.* 4 vols. Trans. Charles Forster Smith. Cambridge, Mass.: Harvard University Press [Loeb Classical Library], 1925–30.

Warhol, Andy. *The Andy Warhol Diaries.* Ed. Pat Hackett. New York: Warner, 1989.

Watt, Ian. *The Rise of the Novel: Studies in Defoe, Richardson and Fielding.* Berkeley: University of California Press, 1957.

Wood, Philip R. *Understanding Jean-Paul Sartre.* Columbia: University of South Carolina Press, 1990.

Index

In this index an "f" after a number indicates a separate reference on the next page, and an "ff" indicates separate references on the next two pages. A continuous discussion over two or more pages is indicated by a span of page numbers, e.g., "57–59." *Passim* is used for a cluster of references in close but not consecutive sequence. Entries are alphabetized letter by letter, ignoring word breaks, hyphens, and accents.

206   Index

Library of Congress Cataloging-in-Publication Data

Schehr, Lawrence R.
Alcibiades at the door : gay discourses in French
literature /
Lawrence R. Schehr.
    p.   cm.
Includes bibliographical references and index.
ISBN 0-8047-2467-9
1. French prose literature—20th century—History
and criticism. 2. Homosexuality and literature—
France—History—20th century. 3. Gay men's
writings, French—History and criticism. 4. Gay
men—France—Intellectual life. 5. Homosexuality in
literature.
I. Title.
PQ629.S33 1995
843'.9109353—dc20   94-46646
                                              CIP